"The science of reading isn't just for the primary grades! In their clear and readable style, Cunningham, Burkins, and Yates examine the research and show teachers of grades 3–5 exactly how to apply it. With zero judgment and endless encouragement, the authors will inspire teachers to rethink current practices and make research-based decisions to help every student."

—Anna Geiger, MEd, Host of the Triple R Teaching podcast
and creator of The Measured Mom website

"With all the noise in the world about reading instruction, Cunningham, Burkins, and Yates discuss a practical, research-driven, and student-based way to shift our reading instruction into balance and clarity. They've done the hard thinking in order to zoom in on what is necessary to teach intermediate readers to succeed."

—Jeff Anderson, Lead author of the Patterns of Power series (pre-K–12)

"As the field of reading instruction continues to reinvent itself, so many of us elementary educators find ourselves in need of a road map. The authors of this second volume of *Shifting the Balance* step in, validate our good intentions, and offer to guide us as we reflect on, reconsider, refine, and reimagine our practice. I look forward to referencing the ideas and resources in this edition (and online) as I continue striving to equip my students for meaningful reading experiences, now and in the future."

—Katie McAlister, First-Grade Classroom Teacher

"Cunningham, Burkins, and Yates clarify misunderstandings, summarize the research in an accessible way, and provide suggestions for what they call high-leverage routines to help teachers enhance their instruction and support students' growth as readers. Thoughtful, well-researched, and teacher-friendly, this book is an invaluable resource for anyone who wants to explore how to implement effective literacy instruction for readers beyond grade two."

—Lisa Maucione, Reading Specialist,
Dartmouth Public Schools, Dartmouth, Massachusetts

"While many of the big conversations about the science of reading research have focused on the foundational skills in primary grades, upper elementary teachers no longer need to feel left in the dark. With this gem, Cunningham, Burkins, and Yates skillfully supply six scientifically-sound shifts—answering the big questions and providing high-leverage instructional routines, while weaving in all five pillars of reading. No matter where you are on your SOR journey, this sensational book is a must-read for all!"

—Michelle Sullivan of The Colorful Classroom and Elementary Literacy Coach

"Teaching reading can sometimes feel like an impossible task. Our classrooms are filled with diverse groups of learners that present all different levels of instructional need. *Shifting the Balance 3–5* gives teachers tools they need to incorporate reading instruction that is purposeful and student-centered. With data-driven techniques and lessons, this book will set up any upper elementary school classroom with success."

—Michaela Durr, Teacher, New York City

"*Shifting the Balance 3–5* brings the science of reading from theory to direct application. This new take on literacy instruction brings forth the hope of long-lasting knowledge and continued growth for students. It is not only a thorough approach but is realistic and, best of all, attainable!"

—Clorasteen Wilson, Structured Literacy Instructor, Associate/OGA

"In *Shifting the Balance 3–5*, Cunningham, Burkins, and Yates go beyond the science of reading being only phonics. Taking a deeper dive into vocabulary, comprehension, fluency, and word identification for upper elementary students, this book helps teachers understand what is needed in their instruction through easy-to-read case scenarios. Thanks to these authors for once again bridging hearts and minds."

—Donna Hejtmanek,
Retired Educator and Creator of the Science of Reading–
What I Should Have Learned in College Facebook Group

Shifting the Balance

3-5

SHIFTING

THE

BALANCE

6 Ways to Bring the Science of Reading into the Upper Elementary Classroom

Katie Egan Cunningham
Jan Burkins · Kari Yates

Routledge
Taylor & Francis Group

NEW YORK AND LONDON

A Stenhouse Book

First published in 2023 by Stenhouse Publishers

Published in 2024 by Routledge
605 Third Avenue, New York, NY 10017
4 Park Square, Milton Park, Abingdon, Oxon OX14 4RN

Routledge is an imprint of the Taylor & Francis Group, an informa business

Credits
Figure 1.2, © Reprinted with permission of The Guilford Press
Figure 1.3, Pierre Vu/Shutterstock
Figure 1.4, Elnur/Shutterstock
Figure 2.1, © 2021. Adapted with permission of John Wiley & Sons
Page vii: Shutterstock
Page 28, Una Shimpraga/Shutterstock
Page 61, Ground Picture/Shutterstock
Page 136, Zurijeta/Shutterstock
Page 165, Ground Picture/Shutterstock
Page 198, Ronnachai Palas/Shutterstock

Library of Congress Cataloging-in-Publication Data
Names: Cunningham, Katie Egan, author. | Burkins, Jan Miller,
    author. | Yates, Kari, author.
Title: Shifting the balance : 6 ways to bring the science of reading into
    the upper elementary classroom / Katie Egan Cunningham, Jan Burkins, and
    Kari Yates.
Identifiers: LCCN 2023017878 (print)
    ISBN 9781625315977 (paperback)
Subjects: LCSH: Reading (Elementary) | Reading, Psychology of. |
    Reading—Physiological aspects. | Cognition in children. | BISAC:
    EDUCATION / Teaching / Subjects / Reading & Phonics | EDUCATION /
    Schools / Levels / Elementary
Classification: LCC LB1573 .C767 2024 (print)
    DDC 372.4—dc23/eng/20230606
LC record available at https://lccn.loc.gov/2023017878

Cover design: Cindy Butler
Interior design: Gina Poirier
Typesetting: Eclipse Publishing Services

ISBN: 9781625315977 (pbk)
ISBN: 9781032673745 (ebk)

DOI: 10.4324/9781032673745

For Jimmy, who shares a birthday with this book

CONTENTS

Contents

SHIFT 4 | # Reclaiming Word-Reading Instruction in the Intermediate Grades

SHIFT 5 | # Revisiting Fluency Instruction

ACKNOWLEDGMENTS

There is no doubt, we three are better teachers, writers, and humans for having navigated the tricky waters of writing this book together. And if gratitude is truly stored in the heart, then there is no question that our hearts have "sized up" as a result of this project. We owe each other, and so many, a debt of gratitude.

First and foremost, we are grateful to be part of a global community of educators like you who keep showing up in this work with open hearts and open minds. You keep bravely reexamining practices, proudly recommitting to those that still hold up, carefully revising those that need freshening up, and courageously letting go of those that simply don't serve children as well as we'd once hoped. You are our heroes.

To our friends who identify as members of the "balanced literacy" community: We commend the ways you have made space for this conversation, showing up with a willingness to continually stretch and grow on behalf of children. We respect the way you have fiercely advocated for practices that preserve student-centered classrooms and teacher decision-making, while also recognizing the need to consider other science-aligned practices, even when doing so has been overwhelming or scary.

To our friends who identify as members of the "science of reading" community: Thank you for your critical but kind feedback, for pushing our thinking, for calling us up instead of out, for patiently sharing your ideas and listening to ours, even when they didn't match up. Thanks for investing in us and fiercely advocating for practices that will make learning to read a reality for more children.

To our critics from both sides of this conversation, you've nudged our thinking and driven us toward deeper understanding and more careful analysis. You have kept us grounded and helped us hone our ability to listen hard for the nugget of truth, despite sometimes finding ourselves feeling triggered or defensive.

To Donna, who saw past labels and discord and dared to advocate for the work of *Shifting the Balance*, even in the face of criticism: Your continued impact on this global conversation astonishes us.

To Rachel, who is a relentless bridge builder: You've generously shared your time, talents, and expertise at crucial points in this and other projects. We're so lucky to have met you and to benefit from your wisdom, not just about reading practices, but about bringing people together, even when they have strong, differing perspectives.

To the entire Stenhouse family: Thank you for saying "YES!" to this project. Your generosity of time, resources, and expertise—not to mention your genuine warmth—have made this project possible. We can't imagine working with a wiser, kinder, smarter team, or feeling a greater sense of support from a publisher. We celebrate you and our good fortune to collaborate with you!

To Terry Thompson, our editor, friend, and mentor: You worked to understand and advocate for our vision from the beginning. You patiently helped us navigate the complexities of a three-way partnership, all the while making us smile (and sometimes laugh out loud). You asked the hard questions and served as our compass whenever we started to lose our way. You worked tirelessly to keep us on track and help us meet our deadlines. You are an amazing human being.

From Jan and Kari to Maggie, Natalie, Rachael, Michelle, and Rosie, who took care of all kinds of important other "stuff" at TheSixShifts.com so we could focus on writing, revising, revising again, and revising some more. We're so grateful for the work you do and for the people you are. Thank you for bringing your talents and your wisdom to the *Shifting the Balance* community, and for being the kind of people who rise to the challenge of living into your values.

From Jan and Kari to Katie: We will be eternally indebted to you. You had the vision to see a gap in the field that this book could help fill, and you took the brave and vulnerable step of reaching out to propose this three-way collaboration. For your giant heart, your patient soul, your humble demeanor, and your astonishing grasp of current research in the field, we love and respect you beyond measure.

From Katie to Jan and Kari: Thank you for taking a giant leap of faith and trusting me to join your *Shifting the Balance* family. Shifting from a duo to a trio took a level of generosity and patience that few people would be willing to give. Partnering with you has been like taking a master class each and every day. You are simply the best thought brokers, writers, and bridge builders out there. I will be forever grateful and humbled that you said yes to all of this and that I gained two dear friends along the way. I am your biggest fan. I love you both!

From Kari to Jan, a mentor, a friend, and the sister I didn't get until later in life: This all began with your tenacious and relentless (but also wise) persistence that we write the first *Shifting the Balance* book. Your ability to see beyond this moment is a true gift. Thanks for trusting me to be your partner and making my days brighter and more meaningful. I'm so glad I found the courage to come along for this wild ride! I love you!

From Jan to Kari, the pinnacle of partners: More than anyone I have ever known, you show up. You show up with grace, kindness, love, and persistence, and all with a level of skill, intelligence, and excellence that I often find incomprehensible. Thank you, Sister, for your constant vision of the possibilities within our shared projects, and within me. I love you.

To our children (there are nine between us!)—and Kari's grandchildren (four)—who keep us grounded in the beauty of life's moments and milestones, and keep us humbly aware of all we still have to learn: You are our inspiration, our joy, and our purpose in life.

To our life partners, Chris, Nate, and John, you never hesitate in giving your complete support to us, even when the intensity of a project, such as this one, constantly spills over into your life, too. For your unwavering patience, your dedicated work, and your stubborn love, we are far more grateful than we consistently show you. None of this would be possible without you.

Finally, from all three of us to children everywhere, especially those for whom learning to read has been a struggle: You inspire us to study more deeply, reflect more openheartedly, and act more bravely, even when our own fears or egos might beg us not to. You are our reason for rethinking, reinventing, and reimagining what is possible in classrooms. You are our most treasured teachers.

Head Work and Heart Work

▼ ▼ ▼ ▼ ▼ ▼

A Bit of Honesty from Jan and Kari

We have a confession to make.

We began exploring the science of reading for selfish reasons. We mostly wanted to be able to argue more effectively in attempts to defend our past practices. We wanted to solidify our own certainty about the wrongness of the criticisms being launched at balanced literacy practices, which had become targets of the "reading war," erupting anew. We were certain that critics were misunderstanding, misinterpreting, and misrepresenting many of the practices we held dear.

But what happened along the way has been profoundly different from what we expected. In writing the *Shifting the Balance* books, we have been humbled, reeducated, and transformed. Our understanding of how reading begins and develops has evolved as well, as we have endeavored to support you in helping children grow into people who can (and want to) read.

Yet as profound as studying the technical aspects of the reading science—doing the "head work"—can be, the process of initiating and maintaining momentum for the shifts often takes more than just learning the science-y stuff. Alongside the head work, most of us also have to make space for some "heart work." We inevitably have to grapple with the vulnerability, uncertainty, and emotional exertion that come with realizing that some of our practices may have been making learning to read harder for children.

So we invite you to join us in this messy and ongoing heart work, shifting from certainty to curiosity, from dismissiveness to listening, from judgment to vulnerability, from all-or-none to nuanced thinking, and from overwhelm (heads in the sand) to action. Student outcomes won't change unless adult practices change, and adult practices won't change unless there is a safe space for examining the problem and owning the solutions.

The Problem: Despite Best Efforts, Too Many Children Still Struggle with Reading and Writing

If you teach in the upper elementary grades, chances are you have some students who have truly taken off as readers and writers. Their skills grow steadily each day along with their confidence. They devour whole series of books and read to learn about the topics that interest them, whether volcanoes, performing magic tricks, or taking care of a goldfish. They write compelling pages to persuade or to entertain and are eager to share them. They take the lead in book clubs and are quick to jump into whole-class discussions. From reading while they wait for the bus, to excitedly telling friends that a favorite author has a new book coming out, to eating lunch quickly in order to have time to "run to the library," they think of themselves as readers and writers and live into that literate identity.

But if you're like most teachers of upper elementary grade students, you also have some students, maybe even many, who keep you up at night. These are students who drag their feet when it's time for independent reading. They guess at unknown words based on the first letter or bits and pieces of the word. They skip or misread whole syllables in multisyllabic words, reading "invention" for *intention* or "elible" for *eligible*. They spend much of their writing time staring at a blank page, and when they do get something down on paper, sentences are choppy and disconnected, and sometimes don't even make sense. What's more, they have a lot of trouble with spelling, writing "goyn" for *join* and "wont" for *want*.

In some cases, their skills are splintered. For example, some children have an impressive speaking vocabulary but considerable difficulty when it comes to decoding or spelling long words. Others have strong decoding skills, but when it comes to comprehension, it's clear that their thinking is surface-level at best. By the time they reach your classroom, many are working to make themselves invisible. And some even rely on a different bag of tricks, including resistance, distraction, and disruption, just hoping to survive what feels like another day filled with reading and writing failures.

It's not that educators haven't been working hard to address the needs of students. We have. But the truth is, some of our practices have actually complicated the process of learning to read, rather than smoothing it out. Unfortunately, this adversely affects some groups of children more than others.

What's more, the academic gaps between the haves and the have-nots just keep widening. The accumulated advantage for some and subsequent disadvantage for others, known as the "Matthew effect" (Stanovich 1986), means that strong readers get stronger and readers who have difficulty with reading get further and further behind.

Many educators—whether "balanced literacy" supporters or "science of reading" proponents—are gravely concerned and committed to disrupting systems that perpetuate reading failures. Some science of reading advocates blame balanced literacy for inequitable literacy outcomes. And some balanced literacy advocates resist the science of reading for fear that it will make access to rich literacy experiences even more inequitable. We would argue that both of these concerns are valid and that neither should be dismissed.

All children, especially those locked into systems that seem to guarantee their failure (Minor 2018), need access to both the secrets of the alphabetic code *and* relevant experiences with texts. They need both explicit information about how reading works *and* immersive experiences that show them how to leverage reading and writing to change the world.

Fortunately, the more we learn, the better equipped we are to make thoughtful changes to practices in order to better serve all children. And the good news is that there is a whole lot of important science about how children learn to read, and consistently implementing this science in classrooms—alongside a continued commitment to providing powerful experiences with worthwhile texts—will enable more children than ever before to lead literate lives.

How Katie Inspired This Book

Shifting the Balance K–2 was dedicated to sharing some critical shifts to practice in the early literacy classroom, where the methodology for reading instruction has been most fiercely debated. The first book was designed to clear up misunderstandings about current practices that might actually be making learning to read harder, rather than easier.

We wanted to share with teachers what we had come to understand ourselves about how the human brain learns to read from the inside out. Our goal was to offer teachers foundational knowledge they could use to provide more science-aligned instruction, basing decisions more on research than on intuition, assumptions, past practices, hunches, or opinions.

But what about readers beyond second grade? And what about K–2 students who *are* making strong progress as readers? These are some of the questions that were on Katie's mind when she approached us in March 2021 with the idea of collaborating on a second *Shifting the Balance* book.

Katie had also taken a deep dive into reading science. As a teacher with years of experience in the upper elementary grades, a college professor, a literacy consultant, and the mother of two children, one in elementary school and one in middle school, Katie was particularly driven to understand the ways reading science could be leveraged for older readers.

Having read our first book, she expressed curiosity and energy for exploring with us how to help teachers address the unique needs of developing readers in light of reading science. We, too, were interested in readers beyond the earliest stages. And, knowing Katie both as a human being and as the author of a book about bringing the science of happiness into the classroom (Cunningham 2019), we knew she would have a lot to offer the project. Truth be told, the book you hold in your hands would never have happened without Katie's initial nudge and subsequent insights, not to mention her hard work and passion for this project.

While it's true that the most heated debates about instructional methods seem to have focused on the earliest grades, there is plenty of confusion and uncertainty about practices with older students, too. And more recently there has been growing concern that excessive attention to explicit phonics in the early grades will eventually result in an over-correction that leads to older readers who don't comprehend well (Wexler 2022; Wyse and Bradbury 2022). So, as a writing team, the three of us settled on an essential, guiding question: *What does the reading science really say about literacy instruction in the upper elementary classroom?*

In response to this question, the shifts we offer in the coming pages hold promise for students who have moved past the "beginning to read" phase and are learning to read with increasing accuracy, automaticity, purpose, and joy. Still, as any writers do, we had to make some hard choices about what to include in this book and what to leave out. We've done our best to distill more than forty years of empirical research into a book that feels accessible and manageable. We've also tried to write the kind of book that you can look forward to reading on a Sunday afternoon on the couch, but which also gives you actionable steps that can make a difference for your students on Monday morning.

Navigating Competing Tensions

Although debates in the field are often presented as "this vs. that"—phonics vs. meaning, knowledge vs. strategies, science vs. joy, structured literacy vs. balanced literacy—the truth is that decisions about reading instruction are more complex than they are binary.

The opportunity for all of us, as a community of literacy educators, is to listen past the noise to hear the signal. We can lean into the dissonance of competing tensions with an open mind, an open heart, and a critical look at the research. For example, as a 3–5 educator, you are probably wrestling with challenges like these:

- Selecting complex texts for knowledge building while also making sure students get word-reading practice that reinforces their developing proficiency.

- Building foundational reading skills while also making instructional decisions that consider children's identities and interests.

- Planning for explicit vocabulary instruction while also making the most of in-the-moment opportunities to develop word awareness—all without dampening enthusiasm for texts and words.

- Offering independent reading practice opportunities that are motivating and engaging while also getting students to do the hard work of stretching into texts that will grow them as readers.

- Teaching important reading comprehension strategies without making reading all about comprehension strategies.

- Leaning into the power of rereading while also making fluency practice authentic and meaningful for students.

- Giving students choices in their reading while also supporting students in reading things they need to read but may not be thrilled about initially.

▲ Filling the gaps for students who have fallen "behind" in reading while also making sure that those who are "on track," or even "ahead," move forward, particularly when they need to demonstrate the same grade-level skills on standardized tests.

In this book, we share a path forward that embraces science *and* balance, applying content knowledge *and* pedagogy to translate research into practice.

How the *Shifting the Balance* Books Connect

There is important connectivity between the two *Shifting the Balance* texts, so we encourage you to interpret their grade-level designations loosely. As you know firsthand, children's reading development rarely fits neatly into grade levels. So in each book there is science that spills across grade levels and is critical for every elementary teacher to understand, regardless of what grade you teach.

For instance, while every 3–5 teacher needs to understand how the reading brain develops, this foundational science is explained in depth only in the K–2 book. Similarly, if you are a teacher in the primary grades, you still need to have a deep understanding of when to teach (and not to teach) reading comprehension strategies, even though this is a shift that is elaborated on only in the 3–5 book.

The following Shifts At-a-Glance table illustrates how the shifts, which are now actually twelve shifts in all, develop across the books. Use this chart to help you consider your learning goals and how each *Shifting the Balance* book can help you adjust your own practices according to your students' needs, regardless of what grade you teach.

In fact, while you might think of the K–2 book as the "first" six shifts and the 3–5 book as the "next" six shifts, each book can also stand alone. Either way, you know the readers in your classroom, so we invite you to design a reading plan that best meets the needs of you and your students.

THE SHIFTS AT-A-GLANCE

The Six Shifts, K–2	The Six Shifts, 3–5
Rethinking How Reading Comprehension Begins	Reconsidering How Knowledge Impacts Comprehension
Recommitting to Phonemic Awareness Instruction	Rethinking the Role of Strategy Instruction in Learning to Comprehend
Reimagining the Way We Teach Phonics	Recommitting to Vocabulary Instruction
Revising High-Frequency Word Instruction	Reclaiming Word-Reading Instruction in Intermediate Grades
Reinventing the Ways We Use MSV (3 Cueing Systems)	Revisiting Fluency Instruction
Reconsidering Texts for Beginning Readers	Reimagining Independent Practice in the Literacy Classroom

How We've Organized this Book

If you have already read the first *Shifting the Balance* book, you will find the organization of this book familiar. Each chapter, referred to as a "shift," is color-coded and focuses on an important facet of reading instruction. The shifts build on one another in cumulative ways and include the sections we describe below.

A Look Inside a Classroom

At the beginning of each shift we step inside a classroom, where you will see familiar literacy practices unfolding with the very best of intentions. These are practices you will probably recognize; they are certainly practices we've enacted in the classrooms we've worked in.

Clearing Up Some Confusion

Here we take a look at some common misunderstandings that might be driving current practices. We draw on important science to help us rethink and revise our mental models for instructional decision-making.

A Short Summary of the Science

Each shift's discussion of misunderstandings and unpacking of science is followed by a research summary in the form of a succinct, bulleted list. This recap offers the key takeaways from the science of that shift and can serve as a tool for review and reference.

Recommendations for Making the Shift

We open this section with a quick-reference table of high-leverage routines. Then we zoom in on a few of these routines in more detail. In a nutshell, this is the super-practical section, offering some simple and scientifically sound instructional moves to consider. Some of these routines will likely be new, while others may be familiar, only requiring relatively simple adjustments to established practices.

Meanwhile, Back in the Classroom . . .

In this section, we step back into the classroom that introduced the shift. Here we get to see how the teacher—after considering additional reading science and adjusting literacy practices—has begun to embrace some key shifts and how the children are responding.

Questions for Reflection

Finally, we wrap up each shift with reflective questions to guide your own thoughtful planning and decision-making as you work to choose next steps for you and your students.

Downloads

To fit in all the science, the instructional recommendations, and the practical tools we wanted to share with you, while also managing page count (our competing tensions while writing this book!), we chose to house additional resources for you at TheSixShifts.com. Throughout the book, we direct you to the site, where you can download tools and resources that expand on the content of this book.

Finding Courage and Community

As you commit to taking an honest second look at your literacy practices with developing readers—working to spot misunderstandings, misinformation, and missed opportunities—we hope the pages of this book will help you find the courage and direction you need to make these shifts on behalf of children.

We also hope that you find a community in your building or district to support you on your journey. This head work and heart work can be intense, and having thought partners who help us process substantive learning can make all the difference. That has certainly been true for the three of us as we've written this book.

As you embark on the journey in the pages ahead, know that we travel with you, holding tight to the Six Commitments we introduced in the first *Shifting the Balance* book (Burkins and Yates 2021).

- ▲ We commit to being kind to ourselves, making peace with the unavoidable reality that *there are* things we have missed, misunderstood, and misinterpreted.

- ▲ We commit to honestly appraising our current practices with an open heart and an open mind.

- ▲ We commit to recognizing and reflecting on our own triggers and biases.

- ▲ We commit to actively working to lower our defenses so we can raise our awareness.

- ▲ We commit to reconsidering, reprioritizing, or simply letting go of less helpful practices, to make space for some that are more effective.

- ▲ We commit to taking action rather than giving in to the paralysis of self-doubt and/or overwhelm.

We invite you to make these commitments with the three of us so that you can build the bridges children need to move from where they are today to the rich and wonderful literacy lives we know you want for them. Along the way, our shared purpose is to give you the information you need to make sound instructional decisions anchored in the best of science, rooted in responsiveness, and relentlessly focused on providing children with experiences saturated with meaning.

It's time for a shift. We are so glad you're here.

1

Reconsidering How Knowledge Impacts Comprehension

Moving into her sixth year as a fourth-grade teacher, Ms. Yang is committed to doing things differently this time around. This year she simply isn't going to let science and social studies get squeezed out of the day as they have been in years past.

Ms. Yang has been passionate about social studies for as long as she can remember. In college, she originally thought she would like to teach high school history. But a volunteer experience coaching youth soccer changed everything, leaving her convinced that she wanted to spend her days surrounded by the energy and enthusiasm of nine- and ten-year-olds!

Yet, while her school is a thriving learning community with aspirations to support every child every day, it also has some of the lowest reading scores in the city. Because of this data, Ms. Yang has felt pressure to structure both her schedule and her instruction to focus primarily on large, uninterrupted chunks of time for reading and writing. And try as she might to design and redesign her schedule to include the kind of time she needs to offer rich social studies and science opportunities to her students, the minutes just never seem to add up.

Her actual schedule only gives thirty minutes daily to science or social studies on a rotating basis, while the language arts block gets ninety minutes every day. And even the time she does have for content areas, which is at the end of the day, always seems to get interrupted for programs or special services or simply serves as a safety valve when she's running behind schedule.

As for reading, she spends most of her instructional time focused on an array of comprehension strategies that she and her colleagues feel will serve students well on standardized tests. She knows that a lot rides on the outcomes of the tests, even though she often questions their use and hates how her students seem conditioned to stress about them.

But even with a big chunk of her schedule dedicated to reading comprehension instruction, Ms. Yang wonders what else she can do to help her students succeed. Although a midyear reading comprehension assessment shows that some students are consistently growing as readers, others have definitely plateaued. Most distressing, it seems that the children who are stuck are the ones who came to her behind in the first place, while the students who came in already reading well have clearly made even more progress. And some students, like Jessica and Reginald, don't seem to really get the more complex strategies, like inferring, no matter how much instruction or guided practice she provides.

Although the curriculum her school uses is designed to give students a lot of practice in informational text that is complex, it's rare that they seem to enjoy the lessons. In fact, on some days, getting students to lean into the work feels a bit like pulling teeth. The topics seem disjointed and not particularly interesting to fourth graders. Spending so much time dragging readers through the texts has made Ms. Yang long for the energy and enthusiasm that made her fall in love with teaching elementary students in the first place. And she often wonders how her students will ever develop a depth of knowledge and a love for science and social studies topics.

Mr. Jackson, the fourth-grade teacher across the hall, is passionate about teaching science in hands-on and exploratory ways. Occasionally Ms. Yang and Mr. Jackson collaborate, pulling their students together and team-teaching so that they can learn from each other.

Because both of them would love to do more of this kind of collaborative content area instruction, they've decided to approach their administrator and advocate for a different model. Ms. Lorrey, their principal, is generally supportive of action research. But they know she is also concerned about reading scores, so they want to make sure to prepare for their conversation with her. The whole endeavor feels like a long shot, but they are hopeful.

A COMMON PRACTICE TO RECONSIDER

▲ ▼ ▼ ▼ ▼ ▼

We underestimate the role of background knowledge in reading comprehension.

M s. Yang's situation isn't unique. All too often elementary teachers and school leaders find themselves making hard choices about instructional minutes, with content area instruction losing out to literacy instruction, especially if reading scores are falling.

In a nutshell, reading comprehension is a reader's understanding and interpretation of what they read. However, a close look at what really makes up reading comprehension can offer some insight into the ways content area knowledge and reading comprehension are actually connected.

To illustrate this connection, we share two related models of reading that shed light on the ways reading comprehension actually *depends* on knowledge about things. These two models are the Simple View of Reading (Gough and Tunmer 1986) and Scarborough's Reading Rope (Scarborough 2001).

The Simple View of Reading

In the Simple View of Reading (SVR), reading comprehension is represented as the product of two essential factors—word recognition (phonological awareness, decoding, and reading words automatically) and language comprehension (the ability to understand spoken language) (Gough and Tunmer 1986; Hoover and Gough 1990). These overarching components are described by Hoover and Tunmer (2021) as "the most important cognitive capacities underlying reading success" (1). This Simple View of Reading equation is presented in Figure 1.1.

Notice that reading comprehension is the *product* of multiplying two variables, not simply a matter of adding the two parts together. So, using the

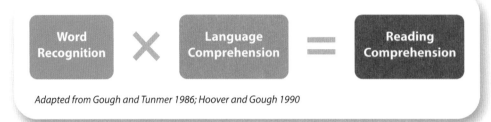

Adapted from Gough and Tunmer 1986; Hoover and Gough 1990

Figure 1.1 The Simple View of Reading

formula in the box above, if you can read 100 percent of the words (1.0) and understand 100 percent of the language (1.0), then your comprehension is also likely to be complete (1.0).

$$WR \times LC = RC$$
$$1.0 \times 1.0 = 1.0$$

But if either word reading or language comprehension is less than complete—less than 1.0—then reading comprehension will be diminished accordingly. Take a minute and really think about how each of the equations below represents reading comprehension.

$$WR \times LC = RC$$
$$1.0 \times 0 = 0$$
$$.5 \times 1.0 = .5$$
$$.5 \times .5 = .25$$

As helpful and insightful as it can be, the Simple View of Reading is just that, a relatively *simple* model that explains the big picture of a very *complex* process. So think of the Simple View of Reading as the forest, not the trees. We can bring in other models to extend this more simple one to help us see the trees. In particular, Scarborough's Reading Rope gives us additional insight into each of the two factors in the Simple View of Reading equation.

Scarborough's Reading Rope

Hollis Scarborough's (2001) Reading Rope is a metaphor that elaborates on the ideas from Gough and Tunmer. Scarborough's Rope provides a model that expands on the two factors in the Simple View of Reading's comprehension

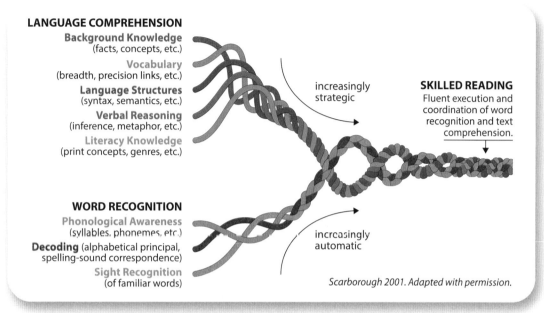

LANGUAGE COMPREHENSION

Background Knowledge
(facts, concepts, etc.)

Vocabulary
(breadth, precision links, etc.)

Language Structures
(syntax, semantics, etc.)

Verbal Reasoning
(inference, metaphor, etc.)

Literacy Knowledge
(print concepts, genres, etc.)

increasingly
strategic

SKILLED READING
Fluent execution and
coordination of word
recognition and text
comprehension.

WORD RECOGNITION

Phonological Awareness
(syllables, phonemes, etc.)

Decoding (alphabetical principal,
spelling-sound correspondence)

Sight Recognition
(of familiar words)

increasingly
automatic

Scarborough 2001. Adapted with permission.

Figure 1.2 The Strands of the Reading Rope

equation—language comprehension and word recognition. Figure 1.2 illustrates the eight strands of Scarborough's Reading Rope.

The strands and substrands in the illustration twist together more and more tightly as a reader becomes increasingly strategic and automatic. Ultimately, they form a rope of skilled reading with comprehension as the *outcome*. A single missing or frayed substrand—such as background knowledge—makes the whole rope weaker and compromises reading comprehension.

Both the Simple View of Reading and Scarborough's Reading Rope illustrate the cognitive demands of comprehending written text. In *Shifting the Balance K–2*, we used these models to support educators in understanding that reading comprehension begins not with text but with our earliest comprehension of spoken language. But when word reading and language comprehension eventually do come together, their interconnectedness continues throughout a reader's lifetime, with each contributing to the growth of the other. In this first shift, we will focus primarily on the language comprehension side of these models. Then we'll explore the word-recognition side in later shifts.

Of course, no single model of reading perfectly and completely captures all of the aspects of the reading process. And there are certainly other frameworks that give us insight into how additional aspects of reading—working memory, executive function skills, text selection, task design, and even sociocultural factors—influence a reader's comprehension, motivation, and disposition toward reading (Aukerman and Schuldt 2021; Duke and Cartwright 2021; Perfetti and Stafura 2014; RAND 2002). We will look more closely at some of these other models in later shifts.

Clearing Up Some Confusion

Most of the background knowledge we have that is relevant for reading is actually in the form of language. And we acquire our background knowledge largely through *language* experiences. This is true even when we gain new knowledge through reading because reading actually *is* a language experience. When we read, our brains translate *all* text into spoken language in our heads, processing it with the very same mechanisms it uses for comprehending *spoken* language. That's pretty amazing!

As an entry point for thinking about the direct relationship between language comprehension and reading comprehension, let's look more closely at the role of knowledge. In the sections that follow, we unpack four common misunderstandings that relate to knowledge building and the role it ultimately plays in reading comprehension.

MISUNDERSTANDING:

Since we live in an age where we can google anything, knowledge building is less important than it used to be.

We definitely live in an information age, and most of us carry around portable computers in our pockets, interacting with them all day long. The internet has revolutionized how we access information and how we create and share our ideas with the world. In part, because we can google any topic and get the information we're looking for—from what to pack for a trip to who won the Battle of Thermopylae—it is intuitive to think that time in the classroom should be spent teaching students strategies for *how to learn* information rather than teaching them specific content. Yet cognitive science and reading research show us that background knowledge—knowing stuff about stuff—is an indispensable component of reading comprehension. So it seems to us that "background knowledge" has *earned* its spot at the top of the list of language comprehension substrands in Scarborough's Reading Rope.

But why *does* background knowledge matter so much?

Research shows that the ability to read and comprehend a text is highly correlated with what we know about the topic already (Alexander, Kulikowich, and Schulze 1994; Kosmoski, Gay, and Vockell 1990; Shapiro 2004). Basically, the more we know about something, the better we can comprehend when we read about it. In fact, recent research by Kim and colleagues (2023) found that when literacy interventions focused on knowledge building, students not only transferred this knowledge to understand other texts about *related* topics, but they even comprehended more when they read about *new topics.* So our reading instruction should intentionally help students build *background knowledge* about a diverse range of topics for reading. It's important to remember that all students come into our classrooms with *prior knowledge*, although it might not include the particular knowledge they need to make sense of a text. At this point you might be wondering: What's the difference between prior knowledge and background knowledge anyway?

▲ *Prior knowledge* includes all of the knowledge students have accumulated. It can be applied in any situation, whether it is knowledge about how to safely get on base in baseball or knowledge about how to make a sandwich when they are hungry. Children build prior knowledge through personal, educational, and cultural experiences.

▲ When students take their prior knowledge and apply it to reading a text, however, it becomes *background knowledge*, improving comprehension by helping them build a mental model of the situation they are reading about. If children come to a text without the knowledge they need to comprehend, teachers can support them by sharing relevant ideas, information, and experiences. Students can use this new knowledge to fill in gaps in their prior knowledge, which they can then apply as background knowledge to make sense of the text (Brody 2001).

What's exciting about the relationship between these two overlapping terms, is that what we teach as background knowledge today can become part of a reader's prior knowledge down the road. And background knowledge has been found to be associated with higher levels of comprehension (Barnes, Dennis, and Haefele-Kalvaitis 1996; Kendeou and van den Broek 2007). While we can't control the prior knowledge students bring with them into our classrooms, we can help all students build background knowledge, thereby making more texts accessible.

Marilyn Adams (2015) provides us with a powerful metaphor for prior knowledge, explaining that it acts like Velcro in the reading brain. This mental Velcro makes it easier to affix new information in your memory when you already have some knowledge of the topic (Velcro) that the new stuff can stick to (Schneider, Körkel, and Weinert 1989; Walker 1988).

The famed "baseball study" really illustrates this Velcro metaphor. Recht and Leslie (1988) found that when given a reading passage about baseball, poor readers with a lot of prior knowledge about baseball had better comprehension than good readers who didn't know much about baseball. And not only did the less proficient readers score higher on comprehension measures, but they were also better at identifying important ideas in the text and at including those ideas in summaries, two high-level skills that we certainly want students to have.

We found these results surprising at first, but logical in light of the fact that background knowledge is made up of language that is essential for comprehension. The children in the baseball study had prior knowledge about baseball, probably from playing on teams, watching games, talking with others about baseball, and maybe even reading articles. They applied that knowledge, which acted as mental Velcro (Adams 2015; Hennessey 2020), to comprehend a new baseball text with even more success than their peers who were better readers but simply didn't have much baseball sense. Of course, if prior to reading the passage they had had an opportunity to build some background knowledge about baseball, the proficient readers who did not do as well on the text would have been positioned to make better sense of the passage.

Here's another example.

Teachers, like Ms. Yang in this chapter's opening scenario, often express frustration that their students are not making inferences consistently or effectively, despite lots of specific instruction and lots of opportunities to practice inferring.

But difficulties with inferring don't necessarily mean that children need more practice making inferences. Rather, it often means that they simply don't have enough background knowledge about the subject to fill in the missing, or implied, information in a text.

Let us use a couple of photographs to demonstrate what we mean.

If you show even very young children the picture in Figure 1.3 of the boy and the broken vase and ask them why the child is upset, they will likely demonstrate that they can infer. Most children have some past experiences with accidentally breaking something and seeing how others respond. So while the picture doesn't show the child breaking the vase, children can easily

Figure 1.3 The Broken Vase

infer what happened, how the child in the picture is feeling, and even what might happen next. They know a lot about being a kid!

But show the same group of children this second picture—we'll call it "Frustrated Knitter" (Figure 1.4)—and ask why the woman is upset, and they probably won't be able to make the necessary inference. Even if they just demonstrated their ability to infer what was happening with the boy and the

Figure 1.4 Frustrated Knitter

vase in the previous picture, they won't be able to answer comprehension questions about "Frustrated Knitter" *unless* they have some knowledge about those long, pointed sticks in the woman's hands and how frustrating it is as a knitter to realize only too late that you've dropped a stitch.

Children's inability to infer what is happening in this second picture is *not* because they don't know the inferring strategy in general but because they don't have the knitting knowledge they need to make the inferential leap by filling in important information the picture *does not* show them. They don't need more practice inferring. In fact, no amount of inferring instruction or practice will compensate for what they don't know about knitting! What they really need in order to comprehend this picture is help building knowledge about knitting.

So, while you *can* search for quick answers on Google to clarify something you read, in order to comprehend deeply you need knowledge about the topic in your head *before you read* (Willingham 2006a), since the ability to read and make sense of what you are reading is highly correlated with what you *already* know about a topic (Kosmoski, Gay, and Vockell 1990). In Table 1.1 we draw from Daniel Willingham's (2006a) four essential roles of knowledge in reading comprehension, including an example of each. (Perhaps you know more about knitting than we do!)

TABLE 1.1

EXAMPLES OF WAYS KNOWLEDGE SUPPORTS READING COMPREHENSION

Role of Knowledge in Reading Comprehension	Example
Accelerating Knowledge speeds up reading comprehension, learning, and thinking, and it makes them all stronger.	The more you already know about knitting, the more quickly and easily you make sense of an article about the best yarns for cable knitting.
Accumulating Knowledge builds on itself and even grows exponentially.	Knowing a little bit about basic knitting stitches prepares you to make sense of next-level information about the fishbone stitch (cumulative) and to understand increasingly complex knitting directions (exponential).

Role of Knowledge in Reading Comprehension	Example
Filling Gaps Background knowledge enables the inferring that is crucial for understanding a text.	When writing about knitting, the author has to assume you know something about the topic. There isn't space to explain everything. The stronger your background knowledge, the more you'll be able to fill in those missing pieces of information (infer) when reading a blog post about hiding the loose ends of your yarn when knitting.
Rereading Less Rich background knowledge means you probably won't have to do as much rereading to comprehend, even if the text is complex.	The more you know about knitting and understand specialized knitting lingo, the more easily you'll make the transition from reading a set of complex directions to picking up the knitting needles and making a pair of argyle socks that actually match. The less you know, the more likely you will need to read, reread, and read again to even start knitting.

Adapted from Willingham 2006a

When we learn new things, important changes take place in the brain. The new knowledge sticks to existing knowledge and gets locked in. This stickiness happens when we read aloud books that expose students to new information and ideas. It happens when we engage students in text comparisons that promote rich discussion and deepen their understanding of ideas. It happens when we take a field trip, virtually or in person, to a museum or a planetarium.

Remember, the more hooks you have on your established knowledge strip of mental Velcro, the more places there are for new knowledge to latch on. Basically, already knowing some stuff about a topic just makes it easier to learn and hold on to new stuff about that topic.

MISUNDERSTANDING:

Knowledge is just facts about things.

It might be easy to think of "knowledge" in a very narrow, content-focused way. Facts about knitting. Facts about training dogs. Facts about the Battle of Thermopylae. But, as it turns out, although factual content knowledge does matter for reading comprehension, it's not *just* factual knowledge that matters.

So, what are the different kinds of knowledge students really need in order to comprehend text? Well, there are quite a few of them, and most move beyond the realm of information that you can google. Students actually need knowledge about words, processes, text types, content, *and* experiences (Adams 2015; Hattan and Lupo 2020). Table 1.2 explains some of the diverse forms of knowledge readers use to comprehend.

TABLE 1.2

TYPES OF KNOWLEDGE FOR COMPREHENDING

Type of Knowledge	Description
Cultural and Linguistic Knowledge	Prior knowledge gained from everyday experiences that either directly or indirectly help a reader understand a text, such as experiences related to a reader's cultural background or native language
Strategic Knowledge	Useful processes that can help a reader better decode, read fluently, understand, and think deeply about a text, such as monitoring comprehension
Textual Knowledge	Knowledge of various text types (i.e., narrative, expository, argumentative), structures (i.e., compare/contrast, problem/solution), and features (i.e., headings, captions), which makes it easier for a reader to integrate information and ideas from literature, poetry, nonfiction, multimodal texts, and more
Word Knowledge	Grammar (syntax), sound-spelling relationships (phonemics and orthography), morphology (semantics), and vocabulary (semantics), all of which help a reader build, expand, and leverage connected networks of words to comprehend text
Content Knowledge	Expertise in specific content areas, such as science or history, that makes it easier for a reader to understand new information about that topic

Adapted from Hattan and Lupo 2020

So, what does all this knowledge work look like in action?

Well, to contextualize these diverse forms of knowledge, let's think about Katie's son Jack for a moment. For his fifth-grade research project on ancient Greece, Jack chose to study the Battle of Thermopylae, a fight between the

Persians and a coalition of Greek city-states led by the Spartans. How's that for an obscure topic? How in the world could Jack have knowledge that would help him understand the Battle of Thermopylae? Well, here's how Jack drew on each of the different types of knowledge described in the table above to tackle this project:

▲ Jack applied **cultural knowledge** that he had about the life of the ancient Spartans by thinking back to a Spartan race he ran with his family, where he needed to complete a series of difficult obstacles.

▲ He applied **strategic knowledge** about how to search for relevant research entries and use key terms and headings to gather the information that would best explain the battle.

▲ He used **textual knowledge** to gather a variety of resources about the topic, including maps, timelines, media clips, and research entries. He also used knowledge of text structures—specifically description and cause-and-effect—to discern and consolidate important information.

▲ Jack applied **word knowledge**, including phonology, orthography, morphology, and semantics, to read and understand the domain-specific words in those written texts, like *alliance, conquer*, and *annihilated*. Jack also needed to apply knowledge of how words were strung together in a variety of sentence structures to determine what was most important.

▲ Jack already had a lot of **content knowledge** about ancient Greece, and his work on the project added more (Velcro).

There is a lot of agreement about the complexity of reading comprehension and the diversity of knowledge that deep reading requires. In fact, you may have noticed that many of these types of knowledge are also represented by substrands of language comprehension on Scarborough's Reading Rope. (Nice connection, by the way. You've got some Velcro there!) And while it's clear that content knowledge was critical for Jack to understand what he was learning about ancient Greece, it obviously was not the only type of knowledge that mattered for him to develop his ever-expanding sense of all that he was reading.

Of course, we can't determine what prior knowledge students bring with them when they come to school (Kaefer, Nueman, and Pinkham 2015; Wexler 2019). We can, however, be intentional about the kinds of literacy opportunities students have in the classroom, providing pathways to intentionally accumulate *various* kinds of knowledge that will ultimately strengthen their reading comprehension.

MISUNDERSTANDING:

Content area instruction is less important than reading instruction.

Ms. Yang is certainly not alone in her worries about content area learning. In too many classrooms, science and social studies instruction gets pushed to the side in lieu of reading instruction. Even the few minutes allotted to learning in the content areas are all too often slimmed down (or even squeezed out!) in the day-to-day reality of the classroom.

As a result, many classrooms have become almost "knowledge-neutral." We have focused on literacy foundations and strategies without enough intentional knowledge building (Neuman 2006). Unfortunately, the overemphasis on narrowly defined reading instruction, to the neglect of acquiring knowledge in content areas, actually makes reading comprehension in complex texts *less* likely and exacerbates inequities because it makes comprehension dependent mostly on the knowledge you already had when you arrived at school.

Basically, the "rich get richer" (Stanovich 1986). It's kind of like trying to help a group of children understand the "Frustrated Knitter" photograph on page 19 by teaching them to find the main idea and supporting details of the photo, rather than by providing them background knowledge about knitting! Only those who already knew about knitting will have the opportunity to really understand the picture.

The challenge is finding the sweet spot between these two tensions—intentional knowledge building and reading instruction. But the good news is that what children are learning in science and social studies can serve as prior knowledge for their reading of informational texts during reading instruction, and vice versa. Fortunately, spreading knowledge building across reading instruction and content area instruction in connected ways means that the two have a symbiotic relationship and don't have to be in competition for the same instructional minutes.

So, as it turns out, we can build content knowledge *and* improve students' strategic processes simultaneously via comprehension strategy instruction in content-rich texts (Duke, Ward, and Pearson 2021). Of course, this isn't in place of science and social studies instruction or hands-on exploration in those content areas, but as a complement to it.

In other words, in a knowledge-building context (such as reading about the civil rights movement), teaching a powerful comprehension thinking move (such as monitoring comprehension) is an effective approach to bringing content area instruction *and* reading comprehension instruction together (Cervetti et al. 2012; Willingham and Lovette 2014). This time-saving consolidation means that Ms. Yang and Mr. Jackson can start by choosing texts that are about the things they already want to teach and which provide a foundation for the experiential learning they are doing in science and social studies, rather than by choosing texts because they align with a particular comprehension strategy

When we commit to building knowledge *and* supporting reading development with both content area experiences *and* meaningful encounters with informational texts, a bit of magic happens. It's like when a meal is really delicious *and* it's good for you too. What's more, when a text provides opportunities for both content learning *and* leveraging strategic thinking moves, you have a win-win. We will look more closely at this winning combination of knowledge building and reading instruction in the high-leverage routines in this shift, and then take the exploration even deeper in Shift 2.

MISUNDERSTANDING:

Building knowledge is simply a matter of exposing students to informational texts.

It seems that, wherever we go, more informational texts are being embedded into the language arts classroom than ever before. But even though children today may have more instructional opportunities with informational texts than children twenty years ago (Moss and Newton 2002; Moss 2008; Duke 2000), these texts are often about an unrelated assortment of informational topics that students are guided to "read closely."

The problem is that because these texts rarely build on or relate to one another, children miss the opportunity to systematically accumulate the networks of knowledge essential for the inferential thinking they have to do to read a text closely.

What's the solution? Research suggests that knowledge can be built and leveraged simultaneously through the use of conceptually coherent text sets

(Camp 2000; Cervetti, Wright, and Hwang 2016; Guthrie et al. 2004). Conceptually coherent text sets are groups of texts that deepen learning around a common topic or theme. They also serve as a lens for examining information or events from multiple perspectives (Cappiello and Dawes 2021).

Still, as important as they are for developing the knowledge and language comprehension that support *reading* comprehension in complex texts, informational texts alone are not enough, for two reasons. First, systematic knowledge building requires intentionality in identifying the topics to invest in from grade to grade. School districts need to support teachers in building quality text sets that align with these topics across the K–12 system. In the long run, it's not enough for one teacher or one grade to think about knowledge building. Getting it right requires long-term collaboration and planning within and across the grades.

The second reason informational texts alone are not enough is that if we think about knowledge building solely in terms of informational content, it can lead us toward an overcorrection and cause us to overlook the value of narrative texts. In fact, narrative texts *also* contribute to knowledge building (Biber and Conrad 2019). Stories—both fiction and nonfiction—can actually help us learn factual information. Just think about all we learn about ourselves and others through the power of spoken and written narratives. Stories are a rich format for sharing knowledge about the challenges humans face, how we solve problems, and how we can relate to one another in a social world (Heath, Smith, and Young 2017).

If you've ever read *Charlotte's Web* (White 1952) to a group of third graders, you know that when Charlotte explains to Wilbur how he will go on to enjoy the beauty of the next season but she will not, children have to understand some science about the life span of a spider *as well as* the emotional implications of what it means to be mortal. Stories have the power to connect us to our humanity, while also teaching us all kinds of things about the world.

So, districts do need to invest in high-quality texts for knowledge building, both fiction and nonfiction. But they also need to commit to providing planning time to ensure that knowledge building—within and across grades—is neither haphazard nor dependent on individual teacher resources. Thoughtfully developed text sets will allow teachers to connect interactive experiences across read-aloud, shared reading, and even small-group instruction, building networks of knowledge from one text to another.

When built with an intentional mix of fiction and nonfiction, text sets will not only support content area knowledge building but also offer children opportunities to stretch into new understandings of the lived experiences of themselves and others. These text sets become an essential tool, equipping *teachers* for greater knowledge-building success and *students* for greater comprehension success.

A Short Summary of the Science

▲ The Simple View of Reading and Scarborough's Rope are two impactful models of reading that in combination illustrate the critical relationship between language comprehension and word recognition, two equally important aspects of reading.

▲ Reading comprehension is a reader's understanding and interpretation of what they read.

▲ Knowledge exists in many diverse forms and plays a number of varied roles in comprehension.

▲ Prior knowledge is all the knowledge a reader brings to school.

▲ Background knowledge is knowledge that can be applied to make sense of a text.

▲ Background knowledge is a strong predictor of comprehension of a text on that topic, even more so than reading proficiency.

▲ Teachers can intentionally help students build background knowledge about a topic before reading.

▲ Strategy instruction can't compensate for gaps in background knowledge.

▲ Background knowledge is more than just knowing facts; it serves a number of diverse purposes when it comes to comprehending text.

▲ Content area instruction can play an important role in building background knowledge for comprehending complex texts.

▲ Narrative texts, both fiction and nonfiction, can also build knowledge.

1

THE SIMPLE AND SCIENTIFICALLY SOUND SHIFT

▲ ▼ ▼ ▼ ▼ ▼

Prioritize intentional knowledge building as the driver of text experiences in literacy classrooms.

Recommendations for Making the Shift

More than any curriculum or program, you have the greatest influence on student learning (Hattie 2003). In this section, we offer suggestions for maximizing knowledge building while simultaneously developing reading comprehension. Brain-friendly instructional routines, like those in Table 1.3, offer a path to deeper and more meaningful learning for students. We describe several key instructional routines in the table, and then we zoom in on interactive text experiences and teaching with text sets. We will look more closely at reading comprehension strategies in Shift 2.

TABLE 1.3

HIGH-LEVERAGE INSTRUCTIONAL ROUTINES FOR HELPING CHILDREN BUILD BACKGROUND KNOWLEDGE

The What: *Routine*	The Why: *Purpose*	The How: *Example*
Intentional Planning for Knowledge Building	To carefully plan for knowledge building that supports content area standards and the unique interests of your students	Using curriculum planning resources (social studies and science standards, interest inventories, etc.) to map out a month-by-month plan of the knowledge-building topics you will explore and to inform text selection
Interactive Text Experiences	To build knowledge, to introduce new vocabulary, to think aloud about comprehension strategies, and to provide joyful shared experiences with texts	See "Zooming In on Interactive Text Experiences."
Teaching with Text Sets	To add on to students' mental Velcro (or establish new Velcro) on a specific topic by using texts with overlapping content and vocabulary	See "Zooming In on Teaching with Text Sets."
Kids Becoming Experts	To provide children the time, coaching, and resources they need to develop expertise on topics of interest to them	Sharing *I Survived the Great Chicago Fire, 1871* (Tarshis 2015) with a student who has recently learned that she is moving to Chicago, who then begins to explore the history of Chicago, gathering several fiction and nonfiction titles about the Windy City

continues

The What: *Routine*	The Why: *Purpose*	The How: *Example*
Building Knowledge with Images and Multimedia	To scaffold or activate students' knowledge before reading or to extend understanding after reading	Prompting students to watch a video clip (look at an image/ listen to an audio clip/etc.), to think about a text they recently read about the Dust Bowl and notice new information, vocabulary, and questions they have

Zooming In on Interactive Text Experiences

For many students and teachers, read-aloud is their favorite time of day, and for good reason. The power of read-aloud comes from the emotional spark created between the book and our collective experience with it. Through read-aloud experiences, we can immerse students in rich content, precise vocabulary, and complex language structures—all of which help build the language comprehension and background knowledge essential for proficient independent reading.

But read-aloud isn't the only interactive text experience at your disposal. Shared reading, which adds the element of students having their eyes on a copy of the text, can also offer rich opportunities for knowledge building, with the benefit of decoding practice. And while even small-group instruction and one-on-one conferences can also give students opportunities to learn new knowledge about the world, this "zooming in" section focuses on whole-group experiences.

Whether planning for read-aloud or shared reading, the way you shape the interactive text experience can help students build knowledge *and* practice the micro-skills that lead to comprehension. So, what are the considerations for planning a brain-friendly interactive text experience? We offer four factors to think about.

▲ **Choose a text.** Selecting worthwhile texts—texts that matter—is at the heart of powerful interactive text experiences. We recommend considering the quality, complexity, and utility of the texts you use (Cappiello and Dawes 2015). As you do so, try to select a range of texts that engage students by exposing them to content about the natural world, historical topics, and influential historical figures, as well as to stories with compelling characters that they can both identify with and learn from (Sims Bishop 1990). It would be difficult to overstate how much the information or story that makes the text compelling becomes the heart of the lesson, the driving force for a meaningful learning experience.

▲ **Get ready to read.** Plan the interaction that will take place *before* the actual reading begins. This may include identifying the reason you've chosen the book, activating or building background knowledge, and pre-teaching essential vocabulary (another form of background knowledge). Pre reading work may also include letting children know which strategies, or thinking moves, will be most important in the lesson. (More about thinking moves in Shift 2.)

▲ **Unlock the meaning of the text.** Make note of key stopping points you want to leverage *during* the lesson, making it interactive and guiding students to deeper understanding. This support will primarily focus on asking connected questions, modeling (thinking aloud), or practicing thinking moves (we zoom in on both of these in Shift 2). You might also include defining key vocabulary on the run, noticing sentences with complex language structures, stopping to study illustrations, and more. Your planned stopping points are opportunities to ensure that students actively engage with the content of the text, building both their cumulative understanding of the text and their toolkit of strategic moves.

▲ **Put it all together.** You've come full circle! This is the time to make space for students to put the pieces together to help them really understand the text. Engage students in reflecting on their experience with the text. What did they learn? How has their thinking changed? What surprised them? What's worth thinking (writing, reading, talking) about some more? With this step, you strengthen those Velcro connections, ensuring that students leave the experience equipped with new knowledge that will serve them down the road. This is also prime time to extend the text experience by connecting it to upcoming reading, writing, speaking, and/or listening experiences.

In Table 1.4 we illustrate the way an interactive text experience might unfold, considering the four parts described above. The example we provide is a read-aloud, but if you have a way for everyone to see the text using multiple copies or a document camera, it could easily be modified for an interactive shared reading lesson.

This sample read-aloud lesson focuses on the deep understanding that our actions matter when it comes to saving endangered animals. This lesson also gives students opportunities to *practice* previously learned reading comprehension strategies (see Shift 2), as well as to expand their vocabulary (see Shift 3). The lesson will typically stretch across a couple of days. Related work around the content can even spill into other parts of the day, such as science, vocabulary instruction, and independent reading.

TABLE 1.4

HOW AN INTERACTIVE READ-ALOUD LESSON CAN UNFOLD

Choose a Text: **What text will you select and for what reasons?**
Text: *Can We Save the Tiger?* by Martin Jenkins (2014) **The Deep Understanding:** Our actions matter when it comes to saving endangered animals. **Reasons for Choosing *This* Text:** • Complex language structures and rich vocabulary (language development) • Interesting information and engaging illustrations (engagement) • Introducing science focus: animals on the verge of extinction (background knowledge) • Supports "Keep a Close Eye on Comprehension" (comprehension strategies) (see Shift 2)
Get Ready to Comprehend: **How will you engage students in thinking before reading the text?** **(engagement, essential vocabulary, background knowledge)**
Show students the cover of the book and the title. **Activate and build knowledge:** "Let's switch on what we already know. What do you already know about why animals become extinct?" Jot on a chart any key terms that students mention. Ask them to listen for these words during the read-aloud.

Pre-teach essential vocabulary: Explicitly introduce the words *extinct*, *endangered*, and *species*—if they weren't already addressed in the last step.

Introduce the focus Thinking Move: "Today we are going to read a fascinating book, with a lot of information to sort through. We've been practicing how to Keep a Close Eye on Comprehension by monitoring, clarifying, and rereading when necessary. Today you will keep an eye on your comprehension by making sure you are really understanding this book as we read it. We'll stop along the way so you can have the chance to think about what you understand, as you build your mental model about endangered animals."

Unlock the Meaning of the Text:
How will you engage students in thinking during reading?
(think aloud, thinking moves, connected questions, vocabulary on the run)

(p. 2) Define *jostling* on the run: "Jostling means that everyone is moving around and bumping into each other."

(p. 2) Ask students how they can use context to figure out the word *coped*.

(p. 14, end of page) Think aloud: "It's time for us to check in on our understanding for this chunk of text about why the tiger has become endangered. Listen as I think about the important ideas: You know, as I look at the text, I notice the author gave us some clues about what parts are especially important. Do you see these big, bold words—'they're big . . . they're beautiful . . . they're fierce'? I'm thinking about how those adjectives are related. Hmmm . . . I remember that these are three reasons that tigers get killed and therefore have become endangered."

Turn and talk: "Share with your partner what you are understanding so far about why these characteristics of tigers—being big, being beautiful, and being fierce—put them at risk of getting killed." Listen in to partners and summarize responses for the whole group.

(p. 20) Define *crops* on the run: "Crops are plants that farmers grow in fields and then sell to make a living."

(p. 23, end of page) "Let's stop and check in on our understanding again. Turn and talk: What do you understand about how the partula snail became so endangered?" After students discuss with a partner, let some share their responses.

(p. 26) Think aloud about the context clues in this sentence: "They eat carrion—the bodies of animals that have already died—which means they do a very good job of keeping places clean."

(p. 30) Define *persuade* on the run: "To persuade is to talk someone into something."

(p. 38, end of page) "Let's check in on our understanding for this section of the text. Turn and talk: What big ideas sum up what you've learned in this chunk and how it is different from the previous sections? Is there anything you need to clarify at this point?"

(p. 46, end of page) "Now we are going to check in on our understanding one last time. What have you understood about why the kapapos almost became extinct and what people did to save them? Turn and talk."

continues

Put It All Together:
How will you engage students in thinking *after* reading the text?
(reviewing, reflecting, extending, and connecting;
arriving at the deep understanding)

Arriving at the Deep Understanding: "As you reflect on this text, what have you learned about how we are connected to endangered species? Turn and talk."

"Tomorrow we'll extend our thinking about endangered species with a shared reading from *A Wild Child's Guide to Endangered Animals* by Millie Marotta."

Other Options for Extending the Learning:

• Allow children to put dots on a world map or globe to show the locations of the endangered animals described in the book.

• Add vocabulary to a chart or a vocabulary word wall (see Shift 3).

• Let students reread the text in shared reading, small-group reading, or independent reading.

• Place books about endangered species in the classroom library.

• Use articles about extinction in shared and small-group reading lessons.

• Integrate Precision Words (Tier 2; see Shift 3) from the text into the week's vocabulary lessons.

• Encourage students to use new Precision Words in everyday conversation and to be on the lookout for them when reading.

For a PDF of a template of this lesson format, go to TheSixShifts.com/Downloads.

Of course, the read-aloud lesson above is just one example of how an interactive text experience can unfold. There are as many different ways to design a lesson as there are books worth sharing with children! The nuances of the lesson will change depending on the topic at hand, the unique characteristics of the text, and the ways you wish to connect the text to the learning experiences that come before and after reading it.

In Shift 2, we'll refer back to this lesson as we zoom in on thinking moves and on asking connected questions, the two main components of the "Unlocking the Meaning of the Text" portion of an interactive text experience.

Zooming In on Teaching with Text Sets

As you take stock of your classroom or school library, consider the core texts that drive your instruction. What topics and themes are most important for students to explore more deeply? Gather picture books, fiction, nonfiction, images, and multimedia that can enhance student knowledge and spark new directions for learning. As you look for connected titles, it is helpful to follow blogs like *The Classroom Bookshelf* (www.classroombookshelf.wordpress.com), where Katie and her colleagues Mary Ann Cappiello, Denise Davila, Erika Thulin Dawes, and Grace Enriquez write about recently released children's literature. Whatever your sources for finding titles, there are many ways to connect texts in your instruction and build the background knowledge and language comprehension children will need to read complex texts. The list below offers a few ideas:

▲ You **select nonfiction read-alouds** for the week that explore endangered animals, taking care to think about how the vocabulary and the ideas across the week build on one another.

▲ After reading aloud *Can We Save the Tiger?*, you **choose portions of the text to project with a document camera** to engage students in shared rereading and deeper thinking about the text. In particular, you challenge them to think about both sides of the issue.

▲ You **put extra copies** of *Can We Save the Tiger?* in the classroom library so that children can reread it during independent reading, making a meaningful and scaffolded connection to independent practice with this complex text.

▲ In groups of four, **children choose** an animal to read about from the gorgeously illustrated and beautifully written book *A Wild Child's Guide to Endangered Animals* by Millie Marotta (2019). Children spend time reading closely in groups, summarizing and questioning chunk by chunk. They then practice repeated reading individually, scaffolding each other as needed.

▲ For shared reading, you **read a poem** about tigers from *The Book of Animal Poetry* (Lewis 2012).

▲ Each child finds a poem about an endangered animal to practice during fluency practice (see Shift 5) and perform on Friday.

▲ You share the PBS Science Trek **video** *D4K: Endangered Animals*, approaching it as an **interactive text experience** by preteaching some vocabulary and pausing the video at key stopping points for discussion or to offer additional explanation.

▲ During small-group instruction, you give students **different but closely related articles** about endangered species and support them in connecting the articles to their growing body of knowledge about the subject.

▲ After an interactive read-aloud of *Can We Save the Tiger?*, your shared **close reading** for the week is the *National Geographic for Kids* article "Endangered Species Act: How This 1973 Law Protects Animals" (Hilfrank 2022). All students have their own copy to annotate.

▲ At the end of the day each day, you **read aloud a chapter** from *Endangered: A Sam Westin Mystery* (Beason 2016). You ask students to share any connections they make between the story and the information they are learning about endangered species.

▲ You begin to create a **collection of varied texts** related to endangered species **for the classroom library**, labeling it, giving it a place of prominence, and introducing it to students.

▲ You support students in identifying a specific endangered or extinct species of interest and in **building their own text sets** for meaningful reading practice in and out of school.

The work of building a text set involves looking for worthwhile texts—beautiful, accurate, culturally affirming, well crafted, and interesting—and then considering how they connect to one another. While you may cast a wide net for the texts you put into your independent reading library, you'll want the texts you choose for instruction to connect in ways that are more substantive. For example, if students are learning about endangered animals, then an article about threats to tigers will offer stronger connections and add more to the mental Velcro you established during the read-aloud than an article about how tigers hunt.

These collections of texts can include many genres, authors, and formats, providing students the opportunity to consider a topic from different perspectives. And the work of creating text sets isn't just for teachers. With support, children can pursue personal inquiry by systematically searching for and assembling collections of texts that help them explore any topic that piques or builds on *their* interest. These sets create stronger mental Velcro (Adams 2015; Hennessey 2020) with more hooks for attaching ever-expanding knowledge. One book can change a reader's life, but personal text sets have the capacity to reach more children, expanding their thinking in connected and intentional ways, while showing them how to pursue both knowledge and passion.

Meanwhile, Back in the Classroom . . .

After spending time gathering insights from colleagues in other districts and digging into some recommended professional reading, Ms. Yang and Mr. Jackson are energized by what they've learned. The connection between background knowledge and reading comprehension is strong, and they want to leverage it in service of more engaging instruction. As a result of their research, they've decided on three initial action steps.

First, they plan to revisit their grade-level social studies and science standards, identifying a few key topics to prioritize as they try out a revised approach to teaching comprehension. Second, they want to scour their own text collections and work with the media specialist to build text sets related to two upcoming content units, one about microbiology and one about economics. Finally, they will use these text sets for read-aloud and shared reading, replacing the texts from their reading curriculum during the time they are focused on each of the chosen content area topics.

When they meet with Ms. Lorrey, the school principal, to share their findings and ideas, she is predictably supportive. Like them, she is concerned about reading comprehension, and she appreciates their initiative. She even offers to dedicate funds to the purchase of new texts if they don't find what they need on the library shelves.

Feeling upbeat about their plan, Ms. Yang and Mr. Jackson set to work and quickly identify a specific topic for each of their two units: *viruses and bacteria* (microbiology) and *the production, distribution, and consumption of goods and services* (economics). They divide the work, with Ms. Yang researching the economics topic and Mr. Jackson searching for texts to support the microbiology exploration. They meet to share ideas, talk about books, and think about how to shift their practice.

Ms. Yang sees some possibilities for using the *Business Basics for Kids: Learn with Lemonade Stand: Profit and Loss* (FintekCafe 2021) as an entry point for some conversations about economics, even though the pictures are somewhat juvenile. She feels it is a nice primer for the more complex text, *Make Your Own Money: How Kids Can Earn It, Save It, Spend It, and Dream Big* (Jackson 2021), which also uses a lemonade stand to talk about profit and loss. She also brings in a copy of *National Geographic Kids Everything Money*

(Furgang 2013) and points out the profit-and-loss sections that directly align to the social studies standards. Since they won't have individual copies of the book for all of their students, they decide they will put some sections under a document camera for shared close reading.

For building knowledge about science, Mr. Jackson is thrilled with the ways that *Tiny Creatures: The World of Microbes* (Davies 2016) is both engaging and informative. He also reads aloud to Ms. Yang from *Horrible Histories: The Measly Middle Ages* (Deary 1998). They are both horrified by the ghastly accounts of history before hand-washing and are certain that students will be fascinated by the grotesque descriptions of the period in history when bacteria and viruses went unchecked.

As optimistic as they are about a different approach to text selection and building knowledge, they spend some of their time together thinking about how to preserve the application of the science and social studies content. They understand that not everything intrinsic to content area study can be integrated into reading lessons. They decide to dedicate most of the instructional time actually allotted to science and social studies to engage in some kind of hands-on exploration.

With her passion for social studies, Ms. Yang has found a simulation for students who will start pretend small businesses and work through various obstacles and advantages that will impact production and distribution. Mr. Jackson, with his years of teaching about microbes, knows some activities and experiments that make learning microbiology engaging. From using glitter to show how germs spread to growing yogurt cultures, he isn't short on ideas for extending students' learning beyond books.

Ms. Yang and Mr. Jackson feel like they are off to a good start, although they know there is still a lot to figure out. They understand that the payoff for their investment in knowledge building may not be immediately evident. They also realize that their text sets have some gaps, so they will still need to rely on their science and social studies texts, at least in the short run. Still, one thing *is* clear: their students will have more opportunities to build knowledge, while also practicing reading for deep understanding.

Questions for Reflection

Checking In with Yourself: Which of the misunderstandings in this shift did you find yourself thinking most deeply about? What might be the next step for you to help your students acquire more knowledge?

Building Knowledge: What drives your current plan for knowledge building? How do you leverage texts connected to science or social studies topics to intentionally build students' knowledge alongside reading and writing instruction?

Interactive Text Experiences: How do you utilize instructional contexts (read-aloud, shared reading, small groups, independent reading) to design interactive text experiences for students?

Text Sets: How can you develop text sets to support knowledge building across interactive experiences with texts? How will you connect experiences with both fiction and nonfiction texts, including both print and multimedia options?

Language Development: How do you make space for student conversation and contributions during interactive text experiences? Do the texts you select include rich vocabulary and varied language structures? How do you teach routines for student interactions?

Differentiation: Who do your current practices serve? Who will benefit the most from a shift in the ways you support knowledge building? Which techniques from this shift could you incorporate to differentiate your knowledge-building efforts?

Rethinking the Role of Strategy Instruction in Learning to Comprehend

SHIFT

2

Mrs. Bueno is hard working and well respected by her colleagues at Riverview Elementary. Her third-grade classroom is a match for her bright and cheerful disposition. When you walk into her classroom, one of the first things you notice is her carefully curated anchor charts that remind students of the strategies they can use to grow more independent as readers and writers.

Mrs. Bueno lives a rich reading life herself and wants her students to love reading too. Each day she teaches carefully planned lessons for both read-aloud and small-group instruction. She works to honor student strengths while also equipping them with strategies for comprehending increasingly complex texts.

Her Sunday nights are spent preparing for the week ahead, making deliberate decisions about which reading comprehension strategies to focus on with the whole class and which to highlight with each of her small groups.

Next week Mrs. Bueno is teaching students how to find the main idea and supporting details in nonfiction texts by paying attention to the title, headings, pictures, and repeated words. She'll model this main idea work across the week, beginning with a text about the history of pizza and then moving to an article on training dogs. She's chosen these texts for their many headings, subheadings, and captioned photos. She's made an anchor chart that uses a pizza-and-toppings metaphor to help students understand the relationship between the main idea and supporting details.

Once she's identified a strategy, Mrs. Bueno spends most of her remaining planning time looking for short texts that will provide students with opportunities to practice applying the particular strategy. Because engagement is a priority, she tries to keep things interesting by varying the topics students are reading about. But Mrs. Bueno has to admit that sometimes she feels overwhelmed by the open-endedness of the task. So many texts! So many possibilities! By the time she is finished, she often feels like her text choices represent a hodgepodge of disconnected topics without a common thread holding them together.

In fact, more and more, Mrs. Bueno finds herself wondering if the strategy instruction she has been providing is really paying off for all of her students. Her one-on-one conferences during independent reading time seem to confirm her concerns. While many students can name strategies, and even tell her which strategy they could use in a certain situation, few actually apply the strategies on their own consistently. And thinking about strategies—looking at anchor charts, deciding which strategy to use, trying something, trying something else—often distracts from the actual reading.

Students like Marcus and Aiyana still seem to "read" with little attention to the meaning of the text, despite all the reading comprehension strategies Mrs. Bueno has taught them. And even though she's spent lots of time teaching various text structures and how to spot them, her students still don't seem to understand that these structures can help them comprehend the text, rather than simply identify a compare/contrast paragraph by finding the clue words *similar* and *different*.

In her conversations with readers during conferences, Mrs. Bueno often struggles to get a meaningful interaction going. Questions like "What are you working on as a reader?" or "What strategies are you using to find the main idea?" lead to blank stares, compliant one-word answers, or wordy attempts to say something that sounds "right."

Mrs. Bueno finds herself longing for higher levels of engagement, deeper thinking, and more memorable learning for all of her students. Although she has always been committed to what she has understood to be "best practices," something just seems off.

A COMMON PRACTICE TO RECONSIDER

We treat comprehension strategies as though learning them is the point.

Mrs. Bueno knows that comprehension is the ultimate goal of reading instruction. But one thing that might be getting in her way is thinking of reading comprehension mainly through the lens of explicit strategy instruction.

Mrs. Bueno is not alone. Many of us have given strategies the biggest slice of the instructional pie when it comes to 3–5 reading. But it seems that this concentration on strategies, as important as they are, has sometimes distracted us from both the purpose of reading instruction and from other, equally essential contributors to reading comprehension.

Fortunately, it is possible to redistribute our instructional efforts. Cognitive scientists and psychologists have been studying the comprehension process closely for decades. And they have found some powerful understandings about how the human brain comprehends language. One important conclusion is that strategy instruction is essential, but *insufficient* (Duke, Ward, and Pearson 2021).

As it turns out, comprehension is complex and multilayered. In addition to needing both specific strategies and the kinds of knowledge we described in Shift 1, in order to comprehend, readers also need the following:

▲ Vocabulary knowledge (understanding word relationships, subtleties, and nuances)

▲ Executive function (task initiation, persistence, thinking flexibly, planning, reflecting, and knowing what to pay attention to)

▲ Working memory (temporarily holding on to bits of information until we can figure out how they fit; a type of executive function)

2

▲ Familiarity with language structures (understanding syntax, or the conventions of how a language works)

▲ Knowledge of text structures (noticing familiar hierarchies and relationships between bits of information)

▲ Verbal reasoning (using words to process information and to figure things out)

▲ Motivation (bringing energy to the reading experience)

To further illustrate what goes on in the reading brain *in addition to* using strategies, we share the Active View of Reading model (Duke and Cartwright 2021), illustrated in Figure 2.1. Notice that it includes both word recognition and language comprehension, as well as bridging processes (such as fluency and morphology) and active self-regulation (including executive function skills and strategy use).

As you study this model of a reader, look for the ways it overlaps with the Simple View of Reading and Scarborough's Rope (see Shift 1), as well as the ways it illustrates how comprehension depends on a lot more than just using strategies.

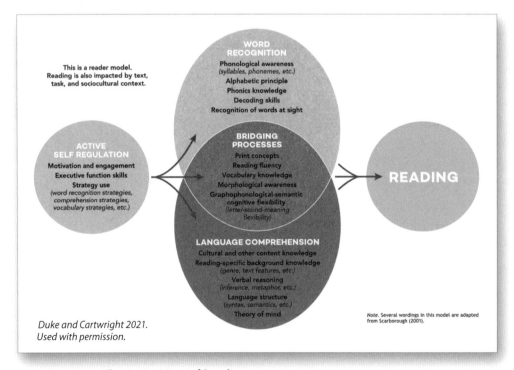

Figure 2.1 The Active View of Reading

Texts, especially complex texts, place a constellation of comprehension demands on a reader. And let's not forget that reading is influenced by what we each bring to a text from a life full of lived experiences. Figuring out how to teach reading comprehension requires both knowledge about the reading brain *and* a deep understanding of the children in front of us.

Clearing Up Some Confusion

Since the National Reading Panel Report in 2000 (National Institute of Child Health and Human Development [NICHD]), comprehension strategy instruction seems to have been the focus of, and often even has dominated, literacy instruction in many intermediate classrooms (Wexler 2019; Willingham 2012). While this focus has been driven by sincere efforts to help children learn to comprehend what they read, some of the ways we have overemphasized strategy instruction may actually make it harder for children to comprehend. Let's untangle five common misunderstandings about strategy instruction.

MISUNDERSTANDING:

Comprehension is a skill.

While it may seem logical to treat comprehension as a skill, reading comprehension is actually an *outcome* and not a single skill (Catts 2021–2022). Of course, the million-dollar question is, an outcome of what?

Well, as you now know, comprehension is an outcome of a lot of things, because comprehending written text is a multifaceted and interactive process by nature (Castles, Rastle, and Nation 2018; Perfetti and Stafura 2014). Children comprehend by drawing on an interplay between word-recognition and language comprehension skills, as well as other cognitive resources like attention and working memory, that are activated and applied to create the outcome—reading comprehension.

Together these processes help readers construct representations in their minds of what was originally in the mind of the author—ideas, events, information, experiences, and so on (Johnson-Laird 1983; Kintsch and van Dijk 1978; Zwaan and Radvansky 1998). These reconstructions are called mental models, and we build them whether we are reading to enjoy a novel or to understand how electricity works. So, understanding written language (and actually the spoken language first) involves constructing in our minds a model of the text's ideas. Of course, readers bring their own interpretations to the text, but still, the stronger this mental model, the better our understanding of what the author is trying to communicate.

Because of the way comprehension processes help us translate language into a model in our minds, whether we are reading or listening, Jan didn't have to be there when Ruby, Kari's pup, found a splintered chicken bone while out on a walk. The language Kari used to recount the moment—"Before I knew it, her jaws were clenched around it and she had all but swallowed it!"—helped Jan paint a picture—or build a model—of what happened, as Kari tried to prevent Ruby from swallowing her dangerous treasure.

Jan had a lot of relevant prior knowledge—she knows Kari, she's met Ruby, and she understands how risky eating a chicken bone can be for a dog. So Jan automatically filled in some gaps without having to stop and say, "I think I should make an inference now" or "Maybe I could use what I know to visualize what happened." With automatic use of her skills, Jan was able to build a robust (and probably pretty accurate) mental model of the event. What's more important, Jan could feel Kari's panic, even though Kari never explicitly described how she was feeling.

Now it's your turn. Here's another example. Read this little story and see how complete a mental model you can build and how your comprehension processes relate to that mental model.

> Victor did not come in on time today, which made Errin late.
> She was so embarrassed! But he felt really bad and apologized,
> so she didn't give him a hard time about it.

How well were you able to construct in your mind a model of this story? You probably noticed that we didn't give you enough information to develop a very complete representation. So, you could really only pull in whatever prior knowledge *seemed* relevant. Because of your automatic use of comprehension monitoring, you may even have had to slow down and intentionally engage some strategies.

For example, because Katie worked as a waitress during college, when she first read the sentences above, she assumed that the phrase "did not come in on time" referred to shift work. Basically, Katie filled in the inferential gaps with some *irrelevant* prior knowledge. This is what readers have to do when they can't build a complete mental model from the text, whether they can't read all the words, lack proficiency in other skills that lead to comprehension, or they just don't know enough about the topic.

But the story above is actually a text message from Jan's husband, Nate, who was watching a play rehearsal that day. It is about how their son, Victor, didn't come in on time with his lines, which threw off Errin, his castmate, causing her to stumble through her lines. Because Jan understood that the story was an anecdote from Victor's play practice, she was understandably able to build a stronger mental model than Katie.

As you can see, we automatically revise and adjust our mental models with each new bit of knowledge we acquire. So reading comprehension itself is not a single skill. It is an outcome that results from the interplay of lots of skills and processes that support us in building a mental model of what the writer was thinking.

MISUNDERSTANDING:

Students need a lot of different strategies to comprehend well.

It's true. Knowledge of comprehension strategies and when to apply them *is* important for making sense of text. But they are not more important than some other things, like background knowledge and working memory.

Daniel Willingham (2007) writes, "Teaching reading strategies is a low-cost way to give developing readers a boost, but it should be a small part of a teacher's job. Acquiring a broad vocabulary and a rich base of background knowledge will yield more substantial and longer-term benefits" (45).

Still you might be wondering, "What is the distinction between skills and strategies?" Well, depending on the text, some students seem to acquire and apply comprehension's mental processes, or thinking moves, with minimal effort—slowing down, rereading, predicting, making inferences—automatically.

But many students will need explicit instruction in how to use strategic thinking moves before, during, and after reading. They need to be taught some strategies (Block, Gambrell, and Pressley 2002; Duke and Pearson 2002). Shanahan (2018) describes such intentional strategy use as "actions that a reader takes to keep his/her head in the game."

Confused? You're not alone. In fact, researchers have been trying to tease out this distinction between strategies and skills—those not-automatic vs. automatic comprehension processes—for decades. More than thirty years ago, Pressley and colleagues (1989) explained, "The short term goal is to teach children facilitating cognitive processes and when to use them to read for understanding. The long term goal is to encourage 'automatic' application of appropriate strategies" (16).

But which reading comprehension strategies are supported by the science about how the brain comprehends? Well, there are a few strategic moves that really stand out in the research—actions that readers can take to help themselves comprehend. These are the moves that proficient readers constantly make but that less proficient readers may need more time to practice. In the list below, we've summarized six of these science-supported thinking moves, giving them kid-friendly labels, and providing a brief description of what they require of readers. We refer to them as the Strategic Six Thinking Moves, or the Strategic Six for short (illustrated list at TheSixShifts.com/Downloads).

The Strategic Six: High-Leverage Thinking Moves to Unlock Comprehension of Any Text

▲ **Switch on What You Know (Activate Prior Knowledge)** Think about the text and what you already know (or don't know) about the topic based on what you've read or experienced before (Alverman, Smith, and Readance 1985; Hattan 2019; Hattan and Alexander 2020; Hattan et al. 2015; Kostons and van der Werf 2015; Rowe and Rayford 1987).

▲ **Map the Text (Notice Structures)** Pay attention to structures, patterns, and features that reveal relationships within and across the text, including signals from text structure, paragraph structure, and even sentence structure (Boon et al. 2015; Burns et al. 2011; Denner, Rickards, and Albanese 2003; Englert and Hiebert 1984; Graves, Cooke, and Laberge 1983; Hall, Sabey, and McClellan 2005; Pyle et al. 2017; Williams, Hall, and Lauer 2004).

▲ **Keep a Close Eye on Comprehension (Monitor and Clarify)** Build understanding chunk by chunk (even phrase by phrase or word by word), stopping when meaning breaks down, and rereading to clear up confusion (Bauman, Sieffert-Kissell, and Jones 1992; Gambrell and Bales 1986; Hilden and Pressley 2007; Meier 1984; Wagoner 1983; Yeomans-Maldonado 2017).

▲ **Dig Below the Surface (Ask and Answer Questions)** Read actively—remain curious, and ask and answer important questions as you read (Cohen 1983; Davey and McBride 1996; Rosenshine, Meister, and Chapman 1996).

▲ **Fill in the Missing Pieces (Infer)** Pay attention to what the author is *not* saying, and add your own knowledge to make inferences— that is, fill in gaps—by visualizing what the author is describing, interpreting a metaphor, or making predictions (DeWitz, Carr, and Patberg 1987; Elbro and Buck-Iverson 2013; Elleman 2017; Graesser, Singer, and Trabasso 1994; Hansen and Pearson 1983).

▲ **Sum Up Core Ideas (Summarize)** Along the way, actively work to connect ideas and/or events across phrases, sentences, paragraphs, and sections. Connecting what is most important is essential for thinking, talking, or writing about the prominent ideas in the text in precise and thoughtful ways (Hare and Borchardt 1984; Rinehart, Stahl, and Erickson 1986; Taylor and Beach 1984; Winograd 1984).

The Strategic Six Thinking Moves is not a definitive list of every process that texts require of readers. Rather, it is a prioritized list of those processes (which draw on clusters of strategies) that research has consistently found to have high utility when it comes to helping readers make sense of text. Proficient readers use these strategies in automated, active, ongoing, recursive, and nonlinear ways *to help them comprehend*.

If children have adequate language comprehension skills, can fluently read the words on the page, and *want* to read, then also applying this handful of integrated thinking moves—whether they are automatic or require intentional effort—will equip them to build a robust mental model to help unlock the meaning of any text (Kintsch 1998; Zwaan and Radvansky 1998). Proficient readers use most of the Strategic Six *throughout* a "conversation" with a text to help them think more deeply about meaning.

The bottom line is that children simply don't need to learn a long list of reading comprehension strategies (Berkeley, Scruggs, and Mastropieri 2009; Elbaum et al. 2000; Fukkink and de Glopper 1998; Gajria et al. 2007; Rosenshine and Meister 1994; Rosenshine, Meister, and Chapman 1996; Suggate 2010; Talbott, Lloyd, and Tankersley 1994; Willingham and Lovette 2014). This is especially true if teaching all those strategies takes time away from efforts to build background knowledge, develop vocabulary, or learn about text structures, all of which are even more critical in the long run as texts increase in complexity.

2

MISUNDERSTANDING:

If my students can identify the basic underlying text structure, they've got what they need for understanding how ideas are connected across a text.

Most of the Strategic Six Thinking Moves probably feel familiar to you. But when it comes to leveraging text structure (Map the Text), there's often uncertainty or confusion about what's most helpful to students.

Since the arrival of the Common Core State Standards, text structure has received a fair amount of instructional attention, mostly aimed at helping children recognize signal words and the text structures they hint at. Teaching children to recognize such cues in text can be a great help to them. But when it comes to the organization of written language, there is more to consider than just a focus on signal words and the structures they connect. It's important that students are clear that the point of noticing structure is to make understanding the text easier, not just to be able to spot signal words or label the structures they indicate.

As an upper elementary teacher, you probably have taught your students about common text structures—chronological, sequential, cause-and-effect, compare/contrast, description, and problem/solution. These structures make it easier for us to process the relationships between chapters, sections, and ideas in the text so we can build a strong mental model.

For example, even when we've only read an opening sentence like the one below, we already see clues about the structure to come:

> *To make a peanut butter and jelly sandwich, first gather your ingredients: peanut butter, jelly, and two slices of bread.*

When you read the word *first*, as well as the context around it, you immediately start to anticipate an upcoming sentence that will probably include the word *second* or *next*. The signal word *first* cues up your expectation of a sequential text structure.

For children who are still learning how texts work, however, utilizing signal words or text features to notice the structure of a paragraph, or even the whole text, takes some intentional effort, and often some instruction. But this is not news to you!

There's also a whole lot more to learn about a text's structures than their common labels. As a matter of fact, there are at least three different levels of structure that build on each other in well-written texts and that can support readers in understanding what they are reading. (Did you notice that your brain got ready for a list of three nested ideas just now? You are tuning in to the structure to come!)

▲ **Language Structures: How a Sentence Is Organized**
Sentences are the first type of language structure that readers need to be able to unpack. And there's lots to know about the structure of sentences, or syntax. For instance, all sentences are made of words that connect to communicate a complete thought. Sentences also come in some predictable varieties, including declarative (*There is a lot to learn about sentence structure.*), imperative (*Please think about what you already know about sentence structure.*), interrogative (*Do you have any questions about sentence structure?*), and exclamatory (*Wow! This sentence structure stuff is more important than we realized!*).

And although some written sentences are very simple or very similar to the sentences we hear in spoken language all day long, many other written sentences—especially in rich, complex texts—have structures that communicate complex ideas, often in ways that are very different from everyday conversation (much like this sentence!). Studies have shown that an understanding of syntax—how words and phrases form sentences—is correlated with reading comprehension (MacKay and colleagues 2021; Mokhtari and Thompson 2006; Scott and Balthazar 2013; Sorenson and colleagues 2021). So, having the chance to regularly unpack—or dissect—interesting, unusual, confusing, or complex sentences is a promising way to help students strengthen their sentence-level comprehension and their overall reading comprehension.

▲ **Paragraph Structure: How a Paragraph Is Organized**
Just as the words in a well-crafted text are woven together in thoughtful ways to construct sentences, authors purposely weave sentences together into paragraphs. Paragraphs, as you know, are sections of a text dealing with a single theme or idea. Although it is possible to find plenty of paragraphs that follow the predictable pattern that includes an introductory sentence,

supporting details, and a concluding sentence, paragraphs also come in many less predictable varieties, and they range in length from one to many sentences.

And just as there are types of sentences, there are also specific types of paragraph structures. These have the same labels as whole-text structures, such as descriptive, sequential, cause-and-effect, comparison, and so on. Because you and I might know a lot about paragraph structures and the importance of being tuned in to them, it is easy to assume our students do too. But many may not. And since paragraphs are a collection of interconnected sentences that both communicate an important idea and bridge the preceding and following paragraphs, understanding their structure isn't so simple for most children. So, teaching them how to unlock the meaning of text includes helping them understand how paragraphs work and the role they play in a larger text.

▲ Superstructure: How a Whole Text Is Organized

Beyond sentences and paragraphs, every skilled author of a text has a plan for how a text is organized, or a *superstructure* (Sanders and Schilperoord 2008). If we can tune in to the superstructure and figure out what the author's organizational plan was, then we give ourselves a head start on being able to organize our *own* thinking as we work to digest the content of the text. For some texts, it's easy to spot and label the superstructure. Consider these examples:

- A book about the history of telecommunications that is organized around descriptions of a series of events (chronological superstructure)

- An article about the causes of global warming that is organized by harmful human actions and the damage they cause to the natural world (cause-and-effect superstructure)

- An article that compares octopuses and squid, offering a paragraph for each across a series of topics, such as habitat, predators, prey, life span, reproduction, etc. (compare/contrast superstructure)

Quite often, superstructures don't neatly fall into the conventional text structure categories. Nonetheless, every text (at least every well-written text) is built with a cohesive plan (skeleton) for how the content will hang together. Noticing how the sentences, paragraphs, sections, chapters, and features pull together in purposeful ways allows us to make better sense of the content within the text. It also gives us a bit of a frame for our brains to use to organize the important ideas from the text so that we can remember them. That is the superpower of superstructures!

In well-written texts, every word matters because of how it contributes to the nesting dolls of language—a word, inside a sentence, inside a paragraph, inside a section, inside a whole text. For example, you may or may not have noticed the structure we used to organize the book you are holding in your hands. But once you do, it will most certainly make it easier for your brain to understand and hold on to the information we share.

The superstructure of *Shifting the Balance* is organized around misunderstandings (problems) and high-leverage routines (solutions). More specifically, each chapter has the same predictable problem/solution skeleton, and all the parts of each chapter—from opening scenarios to short summaries of the science and closing scenarios—hang on this same skeletal frame. The only difference from chapter to chapter is the content we develop within this frame.

Yet on a paragraph or even section level, there's a bit of every type of structure in this book, from chronological scenarios to the cause-and-effect structure of some explanatory paragraphs.

As a proficient reader, you are constantly noticing how these structures relate to each other. This continuous processing of a text's structures—from its superstructure to its language structures—is like noticing how those language nesting dolls fit one inside the other.

So we don't want to *define structure* too narrowly when it comes to helping students understand the levels and varieties of organization within a written text. And we also don't want to *think* too narrowly about the teaching opportunities within a text by limiting our instruction to what is most obvious. If we do, we are likely to overlook the critical but subtle comprehension demands that warrant a reader's attention.

For example, let's look at Gail Gibbons's classic informational book *Alligators and Crocodiles* (Gibbons 2000). While our first instinct might be to look for opportunities to analyze the compare/contrast structure the title implies, right out of the gate comprehension of this particular text hangs on noticing and understanding a lot more about the way Gibbons weaves words together. In fact, as you can see in this first paragraph of the text, there aren't any of the obvious clues or key words that we would typically expect or teach children to look for in a compare-and-contrast text!

> *Something glides slowly through the water, barely making a ripple. It is well hidden and looks like a bumpy drifting log. Two eyes and a snout appear above the water. It is an alligator or a crocodile.*

This chronological opening paragraph is narrative, opening this informational book more like a story. Such narration is familiar and might seem easy enough to understand. But upon closer inspection, you might see some real complexities.

For example, notice that the very first sentence introduces "something," leaving us to remain alert as we read on to discover what that "something" is (readers have to navigate these *cataphoric* references frequently). Meanwhile, we have to infer that the thing gliding through the water is an animal because it has eyes and a snout, and we have to process the simile that compares the "something" (we don't yet know what) to a bumpy log. It's not until the last sentence that we find out that the "something" is either an alligator or a crocodile, which reveals that this paragraph is describing two things, not one!

You can see, even in this first paragraph of Gibbons's book, how the subtle and varied language structure demands within a text could sneak up on readers. Processing aspects of a text's structure—from the sentence level to the paragraph level to the superstructure—is integral to pretty much all the other Strategic Six Thinking Moves.

Of course, we can't explicitly break down every sentence for children, point out every cataphoric reference, or stop to highlight every signal word related to the text's structures. That would make the reading experience drudgery! However, we can select key structural elements—from sentences to the superstructure—to highlight and unpack, clustering those that are most important for unlocking the meaning of a particular text while drawing attention to the careful ways the author has organized the reading experience for the reader.

MISUNDERSTANDING:

Children need lots and lots of practice with each comprehension strategy.

Now that you know you don't have to teach dozens and dozens of comprehension strategies, you might be wondering *how* to effectively teach the strategic moves that really *do* matter. Of course, it certainly seems logical that students would need a lot of practice with each individual move over time to get better and better at applying them, doesn't it?

Well, as it turns out, not so much.

Research demonstrates that students can actually learn these thinking moves quite quickly. In fact, the benefits of teaching them can emerge with relatively little instruction (Willingham 2007). What's more, there just isn't much evidence that longer or more intensive strategy interventions help readers get stronger (Castles, Rastle, and Nation 2018). In other words, continued explicit instruction and practice do *not* necessarily make students better at applying comprehension strategies.

Strategy instruction is a little like vitamin C. It is tempting to think, "A little is good, so a lot must be even better!" But as intuitive as this idea may seem, neither vitamin C nor reading comprehension strategies work that way. Turns out, "just enough" is plenty.

So strategies don't need to be taught and taught and taught. Applying a reading strategy is not like learning to play the ukulele or cook, which are progressive skills that develop over time. Reading strategies are more like learning to fold a shirt. Once you know how to fold a shirt, you can fold a stack of them, and your knowledge of how to fold a short-sleeved shirt will help you figure out how to fold a long-sleeved shirt.

It is true that research *has* found that teacher-directed, overt, and explicit teaching of certain comprehension strategies (like the Strategic Six, listed on page 48) is effective—and this holds up for both for core classroom instruction in all grades (see the range of studies cited with the Strategic Six) and for interventions (Lee and Tsai 2017). So, readers will benefit most from explicit strategy instruction that is *limited* (a handful of lessons for each strategy should do), but *only if students have a reasonable level of reading fluency already in place* (Willingham 2006b).

If children don't seem to be learning a strategy, it may not mean that they need more practice. It may mean, instead, that they simply aren't fluent

2

enough with word recognition to free up working memory to utilize comprehension strategies. Or it may mean that they are missing some *other* piece of the comprehension puzzle, such as essential background knowledge. (Remember "Frustrated Knitter" from Shift 1?)

Research suggests that less is more when it comes to strategy instruction, which is good news, but the news gets even better. Not only can we spend less time teaching individual strategies, but research shows that we can also combine or "cluster" strategies by modeling, teaching, and practicing more than one strategy at a time (Okkinga et al. 2018; Palincsar and Brown 1984; Van Keer and Verhaeghe 2005). Clustering strategies—such as in the Strategic Six Thinking Moves—more closely replicates the actual act of reading, where skills are applied in integrated rather than isolated ways.

Whether strategies are applied individually or in clusters, remember the goal is comprehension, not strategy practice. And less time spent talking about strategies will leave more time for thinking and talking about the meaning of a worthwhile text.

MISUNDERSTANDING:

Text selection should be driven mostly by the strategies we plan to teach.

It can be easy to assume that if we are teaching fewer lessons on a specific comprehension strategy, then the most important factor in text selection should be finding the text that will give readers the most and best opportunities to practice that particular strategy. But that is not exactly true, as you probably guessed because you are tuned in to the way misunderstandings are a big part of this book's superstructure.

As you now know, explicit comprehension strategy instruction in small doses helps students learn them. But the purpose of reading is not to practice strategies; the purpose of reading is to *comprehend*. And once strategies are in our toolkit as skills, they're ready to simply *use automatically*. We don't need to teach mini-lessons on their use, take a quiz about them, or jot them on a sticky note to mark the place where we applied them. Rather, our attention can shift full-on to comprehension, with little conscious thought about which strategy to use when.

And here is some really promising news about text selection and subsequent strategy use. Most of the really important strategies—the ones you actually need to teach, such as summarizing, inferring, questioning, and monitoring—can be practiced with pretty much *any* well-written text! This means that we rarely need to go hunting for texts to match specific strategic moves. Instead, we can select excellent texts that address other objectives, trusting that the opportunities for applying the Strategic Six are already there—the implicit invitation of any good writing. We refer to these texts as *worthwhile texts*.

So, dedicating less time to searching for texts to support specific comprehension strategies gives you more time to think about what makes a text worthwhile in other ways, including how it meets the particular needs of the readers in front of you. Whether learning about the impact of natural disasters or enjoying the next book in a favorite series, different texts and contexts for reading make different demands on readers.

As you know from the Active View of Reading, attention and engagement also come to bear on comprehension and contribute to making a text worthwhile. This means that we need to be mindful of and responsive to students, not just with selection of content or strategies but also considering the lived experiences of individual students, and even this unique moment in history. Gholdy Muhammad (2020) writes, "Teachers need to be truth and knowledge seekers. They must know theory and practice and be masterful with science and the art of pedagogy" (15).

Once we understand these ideas about what makes a text worthwhile, we're positioned to take a *text-centric* (and student-centric) approach to our text selection, rather than a strategy-centric approach. Whether developing content knowledge across a topic or moving children with a powerful narrative, placing rich texts front and center can lead to better reading comprehension (not to mention more engaging lessons).

So, as you make text selections for interactive read-alouds, shared reading, and even small-group lessons, ask yourself: *Of all the texts in the world, why this one?* To help you make sense of this enormous question, you can use Table 2.1 (pages 58–59). It presents a list of considerations to make text selection especially purposeful and better meet the comprehension needs of students by shifting away from a strategy-centric approach toward a text-centric approach.

TABLE 2.1

WHY *THIS* TEXT?
QUESTIONS FOR SELECTING WORTHWHILE TEXTS

Knowledge

- What will students bring to this text in terms of prior knowledge?

- What background knowledge will students need to understand the text?

- How does the text support students' knowledge development—knowledge of the natural world, knowledge of history, knowledge of themselves?

- Does this text have a purposeful connection to other texts you will share with students?

Vocabulary

- Are there enough (but not too many) interesting and high-leverage words in the text that will probably be unfamiliar to many of your students?

- Are there context clues that can help students determine the meanings of some of the unfamiliar words?

- Will some of the unfamiliar words give students opportunities to apply their knowledge of morphology to discern their meanings?

Language

- Does the text include varied and interesting sentence structures?

- What are some of the key verbal reasoning demands of the text (figurative language, alliteration, rhyming, repetition, anaphoric or cataphoric references, etc.)?

- How is the text structured, both within and across paragraphs? Is it logical and cohesive?

Relevance

- How does the text connect to students' lived experiences?

- How does the text include representations of your students and of others?

- How does the text depict people, groups, ethnicities, and cultures in ways that are affirming?

- How does the text stretch students' thinking? Does it give students something to ponder or puzzle through?

Accessibility

- What supports, if any, will students need to develop a robust mental model of the text, and are these supports manageable without taking too much time away from reading the text?
- How does the text position students to be agentive as readers?
- Where in the text might some students need to intentionally practice any of the Strategic Six to help them understand it?

Engagement

- What about this book is likely to draw students in?
- What strong emotions, universal themes, or important ideas does the text communicate?
- What in the text will students be eager to think about and discuss?
- What about this text is likely to stay on students' minds long after the reading?

A well-written text, one that is worthy of children's time, gives them something important and engaging to think about. And strategy instruction can easily piggyback on learning content (Duke, Ward, and Pearson 2021), discussing a plot twist (Dymock 2007), or stepping outside of ourselves to understand the experiences of others. The thoughtful selection of worthwhile texts becomes the heartbeat of the reading classroom. These texts both invite and initiate children into the world of reading and the vast possibilities that await them as readers.

So, go ahead. Choose texts not because they match the strategy of the week but for other reasons that matter. Text selection is the vehicle for bringing your students the kinds of topics and experiences you—and they—care about, the ultimate marriage of reading's head work and heart work.

2

A Short Summary of the Science

▲ The Active View of Reading draws on the Simple View of Reading and Scarborough's Reading Rope, but it explicitly includes bridging processes (like fluency) and active self-regulation (including working memory).

▲ Comprehension is an outcome, not a skill.

▲ Readers have to build a mental model of a text to enable comprehension, and the better the mental model, the stronger the comprehension.

▲ Students need only a limited number of comprehension strategies.

▲ Students do benefit from some explicit strategy instruction, ideally as a complement to deep and engaging interactions with texts that matter for other reasons.

▲ A well-written text has multiple and interconnected layers of structure that a reader must understand.

▲ Comprehension instruction is more effective when it is text-centric (rather than strategy-centric), focusing heavily on giving students deep and engaging interactions with worthwhile texts.

▲ Effective strategy instruction mimics the ways proficient readers use strategies, which tend to be nonlinear, recursive, and clustered.

▲ Selecting a worthwhile text involves much more than thinking about which strategy the text is good for teaching, and the quality of a text plays a critical role when it comes to comprehension.

THE SIMPLE AND SCIENTIFICALLY SOUND SHIFT

Teach select comprehension strategies during meaningful interactions with worthwhile texts.

Recommendations for Making the Shift

In this section, we offer suggestions for making the most of knowledge development while simultaneously equipping students with a manageable number of clustered strategies for unlocking meaning.

Utilizing brain-friendly instructional routines, like those in Table 2.2 (page 62), is a path to maximizing learning for all students. We describe several key instructional routines in the table and then we zoom in on the Strategic Six Thinking Moves, asking connected questions, and reciprocal teaching.

2

TABLE 2.2

HIGH-LEVERAGE INSTRUCTIONAL ROUTINES FOR TEACHING READING COMPREHENSION STRATEGIES

The What: *Routine*	The Why: *Purpose*	The How: *Example*
The Strategic Six Thinking Moves	To integrate explicit comprehension strategy instruction into experiences with worthwhile texts chosen mainly to accomplish other specific purposes	See "Zooming In on the Strategic Six Thinking Moves."
Connected Questions	To ensure that the questions asked during an interactive text experience are thoughtfully connected in ways that support the ultimate goal of unlocking critical understandings from the text	See "Zooming In on Connected Questions."
Reciprocal Teaching	To collaborate with peers, teaching one another about content through self-selected application of specific strategies	See "Zooming In on Reciprocal Teaching."
Question Answer Relationship (QAR)	To teach children how to ask and answer questions by analyzing how the questions sort into four categories: Right There and Think and Search (In the Text); Author and Me and On My Own (In My Head)	Prompting students to read a short text about beetles and to write one of each kind of question and let their partners try to figure out (1) which of the four types of questions each one is, and (2) what the answer is
Noticing Text Structure	To teach children to notice the relationships between ideas and/or events within a text by tuning in to the word-, phrase-, sentence-, paragraph-, and section-level clues the author left to help them understand the way the text (parts and the whole) is structured	Taking time to study the table of contents to look for clues about the structure of the book and to begin to build a framework for how the book is organized

Zooming In on the Strategic Six Thinking Moves

Once you have selected a worthwhile text for your lesson, you will be ready to decide on the right-for-the-moment strategic moves that you can authentically model, or prompt students to practice, during your reading of the text.

In the table below, we share each of the Strategic Six Thinking Moves, an icon to help you and your students remember the move, and some sample think-aloud language demonstrating its utility and flexibility. Remember, these moves are not discrete but overlap and connect to each other. And since comprehension instruction is enhanced when we combine the use of multiple strategies in one text, these clustered processes can serve to powerfully deepen comprehension while also saving time.

TABLE 2.3

THINK-ALOUD LANGUAGE FOR TEACHING THE STRATEGIC SIX THINKING MOVES AS STRATEGIES

Strategic Six Thinking Move	Sample Teacher Language
Switch on What You Know (Activate Prior Knowledge) by thinking about the text and what you already know (or don't know) about the topic.	**Think Aloud:** "When I'm getting ready to read, it helps if I think about experiences I've had that are similar to what happens in the story. For example, when I look at the cover of this book, *Zack Delacruz: Just My Luck*, I infer from the illustration that he—probably Zack—is having a bad day. Maybe he's having a run of bad luck. I know how it feels to have a bad day and be really disappointed, so I already feel some connection to him. I'm curious to learn if his bad luck and mine have anything in common."

continues

Strategic Six Thinking Move	Sample Teacher Language
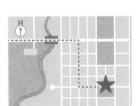 **Map the Text (Notice Structures)** by paying attention to patterns, signal words, and features that reveal relationships—on text, paragraph, and even sentence levels—across the text.	**Think Aloud:** "As I study the table of contents for this book about famous women across time, I can see that each chapter is dedicated to a different woman. As I page through a few of the chapters, I notice consistent headings in the chapter about each woman, for example, 'Early Life,' 'Interests,' 'Challenges and Opportunities,' and 'Contributions.' Now that I know each chapter is set up the same way, I have an idea of what kind of information I will learn about each of these women." **Think Aloud:** "As I read this part of the text—'This all seemed like great news; however, we were about to learn more'—I noticed the word *however*. When an author uses the word *however*, it is a signal that they are about to tell us something that contrasts or reveals a different side of the thing they said before. So when this author uses the word *however*, right after saying 'That seemed like great news,' it helps me get ready, or brace myself to learn why it really wasn't such great news after all."
 **Keep a Close Eye on Comprehension (Monitor and Clarify)** by building understanding chunk by chunk (even phrase by phrase or word by word), stopping when meaning breaks down, and rereading to clear up confusion.	**Think Aloud:** "Every time I read a sentence, my brain is thinking about what it means and how it connects to what I've already read. If I read something that doesn't make sense, I have to stop and *make* some sense of it by rereading and thinking some more. As I read this part about magnets and attraction, I notice myself saying, 'Huh? Something is not making sense to me.' I need to back up and reread. I might even back up a few sentences or study the diagram for clues. Maybe I missed something earlier that was an important idea that is related to this one and would have helped me understand." **Think Aloud:** "When I first read the sentence, 'She shoved a handful of currants in her pocket to snack on later and slipped out the back door,' I was thinking, 'What? How could you slip a *current* in your pocket?' Then I realized this word is spelled differently and it must have a different meaning than current, like the way water moves. I had to ask myself, 'What else could this word mean?' and use context to help me sort out that currants are something small that you eat."

Strategic Six Thinking Move	Sample Teacher Language
 **Dig Below the Surface (Ask and Answer Questions)** by reading actively, remaining curious, and asking and answering important questions as you read.	**Think Aloud:** "Hmm. I'm noticing that in this sentence, 'He was never quite sure what had happened that day,' the author has left lots of missing pieces for us to fill in as we read more. So, I'm asking myself who 'he' is, what day it was, and what had happened on that day. I will have to pay close attention as I read and notice when the author fills in these gaps in information. It's kind of like solving a puzzle, and it really makes me want to keep reading." **Think Aloud:** "The title of this book, *Can We Save the Tiger?*, had me wondering about that question from the start and all through the book. Now that I'm at the end, I need to really think about this question, asking myself if there is anything I can do to help save endangered species."
 **Fill in the Missing Pieces (Infer)** by paying attention to what the author is *not* saying and adding your own knowledge to fill gaps by visualizing, interpreting figurative language, or making predictions.	**Think Aloud:** "The fact that they always take the time to boil the water before using it for bathing or cooking is making me think that they believe the water is unsafe or contaminated. The author doesn't tell me that their water isn't clean enough to drink, but I know that boiling water kills germs, so I can infer." **Think Aloud:** "Wow! When I read this part about the argument between Sabrina and her sister, I could just picture the whole thing. And when I go back and reread, I realize that the author had been leaving little clues so that I could infer that tension was rising between them. I had to fill in some missing pieces, like when Desiree said, 'That's fine!' I had to infer that it really *wasn't fine*. Sometimes each of the missing pieces we need to fill in is small, but they add up to an important moment in the story."

continues

2

Strategic Six Thinking Move	Sample Teacher Language
Sum Up Core Ideas (Summarize) by actively working to connect and prioritize ideas and/or events along the way so you can think, talk, or write about the text in a few precise and thoughtful statements.	**Think Aloud:** "Now that I've read through the text, I'm going to page through the book and use the pictures, captions, and the bolded words to help me review the important ideas and vocabulary before I sum up the core ideas." **Think Aloud:** "After I read a story, it really helps me to think about what I can learn from the characters. The main character, Dakota, faced so many obstacles, but somehow found the courage to keep trying. Persistence is clearly an important theme of this book, because the author keeps giving examples of when Dakota persisted with something that I probably would have given up on."

So, grab a worthwhile text, and spend some time noticing the Strategic Six Thinking Moves that you automatically make as you read it. As you do, consider which ones can serve as the most helpful keys to unlock the explicit (literal) and implicit (inferential) ideas in the text. You will have to be very selective! Proficient readers make many more strategic moves than you can explicitly tackle in a single text. Choose only the most critical opportunities to teach, through modeling and thinking aloud. But remember, explicit instruction in the Strategic Six should diminish over time, leaving more time to discuss the meaning of the text.

As you prepare for the lesson, if you intend to teach one of the Strategic Six, make a note to yourself about the one you will highlight and place a sticky note directly in the book as a reminder. If you're new to thinking aloud, you might even want to script out precise language. A note like this can be a lifesaver when you're in the middle of the lesson and want to remember all the intentional instruction you planned to include. And remember, while the table above offers language for thinking aloud as you model a thinking move, most interactive text experiences will primarily focus on knowledge building, using the Strategic Six *in service of* new understandings and learning from the text, as was illustrated in the lesson in Shift 1.

Zooming In on Connected Questions

Whether you rely on Bloom's Taxonomy, Webb's Depth of Knowledge, or some other structure to help you craft quality questions, one helpful design hack is to connect your questions around a key understanding that you want students to reach. Each individual question might be well written, but if the questions don't work together to achieve the comprehension purpose of the lesson, then the interactive text experience is likely to come up short. As a tool for intentionally supporting students in unlocking a deep understanding of the content or story at hand, connecting questions helps you design a cohesive lesson for your limited instructional time.

As a guide to help you with the work of connecting questions for a text, we offer the following process. This is the path we followed to craft the lesson in Shift 1. Alongside these steps, you may want to review the lesson for the book *Can We Save the Tiger?* from pages 32–34. Look for the ways we connected the questions and how they support students in reaching the lesson's deep understanding—that our actions really do matter when it comes to saving endangered animals.

▲ **Study the Text** Once you have selected a worthwhile text, it's time to really dig into it, thinking deeply about its meaning. This involves reading it carefully—even multiple times—thinking about how it is built and the momentum of the text from beginning to end. Where are there shifts in the text? Where do ideas, information, or events connect, build, and culminate in insight or resolution? How are themes, ideas, or content related in obvious or subtle ways? This is also the time to work metacognitively and notice the text features, text structures, and kinds of knowledge *you* use to understand the text.

▲ **Choose a Deep Understanding** As you are thinking deeply about the text, consider the important insights or information that make reading the text worthwhile. In a few words, sum up what makes the text truly powerful, inspiring, or informative. We refer to this kernel as a *deep understanding*. If it is a narrative text, a deep understanding may be a theme. If it is an informational text, a deep understanding may be a main idea. Oftentimes, the deep understanding is the idea that you hope will stay with children— even change their thinking—after the text has been read. Most worthwhile texts have more than one important message that can serve as a deep understanding. Trust yourself to select one that represents the significant learning you want students to take away from the text experience. By doing this work at the beginning of your planning, you set yourself up to design your lesson with the end in mind, which will be important when it comes to narrowing the questions you plan to ask students.

▲ **Craft Connected Questions** Once you have settled on a deep understanding, it's time to craft a series of questions that will serve as breadcrumbs for students. These questions get at the essential insights or information that students *must* understand in order to get the most from the text. To connect your questions for each portion of the text, think about which ideas, information, or knowledge is essential for reaching the deep understanding. While these text-dependent questions will likely include a mix of both explicit and implicit questions, what is most important about the questions is not the specific type but that each one helps get at some *preliminary* understanding that is essential in eventually arriving at the deep understanding. Basically, these questions help children hold on to the accumulating and connected ideas so that they can, in the end, zoom out and understand the cumulative meaning of the text.

Of course, the quality of the questions we ask is always directly related to the quality of the text, and being able to answer them depends on our ability to engage the Strategic Six Thinking Moves while reading. In a worthwhile text, there is always more to talk about than time will allow. The deep understanding in your lesson is a thread pulling your planning together and ensuring that the interactive text experience has a focus.

Once again, sticky notes will help you remember where you want to stop and what you want to say. Pair your questioning with simple routines—turn-and-talk, stop-and-jot, stop-and-sketch, or think-pair-share—to ensure all students get a chance to express their thinking. These routines allow you to involve *everyone* in the thinking work—rather than just calling on one student at a time—and they are part of what makes the text experience interactive and engaging, ultimately helping to make learning stick.

Zooming In on Reciprocal Teaching

Reciprocal teaching is a powerful way to teach students to both comprehend and monitor their comprehension (Hattie 2009; Oczkus 2010; Palincsar and Brown 1984; Palincsar and Klenk 1992; Rosenshine and Meister 1994). The process involves students becoming the "teacher" for a partner or a small group and leading a dialogue about the reading (especially an informational text), systematically including summarizing, questioning, clarifying, and predicting as they work through the text chunk by chunk (Palincsar and Brown 1984).

Depending on the text, reciprocal teaching may draw on all of the Strategic Six Thinking Moves. Table 2.4 identifies connections between the strategies in the reciprocal teaching process and the Strategic Six. To get started, the "teacher" identifies a segment of a larger text to take through the process. When students work through all four strategies with their segment, they move to the next portion of text, and so on.

TABLE 2.4

THINKING MOVES AND "TEACHER" ACTIONS IN RECIPROCAL TEACHING

Reciprocal Teaching Strategy	Action of the "Teacher" and/or "Students"	Frequency	Connections to the Strategic Six Thinking Moves
Summarizing	Summarize the segment in a single sentence.	Every text segment	Sum Up Core Ideas, Map the Text
Questioning	Ask a question that gets at the heart of what has been learned in the segment.	Every text segment	Switch on What You Know, Dig Below the Surface
Clarifying	Point out anything that was confusing or otherwise requires clarification.	When there is something to clarify	Keep an Eye on Comprehension
Predicting	Make a prediction about the text ahead.	Whenever a prediction is viable	Switch on What You Know, Map the Text, Fill in the Missing Pieces

Adapted from Palincsar and Brown 1984

2

Reciprocal teaching is so named because it begins with explicit teacher modeling and gradually turns responsibility for these four steps over to students, who then take turns being the "teacher" with partners or in small groups. A four-square grid, index cards, or sticky notes in four colors can support students in organizing their thinking when they are eventually ready to teach each other. Table 2.5 illustrates a one-page, reusable four-square grid slid into a page protector. The colored squares represent sticky notes—one for each part of the task—attached to the outside of the sleeve. For each chunk of text, students capture their thoughts on the designated sticky note for each strategy. You can get a copy of this four-square grid at TheSixShifts.com /Downloads.

TABLE 2.5

STUDENT GRID FOR PRACTICING RECIPROCAL TEACHING

Summarize	Clarify
Human actions have an effect on animals.	Had to figure out what "harbor" means. Used the caption and the picture.
Question	**Predict**
Which animals are completely gone because of climate change?	I think the author is going to tell us some things we can do to prevent climate change.

There is substantial research that confirms the benefits of reciprocal teaching (Oczkus 2010; Okkinga et al. 2018; Palincsar and Brown 1984; Rosenshine and Meister 1994). It positions students to support one another in their meaning-making process, while also serving as a form of strategy clustering. However, there are some nuances to implementing reciprocal teaching. We've elaborated on reciprocal teaching tips in a PDF you can download at TheSixShifts.com/Downloads.

Meanwhile, Back in the Classroom . . .

Because of ongoing concerns about last year's third- and fourth-grade reading comprehension scores, the school improvement leadership team has recently provided a series of professional development sessions focused on more intentional practices for knowledge building across the day. Although many of her colleagues have expressed frustration about "one more change" to instruction, Mrs. Bueno has found herself intrigued. In light of her recent wondering about the effectiveness of some of her own strategy instruction, she felt the information came at the perfect time.

In fact, Mrs. Bueno, a voracious reader herself, has found this change a breath of fresh air. Planning for more intentional knowledge development in synergy with research-based reading strategies actually makes a lot of sense to her. And it even seems to save her some planning time—a bonus!

While her colleague next door is uncertain about "jumping from one strategy to the next" within a text, Mrs. Bueno is relieved not to have to jump from one *topic* to the next. She is also finding that drawing on a variety of strategies during a single interactive text experience simply feels more authentic and sets her up to support a deeper understanding of both individual texts and the related ideas across lessons.

Mrs. Bueno's focus has shifted away from overteaching a long list of reading comprehension strategies to more intentionally choosing which particular strategies best support the comprehension of texts that are truly worthwhile for her students. For example, rather than teaching strategies for finding the main idea in short texts that are unrelated to one another, this week she built a text set tied to her science unit on food webs. She included relevant and engaging informational texts, narrative nonfiction, fiction, and even poetry.

Her shifts in planning have also trickled into her practices for conferring with readers. Now, rather than zeroing in on their strategy work, Mrs. Bueno starts by checking in on their comprehension (and engagement). Strategy use has become secondary to the meaning it helps children unlock. She knows that if a student can really talk deeply about a text, then that student is certainly using comprehension strategies already. She's also noticing that her students are more eager to talk with her when she says things like, "Wow! *The Great Shark Escape!* What is this book making you think about?" rather than asking, "What is the main idea of this text?" The change in her intention seems to be a subtle shift with a big payoff.

Last week when Mrs. Bueno said to Mateo, "Tell me about your favorite characters so far. What makes them tick?" he excitedly told her all about the main character, Gavin, whose bike was stolen. Mateo went on to reveal many inferences he was making about what might have happened to Gavin's bike and even offered some text evidence to support his thinking.

Best of all, interactive text experiences for the whole class, both read-aloud and shared reading, have become portals for deep learning about historical events, the natural world, and what it means to be human. And it's clear that her students love developing expertise! They seem more energized and engaged during text experiences and therefore have more meaningful conversations with each other during turn-and-talk. She's also noticing that her students ask more questions and follow more paths into their own inquiry, as they seek out texts to feed their curiosities and interests.

Mrs. Bueno's class has been bitten by the knowledge bug, and it's contagious. Her students are learning more, comprehending more, and finding greater joy in the process.

Questions for Reflection

Checking In with Yourself: Which of the misunderstandings in this shift did you find yourself thinking most deeply about? What might be the next step for you when it comes to comprehension strategy instruction?

Mental Model: How does the idea of building a mental model fit in with your previous understandings about how children comprehend? How might you help students build and strengthen the mental models they form as they read?

Comprehension Strategies: Do you find yourself overteaching or underteaching comprehension strategies? How might you shift your instruction to focus on the Strategic Six Thinking Moves? Which of these moves feels comfortably familiar? Which do you anticipate to be most challenging for children to turn into habits? How will you explicitly teach those moves that need practice?

Text Structures: Which layers of text structure—sentences, paragraphs, or superstructure—are you already including in your instruction? Which of them might need more attention, and what next steps will you take?

Taking a Text-Centric Approach: What processes currently drive your text selection? How might you shift your planning to apply a more text-centric (vs. strategy-centric) approach? What factors beyond strategy instruction are priorities for you in selecting texts?

Differentiation: Who do your current practices serve? Who will benefit the most from a shift in practice? Which techniques from this shift could you incorporate to differentiate strategy instruction to meet the diverse needs of your students?

Recommitting to Vocabulary Instruction

When you walk by his fifth-grade classroom, you'll often find students in the gathering space in rapt attention while Mr. Heitzman reads aloud from his rocking chair. Mr. Heitzman has a long-standing love of literature. He treasures the lyricism of good writing and the power of words to wake up our senses. He reads aloud from a picture book each morning and from a novel each afternoon. He's particularly committed to selecting books that feature topics and characters that represent our diverse world. This year his students have heard books like the Newbery Medal–winning *When You Trap a Tiger* by Tae Keller (2020) and the fantasy series *Amari and the Night Brothers* by B. B. Alston (2021). He has an enviable classroom library that he has painstakingly organized by genre, topic, series, and author.

But lately Mr. Heitzman has noticed that although his students seem interested in learning new words during read-aloud, in small-group instruction some students, like Amal and Maggie, seem to ignore unfamiliar vocabulary by glossing over words, even when it means they don't understand what they are reading. He's pretty sure that if they're skipping words when they read orally, they're doing the same thing during silent independent reading. He also notices that for many students it's rare that they incorporate rich and interesting vocabulary words into their written responses or conversations.

Mr. Heitzman recognizes that some of his students, like Desmond and Fatima, know and use more sophisticated vocabulary, because they came into his classroom with those stores of words in place. But he's feeling uncertain about the ways in which his own instructional decisions have supported students like Dean and Vanessa, whose language comprehension is less developed. He also worries that he may be missing opportunities to support the emerging bilingual learners in his class.

Mr. Heitzman wants to be more intentional about making vocabulary instruction purposeful and engaging for *all* students. He wants his students to have tools for understanding what words mean in context, and he wants them to use more advanced words when speaking and writing.

He wonders if explicit instruction in vocabulary could be effective, but isolated vocabulary drills are definitely not his style. He's also not interested in vocabulary workbooks or spending a lot of time at the photocopier each week duplicating vocabulary worksheets that are boring for students and will just end up in the recycling bin after the lesson.

Instead, he's interested in exploring other, more engaging options. He wants manageable instructional routines that will breathe new life into word learning for his students. But other than thinking aloud about words during read-aloud or having students look up definitions, he's just not sure where to start. With so many words in the English language, and so little time to teach them, Mr. Heitzman wonders how he can maximize the impact of word-learning instruction for all of his students.

He decides to enlist the help of the school's literacy coach. Together they make a plan to dig into the research on vocabulary instruction to see what they discover.

A COMMON PRACTICE
TO RECONSIDER

▼ ▼ ▲ ▼ ▼ ▼

We rely on implicit or "in-the-moment" instruction as the main way to grow students' vocabulary knowledge.

Vocabulary knowledge influences every aspect of a child's life. This isn't news to you. Perhaps you've seen the impact that having a rich lexicon has on students' ability to more easily understand whatever they are learning in science, social studies, and math. Or maybe you've noticed the ways that a broad vocabulary helps students relate to the characters in stories and make inferences about their actions. And, no doubt, you worry about the obstacles some of your students with less robust vocabularies face, not only in their reading comprehension but also in their writing and speaking.

Of course, the goal of vocabulary instruction is not to learn words for their own sake. The goal is for students to apply knowledge about words and their meanings to better understand what they're reading and to expand the possibilities for expressing their own ideas.

For example, one day when Katie was driving with her youngest son to school, they heard a car honk behind them after the light turned green. Matthew proclaimed, "Gosh, Mom, the audacity of that driver!" Katie later realized he had learned the word *audacity* by listening to his favorite podcast, *Myths and Legends*, where the host of the podcast frequently uses the word *audacity* in his retelling of ancient stories. Matthew had multiple exposures to the word and knew it was the right word to use when confronted by the honking of an impatient driver. The audacity!

And Matthew's vocabulary knowledge will do more than impress his mother. Vocabulary gives us access to the mystery and magic of language.

A substantial body of research shows that strong vocabulary fuels comprehension (Cromley and Azevedo 2007; Wagner and Ridgewell 2009), and vice versa—strong comprehension actually helps children acquire more vocabulary (Baumann et al. 2002; Moats 2004; Spencer and Wagner 2017; Stanovich 1986).

In fact, it's a true vocabulary-chicken-and-comprehension-egg situation. Recent research shows that vocabulary can account for as much as 80 percent of students' scores on reading comprehension assessments (Reutzel and Cooter 2015). This makes sense because if you don't know the meaning of enough words, you will come up short when it comes to comprehending what you're reading.

This is in part because as you stop to problem-solve using context, each unfamiliar word slows down your reading process and shifts your focus away from meaning. Of course, we can learn new words as we read, using context to fill in the understanding gap. But when students experience a lot of this start-stop process during reading, it can interfere with active comprehension, demotivate them, and put a ceiling on their access to complex texts. When there is too great a mismatch between students' vocabulary knowledge and the complexity of the text, using context clues isn't enough to help them understand what they are reading (Chall, Jacobs, and Baldwin 1990).

The limits of children's vocabulary and this diminishing support of context appear to contribute to a phenomenon called "the fourth-grade slump" (Chall, Jacobs, and Baldwin 1990). Research suggests that this "slump" has roots in the acquisition and use of vocabulary words (or lack thereof) and the far-reaching effects of insufficient word knowledge as texts become increasingly complex in the intermediate grades.

So how can we help children build the robust word stores they need for success in school and in life? This question is definitely on Mr. Heitzman's mind. And although he loves those in-the-moment experiences when a read-aloud spurs spontaneous vocabulary learning, he isn't really sure how to extend vocabulary instruction beyond teaching words on the fly.

Clearing Up Some Confusion

We've taken a fresh look at the body of science around vocabulary instruction with an eye toward any missed opportunities. In the sections that follow, we share some common misunderstandings, some new possibilities, and some current practices that might benefit from a bit of freshening up. Let's dig in.

MISUNDERSTANDING:

Engaging students in lots of rich classroom conversation across the day is the most important part of their vocabulary development.

Researchers agree that a lot of vocabulary growth happens in a child's lifetime through simple exposure and practice—like Katie's son using the word *audacity*—rather than direct teaching (Nagy and Anderson 1984; Nagy, Herman, and Anderson 1985; Sternberg 1987). This is especially important before children become fluent readers. So, when engaging in conversations with children throughout the day, you'll want to regularly and intentionally use sophisticated language. Their brains are, after all, naturally wired for language learning (Adams 1990; Lyon 1998; Moats and Tolman 2009; Wolf 2007).

But as important as classroom conversation is, success with academics depends on more than conversation. Many researchers have provided evidence that once children develop some reading fluency, the prime contributor to individual differences in children's vocabularies is differences in reading volume, even more so than conversational language exposure (Duff, Tomblin, and Catts 2015; Hayes and Ahrens 1988; Nagy and Anderson 1984; Stanovich 1986). And you've likely noticed that as children grow into experiences with longer and more sophisticated texts, such as when you read aloud a short story that really stretches them, they begin to encounter more and more words that they *haven't* been exposed to through daily conversation.

This, as it turns out, is because written language is typically a richer source of new words than spoken language. And as children move beyond learning to decode, vocabulary development starts to depend more and more on reading volume (Nagy, Herman, and Anderson 1985; Sternberg 1987).

Table 3.1 on page 80 shows the percentage of rare words by type of text (Hayes and Ahrens 1988). We're pretty intrigued by what it reveals! For instance, when you study the table you'll notice that there are over three times as many rare words in newspapers as in television shows. And even comic books have more than three times as many rare words as a conversation between college-educated friends!

TABLE 3.1

RARE WORDS (PER THOUSAND)

Printed Text	
Newspapers	68.3
Popular magazines	65.7
Comic books	53.5
Adult books	52.7
Children's books	30.9
Television	
Prime-time adult television	22.7
Prime-time children's television	20.2
Adult speech	
Expert witness testimony	28.4
College graduates' talk with friends	17.3

Hayes and Ahrens 1988

Pretty remarkable, don't you think? This research illustrates that the lexical richness students encounter through texts is a vital source of new vocabulary. And subsequent research continues to confirm that print material contains more low-frequency (rare) words than spoken language does (Cunningham 2005) and that there is an increase in the complexity of words in texts written for the middle grades and beyond (Carlisle, Hiebert, and Kearns 2015; Hiebert, Goodwin, and Cervetti 2018; Nagy and Anderson 1984).

It turns out that vocabulary knowledge is a lot like the mental Velcro we discussed in Shift 1. It has a sticky quality to it. Every time you have an encounter with a word it connects to your existing networks of words that are constantly growing. So children like Desmond and Fatima from Mr. Heitzman's class, who come to school with large vocabulary stores, have a real advantage when it comes to building background knowledge and learning new vocabulary. Rupley, Logan, and Nichols (1998/1999) explain that "vocabulary is the glue that holds stories, ideas, and content together" and that "it facilitates making comprehension accessible" (117). In this way, vocabulary is partly an outcome of reading comprehension, and reading comprehension is partly an outcome of vocabulary knowledge (Rupley, Logan, and Nichols 1998-1999). In fact, strong reading comprehension depends on already understanding a whopping 90–95 percent of the words in a text (Hirsch 2003; Laufer 1989; Nation and Waring 1997)!

So, knowing that written language in its many varied and wonderful forms is an even richer source of vocabulary exposure than most conversations, we certainly want to lean into high-quality texts as an indispensable tool for word learning and an investment in future reading comprehension. This includes leveraging word-rich texts for interactive text experiences, such as read-aloud and shared reading (remember Shift 1?) and independent reading (more on this in Shift 6).

MISUNDERSTANDING:

I don't really need to *teach* vocabulary if I make sure students get lots of interactions with great books.

We hope we have made clear that we, like Mr. Heitzman, are certainly big fans of read-aloud! In fact, for many reasons, we find ourselves a bit giddy when the value of reading aloud to children—of any age—is affirmed by research (Lennox 2013; Neuman, Copple, and Bredekamp 2000).

And research also clearly supports incidental exposure to words—both through conversation and through interactions with books—as a critical opportunity to build word knowledge and develop word awareness (Schwanenflugel, Stahl, and McFall 1997; Stahl, Richek, and Vandevier 1991). But evidence also points to a need for students to have the chance to learn vocabulary through more explicit instruction (Beck, Perfetti, and McKeown 1982; Marulis and Neuman 2013; NICHD 2000; Stahl 1986; Stahl and Fairbanks 1986). As McKeown explains (2019), "Many learners accumulate high-quality vocabulary knowledge independently, through wide reading and rich language environments that provide abundant practice with words and language forms. However, instruction in vocabulary provides a more efficient way of getting that job done" (466).

Maybe you're wondering whether implicit or explicit vocabulary instruction is a better use of your time. Well, it doesn't seem to be an either/or question. It's both/and. In fact, there is no consensus on the single best, research-based way to teach vocabulary. Rather, a substantial body of research suggests that it is best to use a variety of direct and indirect methods to broaden students' vocabulary (NICHD 2000; Stahl and Fairbanks 1986), especially when that vocabulary is connected to what students are going to read (Cervetti et al. 2023).

The list below presents four brain-friendly methods for vocabulary instruction, which will ensure that your classroom provides a rich variety of word-learning opportunities (Beck, McKeown, and Kucan 2013; Graves 2000; Hennessey 2020; Honig, Diamond, and Gutlohn 2018). Notice how this list includes both direct (explicit) and indirect (implicit) instructional methods, ultimately helping you make the most of your limited instructional time.

▲ Incidental exposure to words

▲ Word awareness and wordplay

▲ Explicit teaching of high-leverage words from texts before reading

▲ Explicit instruction in ways to figure out word meanings

Research shows that children learn more words, and learn them better (NICHD 2000) when the methods include opportunities to actively engage with words and their meanings (Blachowicz and Lee 1991; Rupley, Logan, and Nichols 1998/1999). While (and partly because) there are still things that researchers are figuring out about vocabulary instruction, a mix of instructional methods appears to hold the most promise for students like Dean and Vanessa from the opening scenario. The good news is that research is pretty clear that when we teach students even a little bit about the new words they are about to encounter in a text, it "almost always" leads to better reading comprehension (Cervetti et al. 2023, 702).

So, yes! Definitely continue to read aloud every day. Select books that offer rich stories or information so that students will inevitably have robust vocabulary learning opportunities. But also be mindful about including the other methods on this list as well. We've woven more information about each of these components into other sections of this shift and the shifts to come, including some specific high-leverage routines.

MISUNDERSTANDING:

Explicit vocabulary instruction means that I need to do things like have children memorize definitions, write sentences with the words, or pass a test.

Knowing how to help students grow their knowledge of words in intentional ways can be confusing. Should they look up definitions? Should they write original sentences? Should they record words somehow?

If you're like us, you probably have some memories of the dreaded drudgery of looking up the dictionary definitions for a long word list when you were in elementary school yourself. Worries that traditional practices seem boring and ineffective have kept some of us from really teaching vocabulary in earnest. Not only was the act of finding the word a chore, but too often when you arrived at the definition you found yourself facing even more strange and unknown words.

The truth is, not only does our vocabulary instruction often fall short in terms of quantity (Durkin 1978–1979; Scott and Nagy 1997; Scott, Jamieson-Noel, and Asselin 2003), but it has often fallen short in terms of quality as well. So, what does the research really say about what makes explicit vocabulary instruction effective?

Well, for starters, we have to dedicate some time to it. Then vocabulary instruction must extend beyond offering a single definition (Blachowicz et al. 2006; Marzano 2004; Marzano and Pickering 2005; Newton, Padack, and Rasinski 2008) if we want to help children actually *use* new words and *understand* how they work (McKeown 2019).

We have synthesized the research about explicit vocabulary instruction and prioritized four essential components. The order of these instructional moves may vary based on the particular words you have chosen from the text students are about to read.

▲ **Define the word in kid-friendly terms.** One of the problems with dictionary definitions is that they are often filled with even more words that students don't know! So, offering students a kid-friendly definition—one that uses terms and a tone that connect to their *current* background knowledge and vocabulary—not only makes sense (literally) but is supported by research (Scott and Nagy 1997; Stahl 1986; Stahl and Fairbanks 1986; Rupley, Logan, and Nichols 1998-1999). To create a deeper understanding of a new word and better connect it to current networks of words, you might show students images that represent a word's meaning or have students act it out. Lively and engaging vocabulary instruction will make learning (and remembering) new words easier for your students.

▲ **Analyze the word's structure.** This step is about helping students gain clarity about the phonology (pronunciation of individual phonemes, syllable emphasis, etc.), the orthography (spelling), and the morphology (meaningful parts) of words, including aligning the sounds and their spellings (scaffolding orthographic mapping) (Ehri 1984, 1987, 2014; Ehri and Wilce 1980; Moats 2001). After all, to really know a word means knowing its individual sounds, how it is spelled, how it is used as a part of speech, and its multiple meanings (Juel and Deffes 2004).

Taking time to help students practice pronouncing the word correctly while studying the spelling is especially important for multisyllabic words or those that might be easily confused with similar-sounding words—*invisible* and *invincible*. Although some multisyllabic words may be completely and easily decodable, others will have syllables that adjoin in ways that are not expected or straightforward (more about this in Shift 4).

▲ **Clarify the word's use in context.** Using the new word within the context of a few different sentences—spoken and/or written—provides the brain with information about how the word works in relation to the other words in a sentence. Example sentences can be lifted directly from interactive text experiences, or you can construct supplementary sentences yourself (McKeown 1993; Rupley, Logan, and Nichols 1998/1999). Identifying the part of speech that a word represents can help clarify for students the contexts in which they can use it (Juel and Deffes 2004).

▲ **Connect the word to word networks.** Word learning is enhanced when we help students situate new words within the whole web of words they already know. This is because, in the brain, knowledge of words is organized in networks of meaning (McKeown 2019; Marzano 2004; Marzano and Pickering 2005). So, we can strengthen word knowledge if we teach students to recognize that words have intrinsic categories and that they can make connections within and across these categories (Graves 2006). This might involve identifying synonyms or antonyms, pointing out words that are similar in sound and/or spelling, considering shades of meaning, and exploring morphological word families.

The key practices we described above engage all four parts of the brain's four-part processing system (phonology, orthography, meaning, and context) (Burkins and Yates 2021; Seidenberg and McClellan 1989). Such brain-friendly word teaching makes deeply learning words—how to read them, how to write them, and how to use them—easier for kids. And brain-friendly vocabulary instruction, as you know by now, sets children up for better reading comprehension.

But deep and lasting word learning won't happen if our instruction is heavy on teacher talk and doesn't give students much chance to interact with us, each other, or the words they are trying to learn. Effective vocabulary teaching draws students into networks of words as explorers (Beck, Perfetti, and McKeown 1982; Blachowicz et al. 2006; Newton, Padack, and Rasinski 2008).

In the second part of this chapter, we offer a sample lesson that demonstrates actively engaging students in every phase of a brain-friendly vocabulary lesson.

MISUNDERSTANDING:

Vocabulary instruction should focus on the hardest words in a text.

Now that you know the brain-friendly elements to include in your explicit vocabulary instruction, you're probably starting to consider the million-dollar question: which words deserve this depth of instructional time and attention?

The average dictionary holds about four hundred thousand words. So it's no surprise that deciding which words to focus on can feel confusing or overwhelming. And even with a single high-quality text, no one has the instructional time (or energy) to teach all of the words that may be unfamiliar to students. In fact, trying to do so would leave time for little else!

You have probably heard of Beck, McKeown, and Kucan's (2013) tiered categories for vocabulary. These categories are more than labels. They were created to help us systematically identify and prioritize words worthy of our precious instructional time. So where do you start in making decisions about which words to teach?

Tier 1 words, which we like to call **General Words**, are those everyday words that show up most frequently in speech and in print. Think of these as words we use the most in everyday conversation. Although students who are emerging bilinguals may benefit from more direct instruction related to these words, students typically learn these words through everyday conversation. For example, the word *little* is quite common; it references smallness in a "general" way.

Tier 2 words, which we like to think of as **Precision Words**, are less common but still very useful and versatile. These words show up frequently in print, and many make up the academic language that children must understand to succeed in school. Many of these words don't show up so much in everyday conversation and tend to require direct instruction for students to learn their meanings. For example, the word *minuscule* is a less common word that offers more "precision" than the word *little*.

Tier 3 words, which we think of as **Specialized Words**, require explicit instruction. They are rarely encountered in conversation, and then only in reference to specific areas of knowledge. Some of these are words that help students build domain knowledge in a content area. For example, *subatomic* is a highly "specialized" alternative to the word *little* that requires an understanding of the scientific concept of atoms in order to make sense of it. Table 3.2 provides an overview of the three categories of words as we have introduced them in the paragraphs above.

TABLE 3.2

TIER WORDS

Tier	Descriptive Label	Elaboration	Example
Tier 1	General Words	Words that are most widely used in print and speech, do not have multiple meanings, and rarely require direct instruction for native English-speakers	*mom, dog, see, happy, yellow*
Tier 2	Precision Words	Words that are used more in written language than in every-day talk, often require explicit instruction, and are essential in a variety of situations, including understanding academic content	*cite, evaluate, details, obvious, complex, informed*
Tier 3	Specialized Words	Words that are only used in specific contexts and usually require explicit instruction, including connections to background knowledge	*demagogue, filibuster, isotope, photosynthesis, denominator, quotient*

Adapted from Beck, McKeown, and Kucan 2013

Although it may seem intuitive to spend the most time with Specialized Words because they are often the most difficult, Precision Words turn out to be the words that give us the most instructional bang for our buck (Beck, McKeown, and Kucan 2013; Juel and Deffes 2004). Table 3.3 on page 88 illustrates the general relationship between the type of word and instructional time.

TABLE 3.3

RELATIONSHIP BETWEEN WORD TYPE
AND INSTRUCTIONAL TIME

General Words	Precision Words	Specialized Words
Spend the **LEAST** time here. Most children will easily learn these words through social interactions.	Spend the **MOST** time here. These high-utility words promote success *across* settings and content areas.	Spend **LESS** time here than on Precision Words. Prioritize these words when students need them to understand domain-specific content.

Even if you are spending the bulk of your vocabulary instruction on Precision Words or a few Specialized Words, you're still going to have some decisions to make about which ones are most worth your instructional time. To help with that, we offer three research-based considerations (Beck, McKeown, and Kucan 2013; Juel and Deffes 2004).

▲ **Urgent** Start by selecting the words that are most important at the moment in order to understand the text or topic at hand.

▲ **Uncommon** Next, consider which urgent words are generally uncommon or more sophisticated than those used in students' everyday conversations.

▲ **Useful** Finally, narrow the list by selecting the uncommon words that are most likely useful in a variety of settings and content areas.

We illustrate the use of these three U's in Figure 3.1, The Vocabulary Funnel. By relying on these three considerations to guide you, you'll gradually develop a keen eye for the words most worthy of your instructional time and energy.

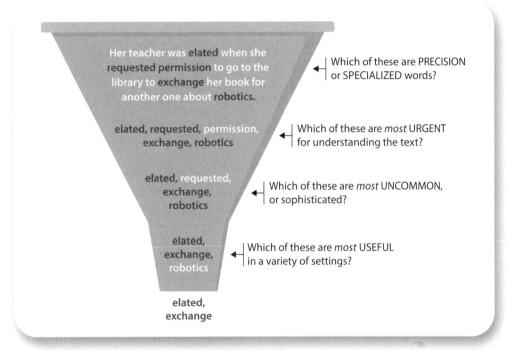

Figure 3.1 The Vocabulary Funnel

5 MISUNDERSTANDING:

Teacher-selected words are the primary source of vocabulary growth for students.

While research points to the value of explicitly teaching words that can be leveraged across many contexts (Beck, McKeown, and Kucan 2013; Juel and Deffes 2004; Marzano 2004; Marzano and Pickering 2005), we won't be alongside our students every time they encounter a new word.

Consider that if a reader—between reading at home and reading at school—reads for an average of 45 minutes a day at 150 words per minute, they will encounter more than 2 million written words in just a year. If 1 out of 30 of the words they read is an unfamiliar word, then they will encounter almost 70,000 new words! In contrast, if we explicitly teach 8–10 vocabulary words per week during a school year, we will only teach 360 words max!

Whoa! Those numbers make a strong case for the importance of empowering readers to be strategic when they encounter unfamiliar words on their own. So, we must equip children—like Amal and Maggie, who tend to skip over difficult words—with the tools they need to strategically puzzle through the unfamiliar words they encounter (Lubliner and Smetana 2005).

We already know that looking up words in the dictionary is often inefficient, not to mention unhelpful. So what can we do to help students get good at unlocking the meaning of the unknown words they encounter when they are reading on their own? Well, we can teach two critical meaning-solving approaches supported by research: using morphological clues and using context clues.

Let's take a closer look at these two kinds of clues and their strategic use, considering how explicit instruction—coupled with lots of agentive discovery—can equip students to teach themselves new words.

▲ **Look Inside the Word (Use Morphological Clues)**

One potentially helpful way to strengthen students' word power is by teaching them to study the interior of the unknown word, drawing on their knowledge of meaningful word parts and comparing and contrasting the new word with words they already know (Baumann et al. 2002; Bowers, Kirby, and Deacon 2010). The smallest *meaningful* parts of words are referred to as morphemes (prefixes, suffixes, roots, and bases), and the study of morphemes is called *morphology*.

While sometimes mistakenly reserved for middle school students, instruction in morphology is actually appropriate—even necessary—for elementary students too (Duke, Ward, and Pearson 2021). Morphological awareness also positively affects reading comprehension (Carlo et al. 2004; Goodwin and Ahn 2013; Kieffer and Lesaux 2007).

So, what's important to know about teaching children morphology?

One important understanding is that morphology instruction typically focuses on one of two types of meaningful word parts:

- **Affixes.** These are word parts that are attached (or affixed) to roots, stems, or bases in order to modify the meaning of the word. Of course, you likely know that affixes also come in two forms:
  - Prefixes, which affix to the beginnings of words (*un-, pre-, in-*)
  - Suffixes, which affix to the endings of words (*-er, -ful, -ly*)

- **Latin and Greek Word Roots.** Different from simple root words, which can stand on their own, Latin and Greek roots are word parts that have consistent meanings across words (*bio, tele, aud*).

So, what makes these two types of word parts so important? Well, affixes and roots act like building blocks that can be used and combined in different ways—think Legos for words. Knowing about the more common affixes and roots can be really helpful in figuring out the meanings of unknown words, especially the academic words students will encounter across content areas.

More specifically, Greek and Latin roots are especially important because they're so often found in words related to science and math content. In fact, it turns out that the majority of academic words—up to 76 percent—contain Greek and Latin roots (Rasinski 2017). So a little time learning morphology can translate into a lot of word learning! Table 3.4 illustrates these two important parts of English morphology—affixes and Greek and Latin word roots.

TABLE 3.4

EXAMPLES OF AFFIXES AND ROOTS
AND THEIR MEANINGS

	Morpheme		Meaning	Examples
A F F I X E S	Prefixes	mis-	wrong, bad	**mis**treat, **mis**guide, **mis**count
		pre-	before	**pre**view, **pre**vent, **pre**cook
		sub-	under, below	**sub**marine, **sub**way, **sub**title
	Suffixes	-er	more	clean**er**, fast**er**, easi**er**
		-ist	person who	dent**ist**, panel**ist**, herbal**ist**
		-ful	full of	art**ful**, hurt**ful**, boast**ful**

continues

	Morpheme		Meaning	Examples
R O O T S	Greek Roots	graph	write	auto**graph**, bio**graph**y, **graph**eme
		path	feel	em**path**y, **path**etic, a**path**y
		tele	far away	**tele**gram, **tele**pathy, **tele**vision
	Latin Roots	aqu	water	**aqu**educt, **aqu**arium, **aqu**atic
		dict	say or speak	**dict**ate, **dict**ator, contra**dict**
		tempor	time	con**tempor**ary, **tempor**al, **tempor**arily

Exploring the similarities between a student's home language and English can be very helpful as well. Cognates are related words in different languages that share meaning and have some spelling or pronunciation characteristics in common. For example, *accidente* in Spanish looks and sounds a lot like *accident* in English. Noticing cognate connections can make learning many words easier. And while cognates aren't helpful with every language, many languages, such as Portuguese and German, share a heavy influence from Greek and Latin, as does English. So cognates can often be a helpful tool for using a primary language to unlock a new language (Calderón et al. 2003).

So, if we want upper elementary students to read grade-level, complex texts (and beyond), then teaching them how to "look within words" to leverage morphology can give them power in puzzling out the meanings of unfamiliar words. What's more, having a strong foundation in morphology not only increases students' understanding of word meanings but also supports decoding and spelling (Nagy, Berninger, and Abbott 2006; Singson, Mahony, and Mann 2000).

Still, it's one thing to understand the important role morphology, or learning to look within words, can play in word learning, and another thing to figure out how to make teaching morphology a manageable part of an already busy day. To download a tool

with specific ideas about which morphemes to focus on, go to
TheSixShifts.com/Downloads.

▲ **Look Around the Word (Use Context Clues)**
The second strategy that can be especially beneficial when figuring
out word meanings is thinking about supportive information
from the text surrounding the unknown word. In other words,
we need to teach children to notice context clues. Readers can
learn to leverage both sentence-level and paragraph-level context
to discover clues about the meaning of an unknown word (Cain,
Oakhill, and Lemmon 2004; Lubliner and Smetana 2005; Nagy,
Herman, and Anderson 1985; Sternberg 1987).

And although chances are you've been thinking about context
clues for a long time already, it might be of interest to know that
authors actually leave different kinds of clues for the reader. In fact,
Baumann and colleagues (2002) identified five types of context clues
that can be helpful in understanding new and unfamiliar words:

- Definitions
- Synonyms
- Antonyms
- Examples
- General information

We elaborate on these different types of clues in this shift's
instructional recommendations, offering helpful questions students
can learn to ask themselves, text examples, and sample think-aloud
language for teachers. Once tuned into these different types of clues,
you might be surprised at how often authors of children's books
leave these hints embedded in the text to help children make sense
of more sophisticated language.

You can be on the lookout for opportunities to teach how to use morphological and context clues during your interactive text experiences, planning
your think-aloud language so that you can point out these hints in ways that
make your thinking *about thinking* accessible to students. We want to be clear,
however, that the usefulness of these clues—both morphological and contextual—does not come from being able to name them. It's not simply about

memorizing a bunch of definitions and rules. Instead, learning words while reading comes from building a more general awareness that the text itself contains lots of different types of useful clues, many of which can empower us to act strategically, puzzling out word meanings so that we can accomplish the goal of all reading—comprehension (Kuhn and Stahl 1998).

A Short Summary of the Science

▲ Strong vocabulary contributes to reading comprehension, and vice versa.

▲ Success with academics depends on acquiring vocabulary that isn't common in typical conversations.

▲ Once children develop some reading fluency, the main contributor to vocabulary growth is reading volume.

▲ There isn't one best way to teach vocabulary; rather, children learn more words when we utilize a mix of instructional methods.

▲ Word learning can happen both incidentally and through explicit instruction.

▲ Research-based explicit vocabulary instruction includes defining the word in kid-friendly terms, analyzing the word's structure, clarifying the way the word is used in context, and connecting it to a network of other words.

▲ To decide which words to teach, it helps to weigh whether they are General Words, Precision Words, or Specialized Words.

▲ Morphemes are the smallest meaningful parts of words.

▲ To figure out the meanings of words on their own, readers can use morphological clues (looking inside a word) and context clues (looking around a word).

▲ Robust vocabulary instruction supports students in interacting with words and their meanings through reading, writing, and discussion.

THE SIMPLE AND SCIENTIFICALLY SOUND SHIFT

▼ ▼ ▲ ▼ ▼ ▼

Balance incidental word exposure with explicit and engaging vocabulary instruction.

Recommendations for Making the Shift

In the chart that follows, we share high-leverage instructional routines that can help you make the shift toward more efficient and intentional vocabulary instruction. We then zoom in on a lesson plan for explicit instruction, interactive vocabulary walls, exploring morphology, using context clues, and shades of meaning.

TABLE 3.5

HIGH-LEVERAGE INSTRUCTIONAL ROUTINES FOR TEACHING VOCABULARY

The What: *Routine*	The Why: *Purpose*	The How: *Examples*
Interactive Text Experiences	To expose and/or introduce students to new vocabulary through interactive experiences with texts, such as read-aloud and shared reading To teach vocabulary on the run	"Let's read this sentence again and try to figure out what the word *exchange* means." "To *observe* something means to watch or study it."
Use Sophisticated Language	To provide incidental exposure to rich and robust language across the learning day and build language comprehension	"Please position yourself on the *perimeter*." (Rather than "Please sit around the edge.")
Lesson Plan for Explicit Vocabulary Instruction	To simplify the design of explicit vocabulary instruction, ensuring it is driven by science-aligned routines and includes opportunities for active engagement	See "Zooming In on a Lesson Plan for Explicit Vocabulary Instruction."
Explicit Morphology Instruction	To develop familiarity with morphemes that students can leverage to help determine a word's meaning by looking within the word	See "Zooming In on Explicit Morphology Instruction."
Using Context Clues	To develop an awareness of different types of context clues and how to use them by looking around the word	See "Zooming In on Using Context Clues."

The What: Routine	The Why: Purpose	The How: Examples
Interactive Vocabulary Walls	To highlight a network of specialized vocabulary related to a content area topic and strengthen understanding of how words relate to one another	See "Zooming In on Interactive Vocabulary Walls."
Word Collection Notebooks	To increase students' word awareness by encouraging them to become "word collectors," noticing and recording new words and exploring their place within word networks	See "Zooming in on Word Collection Notebooks."
Shades of Meaning	To discern relationships between words and encourage precision in language	See "Zooming In on Shades of Meaning."
Meaningful Reading Practice	To expose students to a high volume of new vocabulary words in context	Dedicating time each day to meaningful reading from a broad selection of texts

Zooming In on a Lesson Plan for Explicit Vocabulary Instruction

Once you've identified a specific word from a text students are about to read, you can take a look at the lesson plan on the following page. It includes the four instructional moves described in Misunderstanding 3: defining the word in kid-friendly terms, analyzing the word's structure, clarifying context, and connecting to word networks.

These steps do not necessarily need to unfold in the sequence provided. You may find that it makes sense to shuffle the order, depending on the word. In the example lesson below, we've added some sample teacher language, but you can find a blank version of this lesson structure at TheSixShifts.com /Downloads.

TABLE 3.6

EXAMPLE VOCABULARY LESSON

Lesson Plan for Explicit Vocabulary Instruction Word: *chaos*	
Instructional Notes	**Options for Student Interaction**
Define in Kid-Friendly Terms	
Definition: *a lot of disorganization, confusion, or messiness.* **Sample Sentence:** *A mouse running through the room might create chaos in the classroom.*	☐ Restate definition to partner. ☐ Jot the definition in a notebook. ☐ Illustrate the word. ☐ Create an icon or symbol. ☐ Act it out. ☑ Other: *Describe the opposite of chaos to your partner*
Analyze Word Structure	
Notes about pronunciation: *ch = /k/, long a but short o* **Notes about segmentation (sounds and/or syllables):** *2 syllables: <u>cha-os</u>* *5 letters, 4 sounds* | ch	a	o	s | **Notes about morphemes and/or spellings:** */k/ = ch* *Syllable split between vowels*	☑ Practice pronouncing the word. ☑ Align sounds and spellings with sound boxes. ☐ Mark up a big word (see Shift 4). ☑ Clap syllables. ☐ Explore morphology.

Clarify Context	
☑ Noun ☐ Verb ☐ Other ☐ Adverb ☐ Adjective **Sample sentences:** The heavy snow created chaos during afternoon dismissal. My room is in complete chaos thanks to my baby brother dragging out everything!	☐ Share a sentence with a partner. ☐ Jot a sentence in your notebook. ☑ Other: Share a personal example with your partner.

Connect to Word Networks	
Related words = <u>chaotic</u>, <u>chaotically</u> Synonyms = <u>wild</u>, <u>uncontrollable</u>, <u>unorganized</u> Antonyms = <u>orderly</u>, <u>neat</u>, <u>calm</u>, <u>controlled</u>, <u>organized</u>	☐ Create word web. ☑ Explore synonyms and antonyms. ☐ Explore shades of meaning. ☑ Explore words with common morphology (morphological relatives). ☑ Explore words that sound or look similar. ☐ Add to vocabulary wall.

An explicit vocabulary lesson like this one isn't for every word. It's reserved for those words that are urgent, uncommon, and useful in understanding the text, and which can't be easily taught in passing. The word *chaos*, for example, has some nuances to its use as well as a few spelling patterns that are worthy of a closer look. Once you learn this simple routine, you'll be able to implement it with ease, across content areas.

Zooming In on Explicit Morphology Instruction

In order to increase children's understanding of morphology—the smallest meaningful chunks within words—you need a gradual but intentional plan that begins in the earliest grades with simple morphemes (*-s, -ed, -ing*, etc.) and extends to more complex morphemes (*poly, contra, graph*, etc.) as children grow into increasingly complex texts. But don't worry; morphology instruction doesn't have to be complicated. You can download a multiyear plan for thoughtful and systematic morphology instruction at TheSixShifts .com/Downloads.

Teaching even one new affix or root per week can equip students with a transformative addition to their word-learning toolkit. So, how do you teach a morpheme? In Table 3.7 we offer a five-step process for helping children understand and interact with new morphemes, making them their own. You can also download a template for this lesson structure at TheSixShifts.com /Downloads.

TABLE 3.7

SAMPLE LESSON FOR TEACHING MORPHOLOGY

Step	Purpose	Example Language/ Scaffolds
1. Introduce the morpheme.	Identify the morpheme, its meaning, and its location in a word (prefix, suffix, or base). Note: Even in prefix or suffix form, a morpheme can be more than one syllable.	"Today we're going to work with words that contain the prefix *pre-*, which means 'before.'" | Morpheme	Meaning
---	---
pre-	before	
2. Study examples.	Provide examples of words containing the morpheme. Model the process of stating the meaning of each word.	"To check the meaning of a word containing the prefix *pre-*, say the base followed by the word *before*." preview—to view *before* you view pretest—to test *before* you test precook—to cook *before* you cook

Step	Purpose	Example Language/ Scaffolds
3. Share non-examples.	If relevant, present a few words where the same letters appear in sequence but do not function as the particular morpheme.	Here are some words where *pre-* is not a prefix. We know because it is *not* attached to a base word. pretzel pretty press
4. Build and define.	Provide bases or affixes that students can combine with the morpheme to make other words. Have students work with partners, building words and stating their meaning.	"Here are some bases that might be used with the prefix *pre-*. Practice making a new word and saying its definition. For example, *preview* means 'view before.'"
5. Contextualize.	Using a few cloze sentences, have students provide the missing word for the sentence using a word from the list of example words in step 4.	"Here are some sentences that are missing words with the prefix *pre-*. Fill in the blanks with the word that makes sense." We can _____ the movie to decide if we want to watch it. Since their evening schedule was tight, Dad decided to _____ the pasta for dinner.

For step 4, the "Example Language/Scaffolds" cell contains a table:

pre-	
view	wrap
cook	heat
text	shrunk
wash	occupy

You may wonder how this morphology lesson is different from the vocabulary lesson structure we just shared with you. Well, the lesson plan for vocabulary instruction is for explicitly teaching a specific *word*. Although this lesson often includes some morphology exploration, the point is to learn the single, target vocabulary word. In comparison, the process for teaching morphology focuses on a specific affix or root as the pathway to learning many, many other words. To offer comprehensive and high-quality vocabulary instruction, you need to provide both types of lessons.

 ## Zooming In on Using Context Clues

There are two important ways you can help children develop skills for using context clues, or looking around the unknown word to find hints hidden in the surrounding words in the sentence or paragraph. The first option is to be on the lookout for context clues during interactive text experiences so that you can draw attention to them. These encounters with words give you the opportunity to share your thinking out loud, modeling your own thought process for students: "I wasn't sure what this word meant, but then I noticed . . ."

The second way to teach context clues is to coach children to ask themselves helpful questions as they examine the text surrounding a word: "When you notice a word you don't know the meaning of, you can ask yourself, 'What can I figure out about what this word means?' (Burkins and Yaris 2016)"

In Table 3.8 we elaborate on both of these methods (modeling by thinking aloud and coaching children to ask questions) and provide examples for each of the different types of context clues (Bauman et al. 2002).

TABLE 3.8

TEACHING TYPES OF CONTEXT CLUES

Type of Context Clue	Text Example (with clue italicized)	Sample Think-Aloud Language	Helpful Questions Students Can Ask
Definition	**Sedimentary rocks**, *those that have been formed by layers of silt, sand, dirt, and even animal skeletons*, can be found in the ocean as well as in the desert.	"I'm noticing right after the words *sedimentary rocks*, the text says, 'those that . . .' and then gives an explanation. I know that the word *those* refers to sedimentary rocks. And then the author gave a definition."	"Does the author offer a definition either before or after the word?" "Is there punctuation that can help me find a definition, such as parentheses, dashes, or commas?"
Synonym	The old man was more **chipper**, or *lively*, than we expected.	"The comma, followed by the word *or*, is a big clue that the next word, *lively*, is another word for *chipper*. *Chipper* and *lively* are synonyms."	"Do I know any synonyms for this word, or is a synonym given in the text?" "Is the word followed by a comma and the word *or*?" "If I plug the synonym in instead of the word, is the meaning of the text clearer?"
Antonym	*Easy*? Absolutely not! It was the most **arduous** task I'd ever done.	"When I came to the word *arduous*, I already had a clue because the author told me it was *absolutely not* easy. I think this word means the opposite of *easy*, so it must mean really hard."	"Is the opposite of the word given in the text?" "Does the text tell me what the word is *not*?"

continues

3

Type of Context Clue	Text Example (with clue italicized)	Sample Think-Aloud Language	Helpful Questions Students Can Ask
Example	She always offered **enticements** to get us to clean our rooms, *such as* going out for ice cream when we finished.	"The words *such as* alert me that an example is coming. If going for ice cream is an enticement, then enticements must be the reward someone promises you to get you to do something you don't want to do."	"Does the author give me an example that shows me what the word means?" "Are there clue words—*such as, for instance, for example*—that alert me that examples of the word are coming up in the text?"
General	He didn't make the purchase because the land wasn't zoned for **commercial** use.	"Hmm, I know commercials on TV have to do with selling things. Maybe *commercial* in this sentence means you can sell things there."	"Do I have general knowledge about this word that can help me figure it out?" "Do I know what any part of this word means?"

Based on Bauman et al. 2002

Helpful clues to word meanings can come in many shapes and sizes. But remember, the important work is not for children to memorize the names of different types of context clues or the specific questions in the table above. Instead, the goal is to build word awareness and a reflexive response of scouring the words around an unknown word, looking for anything they *already* understand that can help them figure out the meaning of the word.

Zooming In on Interactive Vocabulary Walls

Vocabulary walls are organized collections of words displayed on a wall or other space in the classroom. They can strengthen content vocabulary and help children notice the relationships between words. Vocabulary walls become interactive when students have an opportunity to move words around and demonstrate their thinking about the connections between and across words.

The first step in creating an interactive vocabulary wall is to select the words you want to include. You'll want to choose a combination of Precision Words (high-utility academic words) along with some Specialized Words (domain-specific words) that are all related to a current topic of study. Write each word on a separate card and post it on the wall as you teach it. In Figure 3.2, we offer an example of a collection of words that might appear on an interactive vocabulary wall—each word on its own card—during a study of animal adaptation. Notice how the words are arranged in columns of related words.

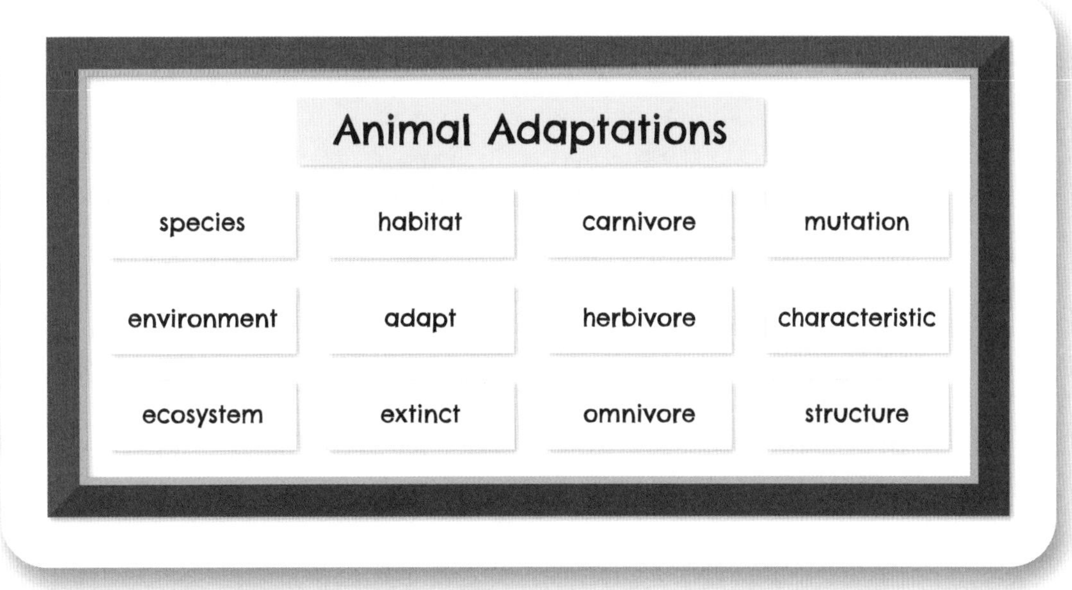

Animal Adaptations

species	habitat	carnivore	mutation
environment	adapt	herbivore	characteristic
ecosystem	extinct	omnivore	structure

Figure 3.2 Sample Interactive Vocabulary Wall

Once you have the vocabulary wall established, there are a number of different ways students can interact with it. Below, we offer just a few ideas to get you started. Any of these options can be varied for use with either the vocabulary wall itself or with copies of the words that students manipulate at tables or on the floor.

▲ **Categorize** Have students organize or group the words in logical categories. Do some words have similar roots? Are any words synonyms or antonyms? Do some words sound the same? After small groups have sorted the words, students can take a gallery walk to see the ways other groups have categorized them.

▲ **Connect** To lift the level of challenge, invite students to use arrows to connect words on the wall or on large pieces of paper, showing the relationships between them. Children can propose connections and then explain their reasoning. Arrows can be permanently added to the wall, or they can change as children make new connections.

▲ **Contextualize** Get students engaged in using the words in context. They can use the word in the context of a sentence, share a sentence explaining the word's meaning, explain an illustration of the word, or write a comparison to a similar or opposite word. You can get creative with the opportunities you give students to think deeply about the words on the wall.

▲ **Compete** You can gamify word learning in a number of ways. One of our favorites is Guess My Word. In this game, one student chooses a word from the vocabulary wall and then offers a definition, examples, or other clues for classmates to guess which word is the secret word.

Categorizing, connecting, contextualizing, and competing not only help children learn individual words but also help them recognize that words have relationships with one another. Language learning is ongoing, and exploring connections between words can be fun.

Vocabulary walls get students interacting with words and with each other and are also a powerful path to knowledge building. This fresh take on the traditional word wall is purposeful, engaging, and science-aligned!

 ## Zooming In on Shades of Meaning

Effective vocabulary instruction involves the gradual shaping of word meanings through multiple exposures. So, once students have a basic understanding of a target word, they can consider shades of meaning as they compare and contrast related words.

One way to do this is to use semantic gradients to arrange words by order of degree in a continuum of words with meanings that vary subtly. To help students determine these shades of meaning:

1. Select a pair of opposite words, such as *large* and *small*. Put each one on its own sticky note.

2. Generate a number of synonyms for each word. Again, use a new sticky note for each word.

3. Manipulate the sticky notes to arrange the words in a continuum from one extreme to its opposite.

For example:

diminutive   tiny   slight   large   massive
   miniature   small   sizable   huge   colossal

This kind of vocabulary exercise teaches students that synonyms can be closely related but still differ in very slight/tiny/small ways. These connections help them both understand nuances as readers and make stronger word choices as writers. Shades of meaning exercises work best with adverbs and adjectives.

You can vary this vocabulary exercise by having students play the game Which One Doesn't Belong? before organizing a set of words in order of degree. In this activity, provide students with four related words and one unrelated word—for example, *small*, *tiny*, *quiet*, *mini*, and *little*. Have students identify which word doesn't belong and explain why. You can extend this exercise by inviting students to rank the remaining four synonyms from strongest to weakest or generate an additional synonym for the word that didn't belong. Students can even create their own versions of the game to play with each other.

You can also use color to help students identify shades of meaning by stopping by your local hardware store to pick up paint color strips. Have students rank words from strongest to weakest by using a marker to write each individual word in its own shade of color. Get out the scissors to cut strips apart, and a whole new set of possibilities for sorting and categorizing the words emerges.

Zooming In on Word Collection Notebooks

There is definitely a lot we can do as teachers to be more explicit in our vocabulary instruction. But we also know that the more students read, the more Precision and Specialized Words they will encounter on their own. Remember those seventy thousand words we mentioned earlier? For children to learn that many words, we need to empower them to become aware of and interested in words (Anderson and Nagy 1992), to notice when they encounter new words (Manzo and Manzo 2008), and to develop what's known as word consciousness (Graves and Watts-Taffe 2002; Lane and Allen 2010), which we refer to as word awareness.

We recommend reading a book like *The Word Collector* by Peter Reynolds (2018) to model for students lots of different ways they can develop their word awareness. If you know the story, you know that the main character, Jerome, loves collecting words. While some kids collect baseball cards or coins, Jerome collects words. He does that by paying attention to words that he hears and reads, and he keeps a record of them in his notebooks. You can download a list of other books that encourage a love of words at TheSixShifts.com/Downloads.

We can scaffold students to keep a record of the words they encounter by using a Word Collection Notebook (or section of their Reader's Notebook) to create a personal collection of new and interesting words. Table 3.9 illustrates one example of what students might include in their notebooks to keep track of a few new words they hear or read over a given week, building both word awareness and accumulating new vocabulary.

TABLE 3.9

SAMPLE ENTRY FROM STUDENT WORD COLLECTION NOTEBOOK

Word	Part of Speech	I Think It Means . . .	Other Word Connections
primatologist	Noun (person)	Someone who studies primates (like apes, monkeys, and humans)	*prime* *primate* *primary* *biologist* *dermatologist*

Adapted from Cappiello and Dawes 2021

You can help students in their quest to become word collectors by setting simple goals about how many words to collect each week. You might even devote time at the end of the week for students to share a favorite word or two with a partner. With encouragement your young word collectors will soon begin to try out these new words in their conversations and writing, delighting in the magic, mystery, and power of interesting words!

Meanwhile, Back in the Classroom . . .

After reviewing some of the research on vocabulary instruction, Mr. Heitzman is excited to try out a few new vocabulary routines in the classroom. He feels his commitment to reading aloud to his students has been affirmed, and he is glad to keep his daily read-aloud routines in place. But one change he has decided to make is to expand his text selections to bring in more informational texts to balance out the fiction he has tended to favor. He hopes this will help support the growth of more academic word knowledge, while also providing a meaningful entry point into morphology instruction and building background knowledge.

He's still committed to texts that represent the diversity in his classroom, and even the world at large. He is working to find more nonfiction texts that can help him meet this goal—like *We Are Still Here! Native American Truths Everyone Should Know* by Traci Sorell (2021) and *Above the Rim: How Elgin Baylor Changed Basketball* by Jen Bryant (2020). His students have loved learning about history, science, and the lives of people.

Another thing Mr. Heitzman is working on is an addition to his read-aloud planning process. Lately, when he selects a book for a read-aloud, he reads it himself with a stack of sticky notes at hand, jotting down words and kid-friendly definitions. He then narrows the words and decides which ones need which kind of instruction.

Some words he just defines on the run. For those words that warrant a little extra attention, he selects two or three that are most critical to understanding the text so that he can pre-teach them just a few minutes before beginning the read-aloud. He adds the remaining priority words to the short list of words he will teach explicitly during a vocabulary lesson the day before the read-aloud. Of course, the students are always excited when they hear their vocabulary words turn up during an interactive text experience.

Another significant shift for Mr. Heitzman is a new commitment to introducing one affix or root each week. As students encounter new words in their own reading, they leverage these morphemes to figure out their meanings more and more easily, and they are especially satisfied when their meaning-solving efforts pay off! They excitedly look forward to the monthly Morpheme Jeopardy competition that Mr. Heitzman has established for morphology review. And some students, including Amal and Maggie, have been excited to share their success with "looking inside" and "looking around" new vocabulary to figure out word meanings when they read independently.

Most importantly, it seems that all of Mr. Heitzman's students have become engaged word collectors. Their notebooks are filling up with interesting words they read, hear, and share. Mr. Heitzman challenged his students to take words from their notebooks and the vocabulary wall and bring them to life throughout the day. Lately, as he listens to their conversations, he catches himself smiling at their increasing confidence with more sophisticated vocabulary. He's been especially excited by the ways Vanessa seems to be so eager to share and try out new words, even in her writing. His students' knowledge of words is growing, and they know it!

The literacy coach is excited about the vocabulary enthusiasm among Mr. Heitzman's students. She's invited Mr. Heitzman to present what he's learned in a professional learning circle dedicated to vocabulary and morphological awareness instruction. The coach's goal is to eventually support a team of teachers in developing and implementing a morphology scope and sequence that spans the grade levels.

Questions for Reflection

Checking In with Yourself: Which of the misunderstandings in this shift did you find yourself thinking most deeply about? What might be the next step for you?

Text Selection: How do the texts you select lend themselves to vocabulary learning?

Selecting Words for Instruction: What is your system for selecting the words that are urgent? Uncommon? Useful? How do you match the words you've identified to the type of instruction (on the run, explicit instruction, vocabulary word wall, etc.) they warrant?

Teaching Words on the Run: How often do you model your thinking about words and their definitions, or pause for some quick word exploration, as a part of an interactive text experience?

Specific Word Instruction: How will you prioritize time for explicit vocabulary instruction? How can you use a science-aligned lesson structure to explicitly teach more Precision Words?

Morphology Instruction: What plan do you have to ensure that children continuously expand their understanding of morphemes? What routines will you regularly rely on to ensure that morpheme instruction sticks?

Engagement: What word-learning routines and activities will you adopt to ensure that children have lots of opportunities to actively engage with words, word meanings, word networks, and each other?

Word Awareness: What strategies will you teach to encourage children to be word collectors, noticing and sleuthing words on their own? How will you inspire and celebrate word awareness, encouraging and enabling your students as they elevate their awareness of words?

Differentiation: Who do your current practices serve? Who will benefit the most from a shift in practice? Which techniques from this shift could you incorporate to differentiate vocabulary instruction?

Reclaiming Word-Reading Instruction in the Intermediate Grades

SHIFT

4

Ms. Schwartz is a beloved teacher in her building because of her sense of humor and her strong connections with her students. Although she did some student teaching in the primary grades, she's always been more comfortable working with older students. And when it comes to reading instruction, she definitely feels more confident supporting students with reading comprehension than with word recognition.

Nevertheless, even though every year it seems that some of her students arrive in third grade navigating unfamiliar words with ease, there are often just as many who can't. Others really stumble and struggle when it comes to oral reading. This year, in particular, the differences in word-recognition skills among her students have her especially perplexed.

Several of her students seem to use only the first few letters before filling in a word that makes sense to them, saying things like "talking nonstop" for *talking nonsense* or "underground" for *underneath*. Even more troubling are students, like Drew, who often make word errors that just don't make sense, like reading *inside* instead of *insect*.

Ms. Schwartz used to think that as long as errors made sense, they were okay because they wouldn't interfere with students' comprehension. But lately she's questioning that logic, because she's become more tuned in to just how unreliable the context of a sentence can be for figuring out words, especially if the text is complex.

In fact, multisyllabic words seem to be at the heart of reading difficulties for many of her students. And it's not just guessing at and approximating words that gets in the way. There are also students, like Macey, who, rather than even trying to decode long words, have developed the habit of simply skipping them. These omissions often leave obvious gaps in the story or information and cause real comprehension difficulties. And then there are students, like Franco, who freeze up with anxiety, seemingly unable to help themselves get a meaningful foothold in the text. Finally, and most concerning are students, like Jaxon, who have developed a whole bag of tricks—avoidance, distraction, disruption—designed to keep his classmates from noticing his word-reading difficulties at all.

And then there is spelling. Yikes! For instance, today Dante wrote, "My ant's fone fell doun in betwene the car seets." Historically, Ms. Schwartz has believed that spelling will work itself out with time. But lately she's begun to question that assumption too, because she's been puzzled by the surprising number of spelling errors some of her most confident readers make. And these patterns don't seem to be improving.

Lately, Ms. Schwartz has really been noticing the broader effect that word-related struggles seem to have on her students' motivation as readers. Drew, for example, is beginning to retreat a bit in the classroom. Macey participates less and less during class discussions and has even begun to resist partner work, something the typically social child has always loved. And it seems the harder the reading gets, the harder Jaxon works to mask his struggles by entertaining himself and others in purposeful but unhelpful ways that are getting more and more disruptive.

So, Ms. Schwartz has tried to incorporate some word work incidentally throughout the day. When she encounters a helpful example of a multisyllabic word during a read-aloud, she sometimes takes a moment to write it on the board and unpack its spelling. And when students have trouble decoding a word during small-group instruction, she's there to provide in-the-moment coaching and looks for patterns that can inform future minilessons.

However, Ms. Schwartz has begun to realize that she has limited knowledge of what her students actually know and don't know about how words work. And although she had some exposure to second-grade phonics during her student teaching, she'd be the first to admit that she feels pretty unsure about how to really help children make progress with decoding and word recognition. Ms. Schwartz is a good speller herself, but still, she often finds herself flustered or confused when coaching students on the spelling of words, especially when it comes to vowel sounds and syllable connections.

In conversation with her grade-level team, it's clear that Ms. Schwartz isn't alone with her wonderings about word-reading instruction for older readers. All of the teachers on the team want to see their students continue to grow as readers and writers, and they decide together to engage in some guided study of the role decoding can play in the reading progress of their students.

A COMMON PRACTICE TO RECONSIDER

▼ ▼ ▼ ▲ ▼ ▼

We aren't intentional enough in assessing and teaching word-recognition skills.

Given the way the brain reads, the complexities of our alphabetic system, and the amount of practice students need to learn to read, it is worth revisiting what learning to decode and eventually recognize words automatically really takes. Ensuring that students establish efficient word-reading skills involves helping them further develop (or begin to develop) their ability to process both phonological and orthographic information—intentionally bringing letters, sounds, meaning, and context together.

In *Shifting the Balance K–2* (Burkins and Yates 2021), we explain in more depth how the human brain has to be rewired to learn to read, offering an explicit process for supporting word learning by scaffolding orthographic mapping. We also describe how the reading mechanisms in the brain—the elements of the four-part processing model (Seidenberg and McClellan 1989)—work together to make reading possible. It is important that all teachers, whatever the grade, understand this learning-to-read process, even though we can't describe it in detail in this book.

4

In a nutshell, however, before their brains will be ready for word reading, children need to have three foundational understandings:

▲ **Phonemic Awareness** The words we say are made up of the smallest units of sound (phonemes), which can be separated and manipulated (segmented, blended, added, deleted, and substituted).

▲ **Phonics Knowledge** Letters and letter combinations (graphemes) are used to represent the individual sounds (phonemes) in spoken English.

▲ **Alphabetic Principle** There are systematic and predictable relationships between phonemes and graphemes, and these sounds and spellings can be aligned to represent spoken words.

And although all three of these understandings may seem obvious and straightforward to us as proficient readers, they are actually anything but obvious for students who are learning to read and write. Because written language is a human invention, reading and writing require work that the human brain is not wired to do. So the rewiring work that is necessary to read and write is not natural.

Clearing Up Some Confusion

One of our primary goals in writing this book is to make it easier, rather than harder, for *all* children to access English's written code—whether they have gotten off to a solid start or not—so that they can engage fully with texts and the world. So, let's take a look at some common misunderstandings about word-reading instruction for older students and the reasons we might want to rethink them.

MISUNDERSTANDING:

By the time they are in the intermediate grades, students should have mastered word recognition.

Given some vocal calls for explicit and systematic phonics instruction in the early grades, it is tempting to hope for (or even assume) that most students will arrive at the doors of their intermediate-level classrooms fully equipped with the word-recognition skills they will need for proficient reading. This would be great news if it were true because it would mean that we could focus solely on things like knowledge building, vocabulary instruction, and teaching a few really high-powered comprehension strategies.

But of course, it isn't true. And that's no surprise to you. Because English is a complex language, all that children need to know about how to read words cannot possibly be taught in the primary grades, even if children's word-reading skills are on track. In fact, in recent years the number of students in intermediate-level classrooms with significant gaps in word-reading skills is on the rise (Kuhfeld, Lewis, and Peltier 2022; Halloran et al. 2021; Lewis et al. 2021).

The National Assessment for Education Progress (NAEP) Oral Reading Fluency (ORF) study from 2018 measured oral reading fluency, word reading, and phonological decoding in 1.27 million fourth graders, and found that 36 percent of them performed below the NAEP Basic level on these skills (White et al. 2021). What we find most alarming about this data is that, on average, students reading below the basic level were likely to misread approximately *one out of every six words*. Think about what this disjointed reading does to comprehension!

But supporting a whole class of diverse readers in achieving the kind of effortless word reading necessary to comprehend complex texts leaves intermediate teachers facing two distinct instructional challenges when it comes to teaching word reading.

▲ **The Filling-the-Gaps Challenge** This challenge requires meeting the needs of students who haven't gotten off to a strong start with word learning by stabilizing basic foundational skills—helping them rewire their brains—setting them up for greater ease with word recognition.

▲ **The Moving-Forward Challenge** This challenge requires meeting the needs of students who are reading "on grade level" by further developing their proficiency with multisyllabic words and helping them increase their automatic recognition of more and more words.

Although these two challenges differ in many ways, their solution is essentially the same: plan for and provide intentional word-reading instruction, not just in third grade but in fourth and fifth as well. Fortunately, there are four common components for word-recognition instruction that teachers at any grade can rely on to assist with both the Filling-the-Gaps Challenge *and* the Moving-Forward Challenge. We describe these in Table 4.1 on the next page.

TABLE 4.1

FOUR ELEMENTS OF INTENTIONAL WORD-READING INSTRUCTION

Element	Description
Scope and Sequence	A research-informed plan for phonics and word recognition that includes *what* will be taught *in what order* and is understood and agreed to by all grades and programs across the school. Figure 4.1 shows an example.
Assessments	Simple word-reading and writing measures that align to your scope-and-sequence and can pinpoint students' strengths and gaps (i.e., spelling inventory, word or sentence dictation, decoding inventory). We suggest the D.I.G. (Decoding Inventory for Growth) available at TheSixShifts.com.
Intentional Instruction	Explicit, evidence-based routines to teach the content of the scope and sequence, driving learning in both whole-group and small-group instruction. (We offer a flexible but explicit phonics lesson template as a free download at TheSixShifts .com/Downloads.)
Mastery Focus	A commitment to mastery of new skills (initial instruction), maintenance of previous skills (embedded cumulative review), and reteaching based on assessment (i.e., targeted differentiation in small groups).

Since an agreed-upon scope and sequence provides the starting point for both the Filling-the-Gaps Challenge and the Moving-Forward Challenge, you may be wondering what a typical scope and sequence for phonics and word study might look like. In Figure 4.1, we offer an abbreviated example of a typical skills progression, beginning with the most foundational skills at the base and building upward to complex multisyllabic words. You can download a PDF of this progression at TheSixShifts.com/Downloads.

As you study Figure 4.1, you'll notice that phonics instruction begins with basic consonants and vowel spellings, applying this knowledge in single-syllable words. As it progresses, the work focuses on increasingly sophisticated skills for navigating multisyllabic words, including syllable junctures and morphemes.

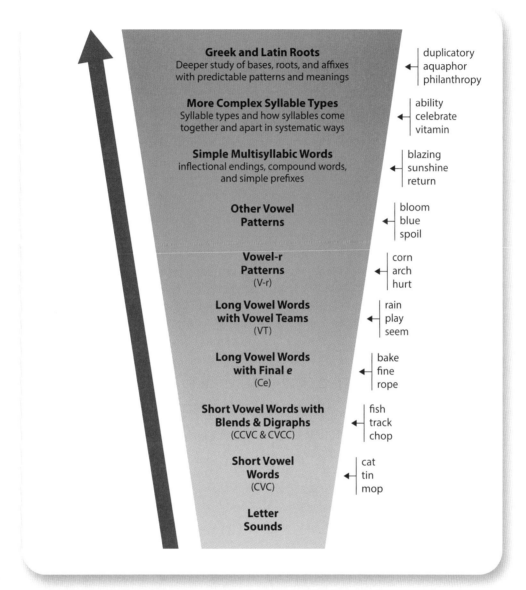

Figure 4.1 Sample Phonics and Word-Reading Skills Progression

Chances are, no matter what the grade, you have some students who still need the most basic phonics instruction, such as firming up all five short vowel sounds in order to efficiently read simple, closed syllable, consonant-vowel-consonant (CVC) words, such as *bin* or *cab* (the Filling-the-Gaps Challenge). Pinpointing student needs and providing students with differentiated small-group instruction is the key to filling gaps.

4

The Moving-Forward Challenge, on the other hand, reminds us that even with basic decoding skills in place, there still is a lot to learn about how to navigate increasingly complex words with confidence and ease. This learning will happen through strong core classroom instruction that continues across the grades.

Any undeveloped word-reading skills will be an ongoing limitation for students because comprehending well requires accurate and effortless word recognition. As Marilyn Adams (1990) explains, "Only if your ability to recognize and capture the meanings of the words on a page is rapid, effortless, and automatic will you have available the cognitive energy and resources upon which skillful comprehension depends" (5).

The four elements described in Table 4.1 above form the foundation of a commitment that teachers in all grades and programs need to make—meeting every child where they are in the skills progression and moving them forward with both patience and urgency.

MISUNDERSTANDING:

Filling in the gaps for children who've fallen behind with word-recognition skills is mostly about teaching phonics skills they have missed.

It might surprise you (it certainly surprised us!) to learn that for most children experiencing reading difficulties, phonics *is not* the primary problem! Believe it or not, insufficient phonemic awareness is the most common cause of word-reading difficulty (Ashby et al. 2022; Kilpatrick 2015). This means that there are many students in the upper elementary grades who will still need intentional instruction in critical phonemic awareness skills—such as how to segment and blend the smallest sounds in words—in order to effectively apply what they are learning in phonics to their reading and writing (Ashby et al. 2022; Brady 2020).

And even though phonemic proficiency is absolutely vital to reading success, it is tricky to teach (and learn) for a few different reasons:

▲ **Phonemic awareness is completely unnatural to the brain.** Prior to human beings inventing written language, there was no reason for the brain to pay attention to the meaningless individual sounds in words. The brain is not naturally equipped to hear and manipulate phonemes. It has to be rewired.

▲ **Phonemes are hard to hear because of coarticulation.** The way individual sounds sort of bump into and bleed onto each other distorts them. This overlapping of sounds, or coarticulation, makes it extra tricky to parse strings of sounds (words) into their individual components (phonemes) because you start forming the second sound before you even finish making the first one. Think of the /t/ and /r/ sounds in *truck* or the /ē/ and /n/ sounds in *jeans*.

▲ **Phonemes are abstract.** Phonemes are invisible. They disappear as soon as we say them. Unless we intentionally use instructional scaffolds to make them tangible and concrete, phonemic awareness work is very abstract and taxing on the working memory.

So ensuring strong phonemic awareness for all children takes a great deal of intentionality. But for linguistically diverse learners, particularly emergent bilinguals, phonemic awareness development has some added layers of complexity. This is because the number and types of phonemes produced in spoken language can vary greatly from one language to the next.

One important instructional consideration is that English contains some phonemes, or sounds, that simply don't exist in other languages. This is especially true when it comes to vowel sounds! For example, Arabic has only eight vowels/diphthongs, while English has more than twice that many unique vowel sounds. This means that many children who are just learning English will likely need extra support learning to produce, identify, and discriminate these new-to-their-brains phonemes.

Yet as tricky as it might be for some children to master, phonemic awareness is a prerequisite for orthographic mapping. And orthographic mapping is the secret sauce of long-term word learning! Orthographic mapping is the in-the-brain process that allows words to be learned in a way that leads to automatic word recognition in the future. Orthographic mapping requires three important skills: phonemic awareness, phonics, and alphabetic insight. The relationship between these skills is illustrated in Figure 4.2 on the next page.

Orthographic mapping is essentially the process of making sense of the orthography of a word by coming to understand the alignment of the word's spoken sounds and written spellings. This "gluing" together of sounds and spellings is a critical step *beyond* decoding that cannot be neglected if words are to get stored in long-term memory for instant and automatic retrieval.

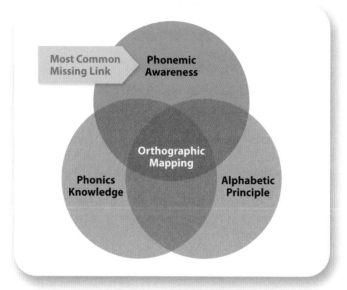

Figure 4.2 Three Understandings Necessary
for Orthographic Mapping

Consider the word *thought* (Figure 4.3). In order to really learn this word, the reading brain must "glue" the three phonemes in the word (/th/ /ŏ/ /t/) to the three graphemes (th-ough-t), which are made up of seven letters (T-H-O-U-G-H-T). So orthographic mapping is the in-the-brain process of permanently connecting sounds to their spellings to lock meaningful letter strings into memory (Ehri 1984, 1987, 2014; Ehri and Wilce 1980; Kilpatrick 2016), as illustrated in Figure 4.3. This is true even if some of the spellings are surprising, as with—*ough*—in the middle of *thought*.

Figure 4.3 Representation of Orthographic Mapping

Phonemic awareness, phonics knowledge, and alphabetic principle come together to enable decoding and eventual orthographic mapping in a chain of learning events detailed in Figure 4.4. The orthographic mapping of more and more words results in a deeper knowledge of words (and their parts) as they get stored in the brain's orthographic filing system, sometimes referred to as the *letterbox* (Dehaene 2013; Ehri 2014). This accumulation of orthographic knowledge has exponentially positive effects, as children can recognize more words instantly and automatically, which leads to increased fluency. This automaticity is cause for celebration because more fluent reading means, of course, that students can redirect more and more attention from decoding to comprehension.

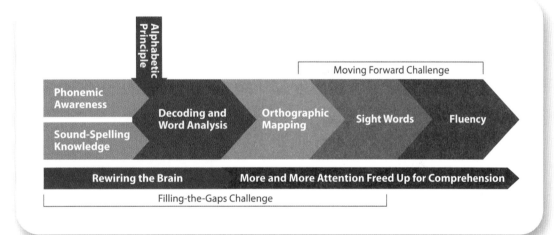

Figure 4.4 Progression from Decoding to Fluency

As you can see, phonics knowledge alone will not get children moving along this powerful chain of increased proficiency. If phonemic awareness is a missing link, then the orthographic mapping necessary for turning any words into sight words just can't happen. So, students won't be able to read fluently, which means they won't be able to comprehend deeply.

4

MISUNDERSTANDING:

Only children who are not reading at grade level need word-recognition instruction in the upper grades.

It seems logical and intuitive to assume that if students have a solid foundation of phonics from the early years, then more sophisticated word-recognition skills will happen on the run, given enough time to read independently. Unfortunately, this assumption won't hold up for a lot of children (Dyson et al. 2017; Tunmer and Chapman 2012).

Without ongoing explicit instruction and a commitment to mastery, we risk weak word-recognition skills and students getting caught in a self-perpetuating cycle. After all, readers who struggle with word identification and decoding tend to avoid reading. They become demotivated by lots of failed attempts and frustrated when it comes to word reading. This avoidance means that they have fewer opportunities to analyze words, scrutinizing those meaningful letter strings less and learning less about how English's sound-spellings work. Fewer successful word encounters result in fewer words learned and even less confidence. Growing frustration even leads to the increased likelihood of avoidance behaviors (McKenna, Kear, and Ellsworth 1995; Moats 2004). Figure 4.5 illustrates this unfortunate self-perpetuating cycle of diminished reading and less word knowledge.

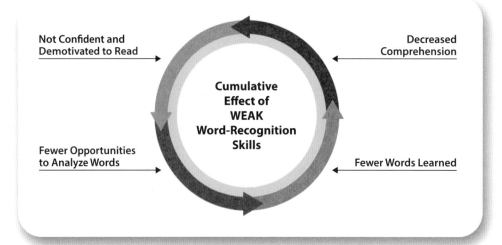

Figure 4.5 Cumulative Effect of Weak Word-Recognition Skills

On the other hand, readers who decode accurately and recognize many words instantly will be more likely to read on their own than peers who are not yet proficient readers (Anderson, Wilson, and Fielding 1988; Moats 2004). This means that they are equipped for more successful encounters with words, analyzing their meaningful letter strings, moving more words into long-term storage, and improving comprehension. This success makes them more likely to read, and the cycle of increasing confidence and motivation continues. Figure 4.6 illustrates this positive cycle.

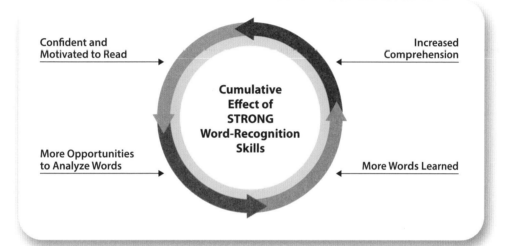

Figure 4.6 Cumulative Effect of Strong Word-Recognition Skills

So, what makes reading English so complex that we need to explicitly and systematically teach how it works all the way through elementary school?

Well, English has what's known as a *deep orthography*, which means that it's not simple or straightforward, because there isn't always a one-to-one match between sounds and their spellings. In all, English has forty-four-ish phonemes that are used to make up all the words in the language, and more than two hundred ways to spell these forty-four sounds using various letters and letter combinations. The phoneme /ā/, for example, can be spelled lots of different ways, as in *cape*, *sail*, and *feign*. These layers of sound-spelling complexity are largely due to the many rich languages that have influenced English. And this deep orthography means that our system has both different (sometimes many) ways to spell a particular sound (see Table 4.2) and different (sometimes many) sounds for the same spelling (see Table 4.3).

TABLE 4.2

DIFFERENT SPELLINGS OF THE
SAME LONG VOWEL SOUND

Sound (Phoneme)	Example Words with Varied Spellings (Graphemes)
/ā/	t**a**me, gr**ai**n, st**ay**, t**a**ble, br**ea**k, r**ei**n, th**ey**, w**eigh**t
/ē/	tr**ee**, g**e**ne, sh**e**, f**ea**t, turk**ey**, fanc**y**, th**ie**f, c**ei**ling
/ī/	p**i**le, t**ie**, tr**y**, l**igh**t, p**i**lot
/ō/	st**o**ne, l**oa**n, gr**ow**, f**oe**, h**o**tel, n**o**, d**ough**
/ŭ/	t**u**ne, z**oo**, d**ue**, fl**ew**, j**ui**ce, y**ou**

TABLE 4.3

DIFFERENT VOWEL PHONEMES SPELLED
WITH THE SAME GRAPHEMES

Spelling (Grapheme)	Example Words with Varied Vowel Sounds (Phonemes)
y	sh**y**, happ**y**
i-e	arr**i**v**e**, act**i**v**e**
ea	h**ea**r, **ea**rly, br**ea**kfast, p**ea**ch, p**ea**r, st**ea**k, h**ea**rt
ow	gr**ow**, c**ow**
oo	f**oo**d, b**oo**k

Adapted from Kearns, Lyon, and Kelley 2022

As you can see from the tables on the previous page, the vowel sounds (especially the long vowel sounds) introduce a lot of trickiness to written English. For example, not only is EA one of at least seven options for spelling the /ē/ sound, but the grapheme EA can also represent up to seven different sounds on its own!

For most children, mastering this complex collection of sounds and spellings—the deep orthography—just can't all happen prior to grade three. It's truly too much! But that's where a thoughtful scope and sequence—paired with a commitment to assessment and mastery—come in, setting students up for an intentional and gradual approach that builds from simple to more complex all the way up through the elementary grades.

But with all this variability in the sound-spellings of our written language, it can be tempting to assume that our orthographic system is just too jumbled and complicated to teach efficiently. We agree that we certainly don't want to confuse kids with all kinds of "rules" that don't hold up.

Yet, despite its complexity, there is a logical system for English orthography (Bowers and Bowers 2017; Coltheart et al. 2001; Eide 2012; Kessler and Treiman 2001). In fact, about 50 percent of the words in English have completely regular or predictable spellings (*computer*, *interesting*, *between*). In another 36 percent of words, all of the phonemes in the word but one—usually a vowel sound—are represented by predictable phonetic spellings (*friend*, *bread*, *again*) (Moats and Tolman 2009). So while our alphabetic system can be intimidating—there is lots to learn—its complexity makes ongoing and systematic word instruction beyond the primary grades especially important. After all, students need to be equipped to read multisyllabic words and comprehend complex texts *as efficiently as possible*.

Of course, some students do pick up on these variations in spelling-sound correspondences mostly on their own over time, but many will not. And while some children may accurately *read* words with diverse vowel representations, their writing samples often reveal that they haven't actually learned them well enough to apply them. In a nutshell, English orthography is hard enough already. Children deserve explicit instruction that makes navigating English's deep orthography—both reading it and writing it—easier, not harder. This commitment means providing dedicated word-recognition instruction throughout the elementary years.

4

MISUNDERSTANDING:

Learning to read multisyllabic words is mostly about learning the rules of syllabication.

Helping students learn to decode multisyllabic words starts by supporting them in becoming confident decoders of single-syllable words. In fact, in English, there are just six basic syllable types to learn, and children need to learn them first in simple, usually one-syllable, words. Table 4.4 lists these syllable patterns in the order in which they are often taught and offers some examples.

TABLE 4.4

SIX SYLLABLE TYPES WITH SINGLE- AND MULTISYLLABLE EXAMPLES

(V = vowel; C = consonant; boldface = example of syllable type)

Syllable Type	Examples
Closed (CVC, CCVC, CVCC, CCVCC, etc.)	**cat**, **chat**, **smash** **pump**-kin, **hid**-den
Final-e (VC-e)	**late**, **bike**, **chute** in-**vite**, com-**plete**
Open (V, CV)	**no**, **he**, **I** **so**-lo, **pre**-vent
Vowel Team / Vowel Diphthong (VV)	**feat**, **paint**, **moon** **out**-bound, **day**-dream
r-controlled / vowel-r (V-r)	**her**, **turn**, **bird** **car**-pet, **or**-gan
Consonant-le (C-le)	ta-**ble**, sim-**ple**, noz-**zle**

Adapted from Honig, Diamond, and Gutlohn 2018

Five of the syllable patterns in the table above are typically taught in the earliest grades and practiced with single-syllable words. In fact, mastering the closed syllable (*cat*, *bed*, *mask*, *crib*, *shop*)—which also happens to be the most common syllable type in written English—is a primary phonics milestone of the kindergarten year!

Eventually, readers start to work with two- and even some three-syllable words that combine familiar chunks and patterns in basic and predictable ways. Once they understand how the patterns for each of these syllable types work in single-syllable words, it's really tempting to think that children will be able to just mix and match these building blocks to read and write big words. But that's only sort of true. There's actually a lot to learn about how syllables work and the role they play in words (Kearns 2020), as the list below illustrates.

▲ Every word has at least one syllable or word part containing a vowel sound (*I*, *a*, *am*, *to*).

▲ Every syllable contains one and only one vowel *sound*, but it can contain more than one vowel *letter* (f*loat*, f*lo*-*ta*-*tion*).

▲ Vowel sounds are the most variable part of the word, so they are more likely to pose decoding difficulty than consonant sounds (*bread*, *broad*, *braid*, *brood*, *bride*).

▲ Unstressed syllables often "break" the rules by replacing the expected vowel sound with a schwa (ə), which usually sounds like a softly spoken short U (eləphant, methəd, cəmplete, dinəsaur).

▲ In multisyllabic words, deciding which syllable gets emphasized plays a huge role in successful pronunciation (*EMphasis*, *emPHASis*, *emphaSIS*).

▲ Sometimes—and usually with good reason—the way syllables are divided in written language (lit-tle) is different from how they are divided in spoken language (li-ttle).

You may be wondering, "If syllable division patterns aren't reliable, is it worth teaching them at all?" Decades of research show us that teaching syllable patterns to assist in decoding has value (Bhattacharya and Ehri 2004; Diliberto et al. 2009; Doignon-Camus and Zagar 2014)—as long as we keep in mind that some syllable patterns are more reliable than others (Kearns and Whaley 2019, Kearns 2020).

4

For example, take a minute to divide these three words, which have a VCCV pattern in the middle, into two syllables.

rabbit

basket

upset

Easy enough, right? Words like these are relatively simple for students to master because the word is broken into two syllables right between the two consonants (VC-CV), creating two straightforward closed (CVC) syllables, which have short vowel sounds.

rab-bit

bas-ket

up-set

And most of the time—70.6 percent of the time, to be exact—the first syllable in this pattern is pronounced with a short vowel sound (Kearns 2020). This level of predictability makes it worthwhile to teach this particular syllable division pattern, for sure. Two-syllable words with this pattern are often the entry point for instruction in multisyllabic words.

But just as some syllable junctures are quite reliable and easy to master, others are not. Take, for instance, words that include a single consonant surrounded by two vowels (VCV). Look at these two words and divide them into their two syllables:

humid

timid

What did you notice? Both words have a single consonant between the two vowels pattern. But did you notice that the word *humid* has a syllable break after the letter U, creating an open first syllable and therefore a "long" vowel sound (hū-mid)? The word *timid*, on the other hand, has its syllable break after the M, creating a closed syllable and, therefore, a "short" vowel sound (tĭm-id).

In fact, for words with *just two syllables* containing a VCV pattern that straddles the syllable break, the most consistent pattern is a syllable split right after the vowel (as in *hu-mid*). But this is still only true a little less than half of the time. And for words with *more than two syllables*, this pattern is even less consistent, holding true for not quite 18 percent of these multisyllabic words (Kearns 2020).

Now, maybe you're thinking, "Ah, so the rest of the time the break in VCV two-syllable words creates a closed first syllable and a short vowel sound." Actually, that's not always true either. A lot of the time the first vowel represents a sound that is neither its long sound nor its short sound but something completely different, such as the schwa in the words *mɘney* and *bɘnanɘ*.

So, what's a reading teacher to do? Well, the bottom line for reading longer and longer words is that students need to know some basic syllabication patterns as a place to start. But they also need to learn to be more flexible in their approximations, as sound-spellings for vowels become more variable and rules become less reliable in longer words (Kearns 2020).

In Table 4.5 we offer examples of simpler to more complex syllable combinations to consider when selecting the type of big-word reading practice to provide. A progression such as this one is often reflected within a scope and sequence. Words with closed syllables created by VCCV patterns are often a starting point, while words containing one or more single-vowel spellings in VCV patterns are typically much more difficult, because of the inconsistency we described above.

TABLE 4.5

SIMPLE TO COMPLEX, SAMPLE SYLLABLE COMBINATIONS

Word-Reading Practice Type	Example Words	Description
VCCV Syllable Junctures (Simplest to Read)	admit, bathtub, catnip, falcon, hundred, investment, Atlantic	When there are two or more consonants separating two vowels, the first syllable will usually be closed.
Closed Syllables + Final e	sunshine, dislike, complete, invite, combine, demonstrate, tranquilize, distribute	The final e is included in the same syllable as the vowel that comes before it, making one long vowel sound.
Mix of Closed Syllables + Vowel Teams	doghouse, freedom, snowman, clueless, playpen	When two or more vowels are right next to each other in the word, they will most likely make one vowel sound within the same syllable.

continues

4

Word-Reading Practice Type	Example Words	Description
2-Syllable Words with VCV Syllable Juncture	human, bison, cabin, atom, robot, unit, habit, gravel, second, behind	If vowels are separated by only one consonant, the vowel sound is most likely long, but it could also be short or even a schwa. You may need to try a few different sounds for syllables like these and see which one forms a word that makes sense. (Requires most flexibility.)
3+ Syllables Containing at least One VCV Juncture	television, helicopter, imagine, celebrate, tranquility, supervisor, vegetarian	

As children store more and more information about English orthography, they enter a phase of word reading referred to as the consolidated phase (Ehri 1995, 2005a, 2005b, 2017), where they can draw on their ever-expanding knowledge of orthographic patterns to spot familiar word parts with greater ease and automaticity (**cat**, **cat**nip, **cat**egory, re**cat**egorize). (You can learn more about Ehri's Phases of Word Development in *Shifting the Balance K–2*, Shift 3.) So, reading big words requires basic decoding, some practice with noticing familiar syllable types, and a commitment to flexibility—especially when it comes to vowel sounds. Whew! Big words, big work!

As children grapple with big words, noticing useful chunks and flexing sounds within syllables, trying one and then another (tee-lee-vigh-shun, teh-lee-vis-i-on . . .), their efforts can still result in some "off-track" word attempts. Yet the good news is that as long as their approximations include every part of the word and offer plausible phonetic attempts, then *set for variability* can help them get the rest of the way.

Set for variability is the mechanism for making the leap from a complete and plausible phonetic pronunciation to the actual word (Edwards et al. 2022; Steacy et al. 2019). It's where, only after decoding sound-by-sound, children need to ask themselves, "Does what I'm saying sound like a word I know?" Set for variability is what prompts students to notice that /teh-lee-vis-i-on/ is not exactly a recognizable word, but it's awfully close to the actual pronunciation, which also makes sense in the sentence *The television was on the fritz, so she couldn't watch her favorite show.*

When decoding words, especially longer words, flexibility is essential. We include more discussion of how to teach students to read syllables flexibly in the "Recommendations for Making the Shift" section.

MISUNDERSTANDING:

Devoting instructional time to word recognition will take away from a focus on comprehension.

It can be easy to worry that time spent on word-recognition instruction will take time away from our main instructional focus—reading comprehension. Of course, our driving purpose isn't to teach decoding or to help children become experts in syllable division! Rather, our intention is to equip learners with the skills they need to get to the meaning *behind* the words they read.

This becomes especially important as the vocabulary in texts becomes more difficult and the language structures become more complex. This moment is when we can see the word-recognition instruction students have gotten either really paying off for readers or, on the other hand, causing inaccuracies in reading and disruptions to comprehension to pile up. Remember the research that said that students reading below the basic level were likely to misread as many as one out of every six words (White et al. 2021)? These decoding errors can be debilitating for readers.

But it's not just a lack of phonics and word study that gets in the way of word-recognition success. We can also actually slow down the accumulation of word-recognition skills when—at the point of word-reading difficulty and with the best of intentions—we treat decoding as the strategy of last resort, prompting students to engage in an array of strategies other than decoding that take them *around* the word rather than *through* it. Some of the prompting practices we've believed in and relied on in the past—asking students to make approximations based on what would "make sense" or "sound right," coaching them to engage in letter sampling, predicting words based on context or picture cues, or even skipping words altogether—turn out to be misguided and to interfere with fluent reading in the long run (Adams 1990; Burkins and Yates 2021; Castles, Rastle, and Nation 2018).

Chances are you've heard about the concerns with "three cueing systems" and the harmful effects this type of prompting can have in the long run (we dedicated a whole chapter to this topic in our K–2 book). It's true that

4

decoding sound by sound can seem like a tedious way to read unfamiliar words. But what we now know is that, ironically, in order to move past needing to do a lot of sound-by-sound decoding and word analysis, readers actually have to first do a lot of sound-by-sound decoding and word analysis (Dehaene 2013; Ehri 1987, 1995, 1998). There's just no getting around it.

Without careful analysis of the whole word, orthographic mapping can't happen, and without the pattern-generating power of orthographic mapping, storage of words for automatic and effortless retrieval can't happen (Ehri 2014, 2017). Without automatic and effortless retrieval, fluency can't happen. And without fluency, comprehension is, well, compromised.

So, supporting readers in the critical (albeit sometimes laborious) work of sound-by-sound decoding *does* support a chain of events leading to the ultimate goal of meaning-making. With every word decoded, the brain learns more about that deep orthography of English, therefore allowing readers to navigate texts with increasing confidence and ease, ultimately leaving more cognitive attention available for (drum roll, please!) comprehension (Duke, Ward, and Pearson 2021).

But without these strong word-reading skills, comprehension will always be a struggle. So, devoting instructional time to word recognition and adopting more science-aligned prompting practices won't detract from comprehension. They'll allow it.

A Short Summary of the Science

▲ Written language is a human invention, so learning to read words requires rewiring the brain.

▲ Readers need three things before they can read words: phonemic awareness, phonics knowledge, and the alphabetic principle.

▲ Weak phonemic awareness is the most common cause of word-reading difficulties.

▲ Phonemic awareness is hard to teach and learn because it's unnatural for the brain, phonemes overlap (coarticulation), and they are abstract.

▲ Comprehending well requires accurate and effortless word recognition.

▲ Insufficient phonemic awareness interferes with orthographic mapping, which is the path to instant and automatic word recognition.

▲ Word-reading instruction should be systematic rather than incidental.

▲ A lack of automaticity in reading can have consequences for students' reading volume and motivation to read.

▲ Understanding how syllables work matters for accurately reading words in English.

▲ The vowels are the trickiest part of words because they are the most variable.

▲ Teaching syllabication has value, but students should be taught how to use syllable divisions flexibly and conditionally (set for variability).

4

THE SIMPLE AND SCIENTIFICALLY SOUND SHIFT

▼ ▼ ▼ ▲ ▼ ▼

Provide explicit word-reading instruction through both whole-group lessons and differentiation to equip children to read increasingly challenging words.

Recommendations for Making the Shift

Making the shift to more intentional word-reading instruction hinges on some basic necessities, including a science-aligned scope and sequence, decodable word lists, and a commitment to periodic assessment that drives both whole-group and small-group instruction. You don't need a huge number of routines to teach word-recognition skills effectively, and you don't need to worry that word-reading instruction means filling students' days with worksheets.

In Table 4.6, we offer a collection of routines that will position you for strong, systematic instruction designed to meet the word-recognition needs of your students for both the Filling-the-Gaps Challenge and the Moving-Forward Challenge. If you use a published program, hopefully these routines are a part of what you are already doing. If not, you can use this list as a guide to revise or supplement your instructional routines. After Table 4.6, we zoom in on scaffolding orthographic mapping, marking up (or writing) big words, and reading long words bit by bit.

TABLE 4.6

HIGH-LEVERAGE INSTRUCTIONAL ROUTINES FOR TEACHING WORD READING

The What: *Routine*	The Why: *Purpose*	The How: *Example*
Scaffolding Orthographic Mapping	To map speech sounds to print, aligning phonemes and graphemes to make their relationships in a word clear, which scaffolds orthographic mapping	See "Zooming In on Scaffolding Orthographic Mapping."
Marking Up (or Writing) Big Words	To scaffold reading and writing multisyllabic words through close analysis of vowels, syllables, morphemes, and even individual phonemes	See "Zooming In on Marking Up (or Writing) Big Words."
Reading Long Words Bit by Bit	To teach students a simple and flexible strategy for reading long words on the run	See "Zooming In on Reading Long Words Bit by Bit."

continues

4

The What: *Routine*	The Why: *Purpose*	The How: *Example*
Practicing Set for Variability	To teach students to engage set for variability, making a leap from their complete sound-by-sound decoding approximation to a word in their speaking vocabulary that *also* makes sense in context	"Let's read the sentence 'The cold water made her /sh/-/ī/-/v/-/er/.' Now let's make a leap from the word I said—/sh/-/ī/-/v/-/er/, which doesn't sound like a word we know—to a word we know that would make sense."
Aligned Reading Practice	To provide readers with opportunities to read texts that are aligned to the current skill focus, including concentrated practice decoding increasingly complex graphemes, syllable types, and multisyllabic words	"Let's practice reading some long words with syllable patterns like the word *compete*. These words have closed syllables combined with syllables that have a final e. We'll warm up with a word list, and then read a short passage that will give you opportunities to practice reading final e in some long words."
Spelling Dictation	To provide students spelling practice aligned to the current instructional focus, including cumulative review and high-frequency words, and to provide the teacher actionable formative data	"Let's write some sentences that include the syllable patterns we've been practicing. Listen to each word carefully and then write the sentence: 'It was a mistake to exclude them from our contest.'"

Zooming In on Scaffolding Orthographic Mapping

Word mapping using sound boxes is a practical and versatile way to support students in aligning the phonemes they hear in words with the graphemes that spell them. This routine helps to scaffold the in-the-brain process of orthographic mapping and can be particularly useful with emergent bilinguals and students who are not yet proficient single-syllable decoders. With consistent practice, students will begin to map more words more easily on their own.

When teaching a new grapheme (EA, -AY) or reviewing a pair of related graphemes (CH, TCH), sound boxes, or Elkonin boxes (Elkonin 1973), provide a way to make the mental work of aligning sounds and spellings clear and concrete. Here are a few simple steps to follow when supporting students as they map words, making organization and retrieval of the word (and its parts) more efficient down the road.

1. **Connect to meaning.** Before mapping the word, take a minute to define the word and use it in a sentence. It can be easy to assume that students already know the meaning, but they may not always know the multiple meanings of words or how they are used in a sentence. Connecting to meaning is an important part of how the brain remembers words.

> Our first word is *choice*. Having a choice means that you get to decide something. I like having a choice about what ice cream flavor I want when I go to the ice cream parlor. What do you like having a choice about?

2. **Segment the word into phonemes.** Prompt students to listen carefully to the individual phonemes in the word, paying careful attention to their number and their order. Students can hold up one finger for each sound they hear.

> Listen carefully to the sounds you hear in *choice*.
> How many sounds in the word *choice*?
> Yes, three sounds—/ch/ /oi/ /s/.
> So we'll use three sound boxes to write the word *choice*.

4

3. **Touch the empty boxes while saying the sounds.** As students say the word, have them touch each empty box, segmenting it into individual sounds. Check to be sure that the pointing and the pacing of the sound pronunciation match.

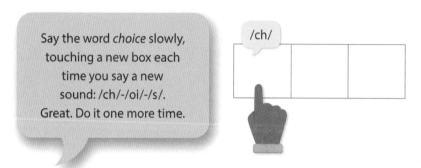

> Say the word *choice* slowly, touching a new box each time you say a new sound: /ch/-/oi/-/s/. Great. Do it one more time.

4. **Write the sound-spellings in the boxes.** Have students write the corresponding graphemes in the boxes that represent them, saying the sounds (not the letter names) as they write them.

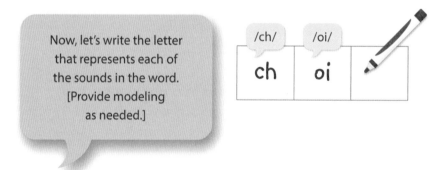

> Now, let's write the letter that represents each of the sounds in the word. [Provide modeling as needed.]

5. **Write the entire word.** Let children practice writing the word, saying the sounds for each sound-spelling as they do, and then checking it.

> Now, let's write the word, without the boxes. As you write it, /ch/-/oi/-/s/, be sure you pronounce each sound slowly. After you've written it, read it to check it carefully, using your finger to touch each sound as you say it.

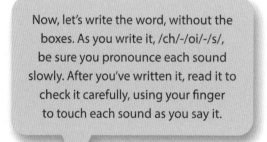

6. **Transfer the learning to new words.** Dictate three to five more words that provide additional practice with the focus skill, as well as some review of past skills. Have students practice reading the list of words.

> Now, let's write another word that has the same sound, /oi/, spelled with the vowel team OI. The next word is *oil*.

ch	oi	ce				choice
oi	l					oil
j	oi	n	t			joint
p	oi	s	o	n		poison
b	oi	l	er			boiler
a	v	oi	d			avoid

> Before we're finished, let's go back and reread all the words together [with a partner, on your own].

To download a blank copy of the sound box tool above, go to TheSixShifts.com/Downloads.

Zooming In on Marking Up Big Words

Sound boxes work especially well for one-syllable words and words with two to six phonemes. But when children are ready to learn how to read and spell multisyllabic (big) words, sound boxes and/or sound-by-sound decoding is not nearly as helpful or efficient. So, in this section, we zoom in on explicit procedures for tackling those big words. The first process—adapted from Moats and Tolman (2009)—will help students read an unfamiliar multisyllabic word, moving it from print to speech. The second process will help you teach children how to *spell* a multisyllabic word, moving it from speech to print.

▲ Reading: From Print to Speech

It can be helpful to teach a process for strategically tackling the pronunciation of a word through close analysis. Certainly, we are not recommending that children use this elaborated process every

4

time they encounter a long word in connected text! Instead, it is a scaffolding routine that you can facilitate during whole-group, small-group, or individual instruction that cumulatively leads to more confidence in tackling big words on the run. The steps below describe the process.

▲ **Student Materials** Each student will need a dry-erase board, two different colored markers, and an eraser.

▲ **Getting Started** Write the target word on the board for students to see, and then guide students through the following steps, providing scaffolding as needed. Over time, students will do more and more of the work.

precipitate

1. **Write the word and highlight the vowels.** Study the word and locate the vowel graphemes. Then write the word on a dry-erase board using one color for consonant letters and another for vowel letters. Notice syllable patterns.

2. **Underline any morphemes you recognize.** Check the beginning and end of the word for any known morphemes (affixes or bases). If you see any you know, draw a line under them with the same marker you used to mark vowel letters.

3. **Do your best to divide the word into syllables.** Study the word again, thinking about vowel placement. Decide where the syllables *could* break. Draw a curved line under each remaining syllable.

4. **Read each of the individual parts.** Read each of the parts of the word in order, blending sounds as necessary. Pay special attention to the vowel sounds.

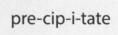

5. **Read the whole word.** Reread the whole word, blending all of the parts together.

6. **Think about the word.** Listen to the word you are saying. Does it sound like a word you know? Is it a word you know? If not, does it sound *close* to a word you know? Try making adjustments to the vowel sounds and the stressed syllable to arrive at a recognizable word.

7. **Bonus Step:** Erase the word and rewrite the whole word without looking at the model. Then check the word carefully and reread it, moving your finger under each syllable as you do.

You may notice how this approach starts and ends by positioning students to be *vowel alert* (Kearns, Lyon, and Kelley 2022), preparing them to be flexible with spelling patterns that may have multiple pronunciations and priming set for variability.

▲ **Spelling: From Speech to Print**

In addition to supporting students to read big words, it will be important to apply a similar process for supporting students to strategically tackle spelling big words. You can teach a parallel process for writing a big word, or moving from speech to print, in just a few steps. For a download of a writing big words routine, go to TheSixShifts.com/Downloads.

English is a morphophonemic language, and this kind of work with big words supports children's development of both knowledge about morphology and sound to spelling connections.

Zooming In on Reading Long Words Bit by Bit

Of course, it's not practical to rely on an involved process like marking vowels and syllable breaks every time a reader encounters a new and complex word in connected text. Students need a quick and flexible strategy that they can apply independently on the run.

A simple, all-purpose strategy for reading longer words in context is to teach children to use a finger to cover and then reveal the word a bit at a time, using *what they know* about orthographic patterns and morphology to come up with an approximation that accounts for every sound-spelling in the word. Here's some teacher language to teach the process, using the word *helicopter* as an example:

1. "Use your index finger to cover up the whole word."

2. "Slide your finger to the right and uncover a bit of the word. Be sure that the part includes one (and only one) vowel grapheme." (Note: The part that is uncovered *does not* have to be a perfect syllable chunk, but it shouldn't be more than one syllable. The image below illustrates two acceptable responses and one unacceptable response.)

3. "Read that part of the word using all the information you know about its sound-spellings." "Plausible" pronunciations for the two examples of "correct" responses (indicated above with green arrows) are:

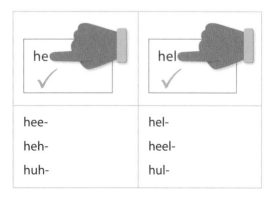

he ✓	hel ✓
hee-	hel-
heh-	heel-
huh-	hul-

4. "Repeat the process with the next part of the word. Each time you uncover a bit, add it to the part(s) you've already read. Continue until you have read the whole word." Here are examples of possible pronunciations of the word *helicopter* using this strategy:

hee-luh-cop-ter

heh-ligh-cop-tear

heh-li-cup-tear

5. "Now reread the whole sentence and think about a word you know that sounds like the word you are saying *and* makes sense in the sentence" (set for variability).

**The helicopter landed on the pad
on the roof of the building.**

This outside-the-brain scaffold can help young readers develop more automatic inside-the-brain processes, like those we have internalized as proficient readers. Coupled with Marking Up Big Words (which helps children become familiar with orthographic patterns) and with set for variability (which helps children take their approximations to an actual word that makes sense), Reading Long Words Bit by Bit can be a powerful in-the-moment strategy for readers grappling with longer words on the run.

What's more, because they utilize their finger to reveal each bit of the word, students who tend to overlook parts of longer words—*presdent* vs. *president*; *organational* vs. *organizational*—can learn to blend all the way across the word without excluding any of it. As an added bonus, covering up the word to focus on a single part at a time makes the potentially overwhelming task of reading long words more manageable and calms the big-word panic that many students experience.

Meanwhile, Back in the Classroom . . .

As a result of several weeks of studying a number of resources, Ms. Schwartz and her colleagues have identified some important revisions to their word study practice that they are committed to making.

Realizing they all needed a baseline understanding of what their students really do and don't know when it comes to phonics skills, the third-grade team has decided to administer a diagnostic decoding inventory. After previewing a few different assessment options, they chose a tool that included both word reading and a short spelling inventory. Everyone was excited about getting more detailed information about their students' decoding skills. In fact, after catching wind of what was happening, the second- and fourth-grade teams decided to participate.

Ms. Schwartz's initial assessment results confirmed her hunch that the difference between her students' knowledge of foundational skills is expansive. She definitely needs to plan for both the Filling-the-Gaps Challenge *and* the Moving-Forward Challenge in her classroom.

To tackle the Moving-Forward Challenge, she and her teammates have collaborated to redesign their daily schedules, claiming ten minutes of the forty minutes that were previously dedicated to independent reading. Dedicating time for explicit instruction and practice with word-reading skills is new and a little scary. But the team is working together to identify a weekly focus to help children build their skills for reading big words.

As for the Filling-the-Gaps Challenge, the decoding and spelling inventory revealed that nearly half of her students still have difficulty decoding and encoding even single-syllable words. On the advice of a special education teacher in the building, Ms. Schwartz decided to also take a quick informal look at their phoneme blending and segmentation skills. This was something she'd never given much thought to before, as a third-grade teacher. Ms. Schwartz knows she has her work cut out for her. But something feels sort of satisfying about being able to put her finger on the specific gaps that need to be filled, especially for students like Macey and Dante, who, as it turns out, need help blending and segmenting phonemes. She also has a clear starting point for students like Maribel and Henry, who still demonstrate confusion about long vowel teams, r-controlled vowels, and even words with final e.

Since she's always been committed to small-group instruction, she already had the structures in place for differentiation. Now, Ms. Schwartz is working to adjust the routines and texts she uses in small groups to connect with the specific word-reading needs of her students. She is also intentional about including opportunities to read *and* write words with the targeted skills. This application work also includes using decodable, or phonics-aligned, instructional texts for those who need them.

The good news is that she's seeing the new skills transfer to reading and writing more and more. Students like Drew seem more engaged and more eager to try new things as readers and writers, not just during small-group

4

instruction but across the day. Now when Drew encounters a multisyllabic word, he's slowing down to read across the whole word rather than guessing based on a few letters. When working to spell unfamiliar words, he is also better able to stretch the word out, phoneme by phoneme, confidently matching each sound to the new graphemes he's learned. Last week, Ms. Schwartz was thrilled to see Drew figure out how to spell the word *incredible* by himself.

And, to her surprise, it seems that for many students, greater automaticity with word recognition has really enhanced comprehension. As they attend to words more closely, her students' understanding of texts is deepening.

Looking back at her past approaches to teaching reading and spelling, Ms. Schwartz realizes that she and her colleagues had taken for granted that their students already had a lot of foundational skills in place. But she's seeing more clearly that the development of her students' phonemic awareness, decoding, and spelling skills can't be taken for granted or left to chance. Rather, she's embracing the idea of becoming more planned and purposeful in her approach to word-reading instruction—both for filling gaps and for moving forward!

Questions for Reflection

Checking In with Yourself: Which of the misunderstandings about word-reading instruction did you find most thought-provoking? Which ones have you believed and how has your thinking changed? How will your word-recognition instruction change as a result?

Purposeful Instruction: Do you have a research-informed plan for phonics and word-recognition instruction that includes what will be taught and in what order? Is it shared by all? What are your next steps?

Dedicated Time: How much dedicated time do you have in your schedule for whole-group or small-group word-reading instruction? Is it enough to allow a truly explicit and systematic approach and to teach to mastery?

Diagnostic and Formative Assessment: What diagnostic tools, such as phonics and phonemic awareness surveys, do you have/need to determine what skills your students have mastered and where they need support? How can you incorporate ongoing, simple formative assessments like spelling dictation, to determine what's sticking for students?

Orthographic Mapping: If orthographic mapping is new to you, how will you learn more about it? How will you design instruction to scaffold grapheme-phoneme mapping more intentionally across instructional contexts?

Teaching Syllabication: What role has syllabication previously played in your instruction? What revisions might you make based on what you've learned?

Differentiation: Who do your current practices best serve? Who will benefit the most from a shift in practice? What next steps will you take to inform your teaching and differentiation? Which techniques from this shift could you incorporate into your small-group instruction to differentiate word-recognition instruction?

Revisiting Fluency Instruction

M s. Stone is a fourth-grade teacher who learned long ago that there is a connection between reading fluency and comprehension. So she values the data she gets from the timed fluency measures that all teachers at her school periodically administer.

But this year, she's noticing more and more students who simply equate fluency with speed. When reading aloud, Aaden and Lamonte both rush through a text as if they are in a race, without so much as a pause between sentences, let alone emphasizing words or phrases to convey meaning.

And reading too fast isn't the only fluency problem Ms. Stone is concerned about. She also notices a number of students who seem to use little or no expression, reading word after word after word in a mostly monotone voice. Some have difficulty with character dialogue, overlooking intonation cues, such as italics and exclamation marks. And others, like Anna and Rosella, sound smooth and conversational when they read fiction but become stilted and disfluent when they read informational texts.

Because of these challenges, and because she wants to make sure that her students are prepared to perform well on oral reading fluency assessments, Ms. Stone has made a commitment to embedding oral reading opportunities across the week, in both whole-group and small-group settings.

When she first started teaching a few years ago, Ms. Stone had students read in a "round robin" style. She would ask one student to read a paragraph aloud while everyone else followed along from their own copy, and then the next student in the line would read. But lately, she has grown frustrated with this method and its unhelpful predictability. After all, it doesn't take much math for the students furthest down the line to realize they can, more or less, coast until their turn to read. And it's easy for those who've already read aloud to get the idea that they are pretty much finished with reading.

SHIFT

5

So, recently, Ms. Stone decided to mix things up a bit in an attempt to make oral reading practice more engaging. Now she uses two different methods for oral reading. The first is "popcorn reading," where one student reads part of a passage and then "popcorns" to the next reader by calling on anyone in the room to go next. For the other routine, she relies on popsicle sticks, one with each student's name on it. She keeps the sticks in a can and randomly draws the name of the person who will read aloud next.

Ms. Stone likes how these methods not only support oral reading practice but have the added bonus of keeping her students on their toes so that they follow along with the text. Still, there are many students who exhibit signs of acute anxiety and distress regardless of the turn-taking method she uses. Some students, like Lucia, are even more nervous about reading aloud now that they don't have advance warning of what they'll have to read or when their turn is coming.

And Ms. Stone has started to notice that understanding the text during these oral reading events is tricky, not only for the students who are having trouble tuning in because they are nervous about their turn to read aloud but also for anyone who is trying to follow along with the oral reading of peers, which is often disfluent or inaccurate.

Recognizing problems with each of the systems she's tried, Ms. Stone is struggling to think of the best way to help students with all of these aspects of oral reading, while also preparing them for success with those more formal, timed fluency measures. Recently she had a conversation with Mr. Sanchez, her teammate next door, and learned that he too is unsure about how to best support fluency. So, they have decided to do a little research to deepen their understanding and to identify methods that might be more effective, engaging, and even joyful for all students.

5

A COMMON PRACTICE TO RECONSIDER

We think too narrowly about what fluency instruction can look like.

Ms. Stone is not alone in her confusion about how to best support fluency development in readers. After all, it can seem logical to have students read aloud one by one as a way to monitor and nudge them on their oral reading. And it can be easy to place all of our attention on reading speed when universal assessments that only measure the number of words read accurately per minute have become a mainstay of reading assessment in the elementary grades.

But, as we will unpack in this shift, fluency is about more than reading rate. Fluency is actually a critical link between decoding and comprehension (Duke, Ward, and Pearson 2021; Pikulski and Chard 2005; Rasinski 2012). Remember the Active View of Reading model (Duke and Cartwright 2021) that we introduced in Shift 2? Well, it positions fluency as a *bridging skill* alongside vocabulary and morphological awareness. In the Active View model (Duke and Cartwright 2021), strong fluency strengthens both word-recognition and language comprehension skills—the two strands of Scarborough's rope (Scarborough 2001). Figure 5.1 illustrates this bridging relationship.

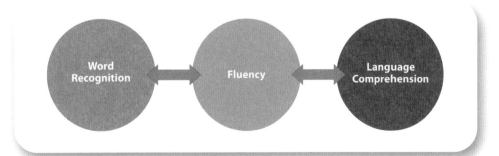

Figure 5.1 The Fluency Connection

Think about your experiences learning a new skill, such as playing an instrument, participating in a sport, or driving a car. All of these require automaticity in order to become fluent. For example, on your first day behind the wheel, you were focused on each discrete part of driving. Checking your mirrors, picking up speed, or putting on a turn signal probably took concentration and effort.

Eventually, though, you became more fluent. Things that once required a lot of attention became more automatic and effortless. You now automatically put on your wipers at the first drop of rain or flip on your blinker before changing lanes without giving either task even a fleeting moment of conscious attention. This automaticity frees up more attention to focus on the podcast you've got playing on the sound system or the conversation you're having with the kids in the backseat. Becoming fluent in any complex behavior requires automaticity (Moats 2004).

We've known for a long time that the same is true for reading (LaBerge and Samuels 1974). For example, beginning decoders focus most of their attention on translating the letters on the page to the sounds they represent so that they can accurately read words. And readers have to do lots of decoding (and orthographic mapping) to develop the automaticity with word recognition that is necessary for fluency (more on this later). But once some fluency develops, readers can navigate the print effortlessly, paying little conscious attention to word recognition, which means they can shift more attention to comprehension. Yay! Because comprehension, of course, is the ultimate goal of reading.

Clearing Up Some Confusion

Fluency and its comprehension benefits don't just develop as a matter of course once children have some decoding skills under their belts (Kuhn et al. 2006). And despite some ongoing confusion about the topic, decades of research show that reading fluency both influences the reading comprehension process (Fuchs et al. 2001; LaBerge and Samuels 1974; Nese et al. 2013; Rasinski et al. 2005) and can serve as a predictor of reading comprehension skills (Kim 2015; Kim, Quinn, and Petscher 2021; Nathan and Stanovich 1991).

In this shift, we'll show you how you can support fluency development using science-aligned methods in order to reach the true goal of reading—comprehension.

MISUNDERSTANDING:

Reading fluency is mostly about reading speed.

As a fourth-grade teacher, Katie often had students who read too quickly, racing through punctuation in an effort to finish first or appear more "fluent." These were often the same students who took great pride in being the fastest ones on the playground at recess. She regularly had to remind them of the tortoise and the hare—that the fastest is not always the best. This is true in many aspects of life, but it can be especially true in reading.

Of course, rate is certainly a critical factor in reading fluency. The Hasbrouck-Tindal oral reading fluency chart (Hasbrouck and Tindal 2006, 2017) shows the oral reading fluency norms of students across grade levels. It's likely you've used a chart like theirs to draw conclusions and make decisions about your own students' oral reading fluency.

However, as helpful as they are, fluency rate charts can also deepen the false assumptions we may carry that reading has to go fast. Reading fluency is about more than rate (Álvarez-Cañizo, Suárez-Coalla, and Cuetos 2015; Elhassan et al. 2015; Hudson, Lane, and Pullen 2005; Kuhn and Stahl 2003). And while reading rate is one important fluency factor, it can be easy to overemphasize speed while underemphasizing other essential aspects of fluency.

Reading fluency is actually complex and multifaceted, with three primary components. Rate is only one of them. Each of these components has subskills that, if weak or missing, can contribute to disfluency. We describe these components in Table 5.1 on the following page.

TABLE 5.1

READING FLUENCY COMPONENTS

Component	Description	Prerequisites for Success
Accuracy	The ability to decode or recognize words correctly	• Knowledge of relevant letter-sound relationships (phonics knowledge) • The ability to blend sounds into words (phonemic awareness) • An understanding of the alphabetic principle • Knowledge of relevant irregularly spelled high-frequency words • Ability to notice when errors are made and to activate self-correction
Rate	The pace at which one reads a portion of text	• Accuracy with word reading • Automaticity with word reading
Prosody	A reader's use of intonation, stress, and phrasing	• Use of pitch in ways that mirror spoken language • Ability to stress the right syllables within words • Understanding which words to emphasize within a sentence • Automaticity with chunking words into phrases or other meaningful groups

Kuhn and Stahl 2003; Álvarez-Cañizo, Suárez-Coalla, and Cuetos 2015; Elhassan et al. 2015; Hudson, Lane, and Pullen 2005

When students increase their accuracy as readers, it usually improves their reading rate. An increase in rate, of course, can also improve prosody, or expression. And improved prosody, whether reading aloud or in our heads, makes it easier to comprehend the text.

The diagram in Figure 5.2 illustrates the path from decoding to language comprehension. This diagram helps us understand why decoding difficulties and word-by-word reading interfere with expression, which in turn compromises comprehension. And of course, until the written language of the text is translated into spoken language—whether aloud or in our heads—we can't comprehend it.

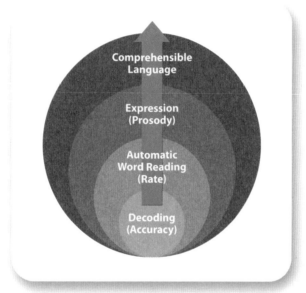

Figure 5.2 The Fluency Path from Decoding
to Comprehensible Language

The fluent reader does all of this work in a way that is seemingly effortless. For nonfluent readers, on the other hand, the work of decoding can monopolize their attention. This means their cognitive resources are less available for making connections between sentences, relating what they are reading to what they already know, and making the inferential leaps a text requires (Pikulski and Chard 2005).

But whether we're "listening" to our own silent reading inside our head or reading a passage aloud, each of the aspects of fluency—accuracy, rate, and prosody—has the potential to either enhance or complicate comprehension (Valencia and Buly 2004). Table 5.2 (page 158) offers examples of some of the kinds of comprehension errors that can be caused by a lack of fluency.

TABLE 5.2

EXAMPLES OF COMPREHENSION
ERRORS CAUSED BY FLUENCY ERRORS

What the Text Actually Says	What the Reader Says	Factors Affecting Comprehension
She did not anticipate the abrupt ending.	"She . . . did . . . not . . . an . . . ti . . . ci . . . pate . . . the . . . a . . . brupt . . . end . . . ing."	*A slow pace* (rate)
That was not her invention. It was his.	"That was not her intention. It was his."	*Inaccurate decoding* (accuracy)
We're listening to the committee.	"We're listening to the comedy."	*Incorrect syllable-level stress* (accuracy)
The BOY is in the house! (Not someone else.)	"The boy is in the HOUSE!" (Not somewhere else.)	*Incorrect word-level emphasis* (prosody)
We're going to watch this again?	"We're going to watch this again."	*Misreading punctuation* (prosody)
We advocated for more information to be published in the book about elephants.	"We advocated for . . . more information to be . . . published in . . . the book about elephants."	*Ineffective phrasing* (prosody)

As you can see, fluency involves a complex interaction of skills. So, when students have low scores on fluency measures, it's important to sort out the root cause. Not surprisingly, the solution isn't always about speeding things up. When children lack accurate, automatic, and/or expressive reading, as described in the tables above, they will need direct and explicit instruction in the prerequisites they are missing.

Fortunately, because the elements of fluency and their subskills are intertwined, supported practice with one element often means students are simultaneously working on another. For example, when students read with a focus on paying attention to punctuation, their voice begins to better match how the character should sound. Hearing how the character sounds can help to better imagine what the character might be feeling. That greater understanding of the character's feelings, in turn, leads to more appropriate expression.

So when students lack fluency, put on your detective hat and dig a little deeper. There can be a number of reasons for a lack of fluency, and different fluency issues will have different remedies. But once you determine what is affecting fluency, explicit instruction and practice aimed at shoring up those skills will be a worthwhile investment in overall fluency and, of course, comprehension.

 ## MISUNDERSTANDING:

Once students have basic decoding skills, silent reading is more important than oral reading.

If you're like many teachers in the upper elementary grades, you may be experiencing some dissonance around the seemingly conflicting priorities of independent *silent* reading and strong *oral* reading fluency. You want students to have a rich reading life and encourage them to read on their own, both in and out of the classroom. You also know that students need eyes on print and that a vibrant reading life is not only about skill building—it's about soul building.

It is easy to see why independent, *silent* reading is the heart of many upper elementary classrooms. After all, comprehension is an outcome that happens in our heads. What's more, silent reading can often be more efficient, allowing students to concentrate on understanding rather than pronunciation, creating pathways for them to read faster, and helping them retain their thoughts about the text (Spichtig et al. 2016).

In fact, there is an emerging body of work on the relationship between comprehension and rate in *silent* reading, a construct that has been labeled as comprehension-based silent reading rate (Hayden, Hiebert, and Trainin 2019; Wissinger, Truckenmiller, Konek, and Ciullo 2023). And in the long run, silent reading becomes the primary mode of reading for proficient readers. So, developing silent reading skills is definitely an important goal. But perhaps you've also started to ask yourself some questions about silent independent reading, like these:

- ▲ Are my students actually reading or just pretending to read?
- ▲ Why do they spend so much of their reading time book shopping, sharpening their pencils, or asking to go to the bathroom?

▲ Why do they tend to stick with only one series, resisting other authors or text types?

▲ Are the texts students choose for themselves giving them what they need to grow as readers?

These are all valid concerns.

And it may seem counterintuitive, but one of the ways to support *silent reading* is to give students more practice with *oral reading*, because when it comes down to it, there's really no such thing as silent reading. All reading is "heard" inside our heads. So if children aren't successfully navigating the multidimensionality of fluency's demands—monitoring accuracy, managing rate, negotiating the melody of the language, and stressing words and phrases in ways that make sense of the text—then what they are "hearing" during silent reading will work against comprehension, confidence, and engagement.

Oral reading is a dipstick, giving us insight into how silent reading is "sounding" inside kids' heads, and what supports, if any, might be needed. In fact, listening to children read aloud is the only way to really check on fluency. So, teaching reading fluency requires more than just silent, independent reading (Hiebert and Reutzel 2010; Reutzel, Jones, and Neuman 2010). It also requires building in time—through whole-class instruction, small-group instruction, partnerships, and conferring—to listen in on reading so that we can provide instructive feedback. When we listen to individual students read, we can offer differentiated and explicit instruction specifically tailored to their developing fluency skills.

MISUNDERSTANDING:

3

Students taking turns reading aloud while everyone else follows along is an effective and efficient way to support reading fluency.

It's not a total surprise that children need regular opportunities to read aloud and get feedback on their oral reading. In fact, that's often been the driver behind having students take turns reading aloud one after the other while their peers follow along. But there are a number of problems with round robin and its instructional cousins (popcorn reading and popsicle stick reading), such as:

▲ The only time students practice oral reading is when it is their turn to read a slice of print for the group.

▲ Opportunities to offer meaningful individualized feedback or teach fluency elements are limited, because it can be tricky to give children feedback on their individual fluency during round robin without making them feel even more put on the spot in front of their peers.

▲ At any given moment, the students who are *not* the designated reader are at risk of disengaging. Some will be listening to the reader and following along, but others will be lost in the text, reading ahead or falling behind. Still others will have a completely different agenda—whether doodling, daydreaming, or even disrupting the class.

▲ Reading aloud while everyone else listens can be excruciating for some students. Those who are still developing automaticity often feel shame about their difficulties with word recognition. But they aren't the only ones. Many proficient readers also have anxiety about being put on the spot in front of all their peers.

▲ Trying to follow along and piece together the meaning of the passage when hearing it read aloud by a mismatch of disconnected readers can actually be more difficult than comprehending while reading the text for yourself (Ash and Kuhn 2006; Opitz and Rasinski 2008). In a way, fluency is the finishing touch that ensures that language entering the brain via reading sounds like spoken language. Without the bridge of fluency, language is simply more difficult for the brain to make sense of.

So if these turn-taking staples for oral reading practice aren't as helpful as we'd hoped, what are the alternatives? Well, based on dozens of studies that have shown its power (including Rasinski 1990; Sindelar, Monda, and O'Shea 1990; and VanWagenen, Williams, and McLaughlin 1994), the National Reading Panel (NICHD 2000) found that repeated reading (Samuels 1979)—originally considered a decoding intervention for less-skilled readers—is an effective tool for improving reading accuracy, rate, prosody, and comprehension. And these benefits are not just for students with reading difficulties (the Filling-the-Gaps Challenge) but also hold true for typically progressing readers (the Moving-Forward Challenge).

When you serve up repeated reading as the main course, with some instructional sides of explicit instruction, modeling, and feedback—all aimed specifically at what your students need to work on—you offer students a powerful and engaging pathway to improved fluency (Kim et al. 2017; Maki and Hammerschmidt-Snidarich 2022; Therrien 2004).

So, what does this fluency main course look like in practice? In its simplest form, repeated reading is the practice of having students intentionally read the same connected text aloud multiple times with the goal of measurable improvements in one or more of fluency's elements. Reading a text multiple times gives children opportunities to work through any decoding obstacles, translating the written language of the text back into increasingly fluent spoken language that the brain can comprehend. Of course, as illustrated in Figure 5.1, on page 156, decoding and automaticity are contributors to expression and comprehension. Even better, research shows that we can integrate the important aspects of repeated reading into independent silent reading for a combined effect that offers many of the benefits of both practices (Stahl, Heubach, and Holcomb, 2005).

Not only is repeated reading powerful—especially when augmented with explicit instruction, modeling, and feedback—but it is versatile, offering an engaging and effective alternative to round robin reading. There are several science-aligned ways to vary repeated reading, differentiating for students and positively impacting their fluency and their reading comprehension (Kuhn 2020; Turner 2010). We will explore some of these in the instructional recommendations later in this shift.

MISUNDERSTANDING:

Fluency practice works best with instructional-level texts.

All this work with fluency depends on one critical instructional tool—the text! So, what kind of texts best lend themselves to fluency practice through repeated reading? Should they be at a student's independent reading level? Instructional level? Content area? Fiction?

Fortunately, research suggests three primary considerations when selecting a text for fluency practice. Careful text selection will support explicit instruction, modeling, and feedback.

▲ **Difficulty** You might be surprised to learn that fluency practice leads to the greatest improvement when texts are somewhat challenging to begin with (Shanahan 2017; Walpole et al. 2020). These are sometimes referred to as "stretch texts" (Vaughn et al. 2022) or even "frustration"-level texts. Basically, if students don't make many mistakes during their first reading of a text, then it is less likely they will make substantial improvements with subsequent readings. Simply put, there needs to be enough to work on from the first reading to the last to make repeated reading worthwhile. Of course, since the first reading will be designed to stretch the reader, we can assist students during the initial reading of the text by choosing from a wide variety of available scaffolds, such as having students follow along with a recording or participate in whole-class choral reading.

▲ **Length** A general guideline for fluency-focused text selection is to use connected texts (rather than lists of words) that are between 50 and 250 words long (Armbruster, Lehr, and Osborn 2001; Shanahan 2017). You can choose poems, passages, excerpts, articles—anything that isn't too long to read multiple times. Texts of this length support short, distributed practice sessions (Gerbier and Toppino 2015) and help keep the hard work of reading a challenging text from becoming onerous. Connected texts require greater skill than reading lists of words because students have to recognize words, integrate what they are reading with their background knowledge, and monitor their comprehension (Foorman et al. 2016). Importantly, connected texts also offer valuable opportunities to practice those melodic features of connected language that enable the listening comprehension mechanisms in the brain to comprehend the written text.

▲ **Engagement** With the freedom to select texts that are beyond what children could read on their own, we can center our fluency instruction around texts with engaging content that provide the added bonus of bolstering students' knowledge. These can include texts with subtleties and layers of meaning that lend themselves to discussion and make rereading worthwhile. As Young, Paige, and Rasinski (2022) write, "When we can use the scientific essentials for fluency and find ways to teach them in ways that are also artful, we are more likely to move students well beyond improving their performance on fluency assessments to finding new ways to make reading engaging and meaningful" (86).

Effective fluency practice unfolds with short but engaging texts that offer children the chance to stretch themselves a bit as readers.

These texts, in combination with repeated reading and relying on research-proven scaffolds from a teacher, a peer, or even audio recordings, position students to experience new levels of success with all of the critical elements of fluency.

A Short Summary of the Science

▲ Fluency is a critical link between decoding and comprehension.

▲ Automatic word reading frees up attention for comprehension.

▲ Fluency both influences and predicts comprehension.

▲ Fluency consists of three components: accuracy, rate, and prosody.

▲ Whether reading silently or aloud, readers must translate text into comprehensible "spoken" language to understand it.

▲ There are different kinds of reading errors that result in disfluency.

▲ Listening to children read aloud regularly gives us important opportunities to provide fluency feedback and instruction.

▲ Repeated reading is a research-based alternative to round robin practices.

▲ The ideal text for fluency practice is short, challenging, and engaging.

THE SIMPLE AND SCIENTIFICALLY SOUND SHIFT

▼ ▼ ▼ ▼ ▲ ▼

Embrace brain-friendly and engaging fluency instruction as a bridge to comprehension.

Recommendations for Making the Shift

Given the importance of fluency development for reading comprehension, it is essential that we intentionally support students through carefully planned fluency instruction, including modeling, practice, and feedback.

The good news is that a few simple but flexible instructional routines can help students develop greater oral reading fluency and, consequently, deeper comprehension. In Table 5.3, we offer a collection of instructional routines that will position you to incorporate strong, systematic fluency instruction. We zoom in on establishing a weekly routine, scaffolding repeated reading, scooping phrases, performance reading, and self-assessing fluency.

TABLE 5.3

HIGH-LEVERAGE INSTRUCTIONAL ROUTINES FOR TEACHING FLUENCY

The What: *Routine*	The Why: *Purpose*	The How: *Example*
Establishing a Weekly Routine	To provide students with a predictable schedule for developing fluency in a particular text across a week	See "Zooming In on Establishing a Weekly Routine."
Scaffolding Repeated Reading	To provide students the supports necessary for initial readings of appropriately complex texts	See "Zooming In on Scaffolding Repeated Reading."
Choral Reading	To hear and be scaffolded by the shared voice of an entire class or group while reading a text—matching accuracy, rate, and prosody	"Today, we're going to read this passage as a class. You'll follow my lead. You might notice that some parts are tricky at first. That's okay. We're going to practice this passage each day this week so that you get stronger and stronger with your accuracy, reading rate, and expression."
Echo Reading	To scaffold fluency as the teacher or a partner reads a sentence and then student(s) read the same sentence (like an echo)	"Today, we are focusing on our fluency by echo reading. Follow along with me as I read each sentence. Then it's going to be your turn to read the same sentence. Notice my reading rate and my expression as I read."
Scooping Phrases	To help students transition to reading in phrases	See "Zooming In on Scooping Phrases."

The What: *Routine*	The Why: *Purpose*	The How: *Example*
Read, Record, Listen	To give students opportunities to hear themselves read as a way to reflect on their fluency	"Let's use technology to help us hear ourselves read. What do you notice about how you sound? What can you do to improve your rate/accuracy/ expression?"
Read-Alouds	To provide students with models of fluent, expressive reading while also building listening comprehension via teacher read-alouds, audiobooks, and podcasts	"Today, we're going back to our read-aloud text from yesterday. But, now that we have a strong understanding of who the characters are and what's happening, this time, as I reread these last few pages, you can pay attention to how my voice matches the meaning and where I pause with purpose. Our voices make stories come to life. Let's listen!"
Performance Reading	To provide authentic and purposeful reasons to engage in repeated reading	See "Zooming In on Performance Reading."
Self-Assessing Fluency	To give students opportunities to reflect on and document their fluency progress	See "Zooming In on Self-Assessing Fluency."

Zooming In on Establishing a Weekly Routine

When it comes to fluency practice, frequent, brief, distributed practice is especially powerful. Think of it as lifting three-pound weights for ten minutes every day versus lifting thirty-pound weights once a week. Short bursts of intentional fluency focus every day can have more impact than random, on-the-fly fluency instruction once in a while.

You can develop a weekly calendar, such as the example in Table 5.4 (page 168), to help you commit to consistently supporting students' fluency development as an integral part of your literacy instruction.

TABLE 5.4

SAMPLE PLAN FOR FLUENCY-FOCUSED
INSTRUCTION ACROSS A WEEK

	Scaffolds	Self-Assessment and Independent Practice
Day 1	**Teacher Reads:** Teacher reads a short text (paragraph, poem, passage, etc.) aloud to students, modeling fluent reading.	**Pre-Assessment:** Students read the passage (1–3 paragraphs) and use a self-assessment tool to reflect on and evaluate their accuracy, rate, and prosody, choosing one or more areas of focus for the week.
Day 2	**Choral Reading:** Teacher rereads the text aloud and students read along, matching rate and prosody.	**Independent Practice:** Students read the text chorally with a partner.
Day 3	**Echo Reading:** Teacher reads the text aloud part by part. After each segment, students read aloud, in unison, *without* the teacher.	**Independent Practice:** Students read the text repeatedly on their own, practicing expressive reading.
Day 4	**Differentiated Scaffolds:** Teacher, partner, or technology scaffolds are made available for those who need them.	**Independent Practice:** Students read the text repeatedly on their own, practicing expressive reading.
Day 5	**Performance:** Some students read the text aloud to the whole class, or each student performs the reading in small groups. The teacher and/or peers may offer feedback.	**Post-Assessment:** Students reread and/or record the passage one last time, using a self-assessment tool to consider their accuracy, rate, and prosody and noticing their improvements.

Adapted from Honig, Diamond, and Gutlohn 2018

This is just one of many possibilities for weaving fluency across a week. For example, not every passage warrants a performance, and sometimes you may have a single short paragraph that you want students to pre-assess, practice, and post-assess on a single day. And you will have to do some differentiation for those students who can already read the designated text fluently on Monday! The point is to teach fluency with planning and purpose so that students get the kinds of varied practice and scaffolded support they need to grow in rate, accuracy, and prosody.

Developing a weekly fluency schedule will not only save you planning time and energy; students will grow to appreciate the predictable routine as well. Practice over time gives students the opportunity to witness and document their own fluency growth. Making their improvement concrete and tangible has powerful implications, both for fluency progress and for life as a learner.

Zooming In on Scaffolding Repeated Reading

You already know the texts for repeated reading need to offer students enough challenge for their efforts across readings to result in demonstrable growth (Misunderstanding 4). Experiencing clear evidence of progress can be one of the most powerful and motivational aspects of repeated reading. However, to get traction with these texts, some less-proficient readers may need scaffolds that provide a higher degree of support. Fortunately, there are a number of options for differentiated repeated reading practice. You may have noticed these built into the sample weekly schedule. Table 5.5 describes, in more detail, three different categories of fluency scaffolds that were mentioned in the weekly routine above.

TABLE 5.5

FLUENCY SCAFFOLDS

Scaffold	Application Examples
Teacher	• The teacher reads the text aloud before the student reads it. This can include breaking it up into smaller parts for echo reading or modeling phrasing for "scooping" words.
	• The student reads the entire text aloud to the teacher. The teacher supports accuracy, rate, phrasing, and expression by prompting the student to reread portions as necessary and modeling sections as appropriate.
	• The teacher and the student alternate reading. This can include the student reading aloud and then pausing when they want the teacher to take over.

continues

Scaffold	Application Examples
Peer	• Students alternate reading *sections* of a passage aloud to each other. While one reads, the other listens and acts as the "teacher." The listener scaffolds the reader by following pre-taught procedures for providing feedback. • One student reads an *entire* passage aloud to another student. The listener scaffolds the reader by following pre-taught procedures for providing feedback. • Students participate in choral or echo reading with partners.
Technology	• Students listen to an audio recording of a text, following along with the print at the appropriate speed. Students read along orally on subsequent listenings. Eventually, the students read the text without the audio assist. • Students record themselves reading a passage, listen to their recording, self-assess, and then reread.

Assists like these allow even the students experiencing the most difficulty with reading to actively participate and witness their own progress. In fact, many times students who struggle through the first read of a text will be the ones to demonstrate the most growth in the final reading. You can use the assists in the table above in combination with one another and, of course, there are other ways to scaffold students. Repeated reading affords you, the teacher, lots of creative license when it comes to scaffolding students and establishing a purpose for repeatedly reading a text.

Zooming In on Scooping Phrases

Luckily, most students easily catch on to natural phrasing during oral reading, assuming that word recognition is not a barrier. But for students who read accurately but simply have trouble breaking sentences into meaningful word groupings, explicit instruction in phrasing is often helpful (Rasinski, Yildirim, and Nageldinger 2011; Hudson, Lane, and Pullen 2005). One of our favorite ways to teach phrasing is through using the metaphor of "scooping" words together into meaningful clusters (Serravallo 2015; Taberski 2011). You might say something like: "Today, we're going to focus on the natural breaks our voices make when we are reading sentences. Paying attention to how words go together in phrases is a way we can help ourselves and any listeners better understand what the author is saying."

We recommend that you display or give students a copy of a text that you have already chunked into phrases for them. For example, if you were reading the opening sentence of the book *Can We Save the Tiger?* by Martin Jenkins (2014), you *could* break the first two sentences into the following chunks:

> *The world's / quite a big place, / you know. / But it's not / that big / when you consider / how much there is / to squeeze / into it.*

Ask students to listen as you model phrasing the text while they follow along. Then let them practice reading the text chorally, with or without you, with appropriate phrasing.

Once students understand the concept of reading meaningful phrases, you can transition to them chunking, or scooping, phrases that they think logically go together in a sentence. We recommend starting with sentences that inherently lend themselves to two- or three-word phrases, such as:

The bumblebee is an insect. Its body has three parts and six legs.

Students can begin by studying a sentence closely and then drawing scoops underneath groups of words that form meaningful phrases. Eventually they can simply use their fingers, making a scooping motion to connect words in phrases *while* reading. In time, they'll be ready to remove the scaffold altogether as reading in meaningful phrases becomes more automatic.

You can integrate scooping practice as a focus for your regular fluency work, building it into your fluency routines. The practice, however, is straightforward enough that many children will be able to quickly put it into practice, enhancing their comprehension almost immediately, while others will need more time and support. So this adaptable and portable instructional move also lends itself easily to one-on-one conferences or small-group work.

 ## Zooming In on Performance Reading

Students often thrive when reading is seen as more than something they do on their own—when literacy is a social practice that invites them to interact with their peers. One way to support engagement, motivation, and fluency development is to give students time to practice and perform readings with and for their peers.

You can introduce this collaborative work as part of a weekly routine where students rehearse the same text Monday through Thursday and then perform that text for one another on Friday, as shown in the example schedule we provided on page 168. You do not need scripts, costumes, or prompts to support performance reading. Rather, you need meaningful texts selected with consideration for their quality, complexity, utility, and cultural relevance (Cappiello and Dawes 2015; Souto-Manning and Martell 2017). With these texts in hand, students can engage in repeated reading to develop the skills and confidence they need to perform in front of their classmates or other audiences. Below, we share a number of simple but powerful ways to make repeated reading joyful and authentic.

▲ **Putting Feeling into Poetry** Rehearsing a poem across a week can take just minutes a day, and it is easy to give every child their own copy, even assembling them over time into a book. Because collections of poetry are plentiful, because poems often fall in the recommended range of 50–250 words, and because poems are highly engaging, poetry is an accessible starting point for repeated reading practice.

▲ **Reading Like an Expert** Nonfiction texts provide the perfect opportunity for students to practice reading like a scientist or a historian, using a great deal of authority in their voices! When you select texts related to the topics you are already studying in science and social studies, you hit a home run with knowledge building, decoding, vocabulary development, and fluency practice all wrapped up in one.

▲ **Becoming the Characters** You can use a dialogue-rich section of literature, having students read aloud only the lines of dialogue. They can search the rest of the text for clues that will help them match their expression to what is happening with the characters in the scene. This type of fluency practice is a chance to let students step into a character's shoes, envisioning exactly how they might express the words if they were that character.

▲ **Reading to Younger Buddies** Pairing older students with younger students in the building as read-aloud buddies gives the older student a purposeful reason to select, practice, and perfect oral reading of a short text.

▲ **Delivering the News** School or classroom news broadcasts are an opportunity for students to engage in performing pieces while also serving the classroom or school community. Students can even read, or report, pieces they have written themselves for specific purposes.

▲ **Reliving Great Speeches** The study of famous speeches is a powerful and often overlooked opportunity to provide meaningful repeated reading practice. For example, you might have a selection of speeches or excerpts from which students can choose. Students can spend several days practicing the speeches with teacher (or other) support, in partnerships, or on their own.

▲ **Singing (or Saying) a Song** Song lyrics can be especially compelling texts for repeated reading. Whether you draw from current pop culture or choose an oldie-but-goodie, song lyrics are both readily accessible and often easy to connect to historical or current events. Students can perform the lyrics as a song or as poetry.

The beauty of integrating performance opportunities like these into your regular routine is that they provide a genuinely authentic reason to practice, practice, and practice some more, developing fluency, comprehension, and confidence.

Zooming In on Self-Assessing Fluency Progress

It's not always possible to listen alongside our students as they read. To help facilitate self-awareness around all three components of fluency, you can use simple tools for students to assess their fluency efforts and document their improvement across repeated readings. Self-assessment can help readers improve fluency skills while also teaching them to be more agentive as readers (Fisher, Frey, and Hattie 2016; Saat and Özenç 2022). Self-assessment also taps into children's natural drive to improve over their last attempt, giving repeated oral reading an additional purpose.

By audio-recording an initial and a final reading of a text, students can use self-assessment to listen for specific fluency strengths, reinforcing the individual components (beyond speed) of fluent reading. Table 5.6 (page 174) offers you an example of a fluency self-assessment rubric. However, you don't have to use this tool; a self-assessment can be as simple as a list of questions you and the students develop together. Either way, careful listening and reflection will likely take some modeling, and even some individual conferring, but it can become a pathway for improving fluency.

TABLE 5.6

SAMPLE COMPLETED READING FLUENCY
SELF-ASSESSMENT RUBRIC

Fluency Self-Assessment Rubric			
Name: Macey J. **Text:** "What's the Big Deal About the American Revolution?"			
1. **Read** 2. **Reflect** 3. **Rate** 4. **Repeat**	**1st Reading:** September 24th **2nd Reading:** September 27th		
	I have a lot of fluency work to do.	**I'm making some progress toward fluency.**	**I'm almost there!**	**I've got it!**
Accuracy: I read the words correctly, self-correcting as needed.		Sept. 24		Sept. 27
Rate: I read at an appropriate rate—not too fast or too slow.	Sept. 24	Sept. 27		
Phrasing and Smoothness: I read smoothly by noticing phrases that go together.	Sept. 24			Sept. 27
Expression: I changed my voice to emphasize words in a way that helped my listener understand the text.		Sept. 24	Sept. 27	
Punctuation: I attended to punctuation across the sentence, including ending punctuation, commas, and dialogue.			Sept. 24	Sept. 27

For a blank copy of this self-assessment tool, go to TheSixShifts.com/Downloads.

Of course, the goal of fluency instruction is not simply for students to become more fluent readers; it's for them to comprehend better and find more engagement in what they are reading. When word reading is automatic and fluent, it frees up mental space to focus on meaning and purpose. In this way, fluency practice can evoke long-lasting positive associations with reading.

Meanwhile, Back in the Classroom . . .

Ms. Stone is excited about her recent fluency exploration with Mr. Sanchez. As a result, she's decided to ditch popcorn reading routines all together. And although she no longer uses popsicle sticks to call on students to read aloud on the spot, she has found lots of ways to repurpose them. She is determined to avoid demotivating students by "cold-calling" on them to read aloud in front of their peers. Rather, she's reimagining her oral reading practices by giving students ample opportunity to rehearse before performing.

Her new favorite part of the day is when students engage in ten minutes of targeted fluency practice. On Mondays, her students get excited to see what poem, song, or passage they will read across the week. She's excited to hear many of them tell her that they practice reading the text at home at night to their siblings (and even to their pets). Each day, the class alternates between choral and echo reading for five minutes before working in fluency partnerships for another five minutes. Ms. Stone has created partnerships using word-reading fluency data and pairing students with similar skills. She's found that the members of each partnership are incredibly supportive of each other and that they get excited to hear themselves, and their classmates, read with increased fluency.

She's also started incorporating direct, explicit fluency instruction into her small-group work. For her students who are effective decoders but struggle with fluency, she's incorporated text scooping to help them improve their phrasing. For students who read without expression, she focuses on texts that support "reading like an expert" as well as texts with lots of dialogue to help them practice "sounding like the character." She's seeing real progress in those students, in both fluency and comprehension. Aaden and Lamonte, for example, are spending less time racing through text and are shifting more attention to phrasing and expression.

Ms. Stone has also been mindful to ensure her students see connections between fluency practice and understanding the text—not just performing texts. She makes sure every lesson emphasizes the ways reading is about meaning and that automaticity frees up our brain space to focus on what the text is about and what we think.

This connection between comprehension and fluency has been very prominent for Anna and Rosella. Repeated reading, with attention to comprehension and performance practice, has helped them read more fluently in the kinds of informational texts that previously gave them trouble. They recently collaborated to perform a piece about microbes that they had adapted from their science text. Anna and Rosella are both quite proud of their progress in fluency, not to mention their development of science expertise!

Ms. Stone and Mr. Sanchez have engaged other colleagues in working more intentionally to help students build fluency. They're all working together to develop fluency text sets that they share with one another. They're also planning a unit on famous speeches to give even greater purpose to the performative aspects of fluency instruction. They're excited to see the speeches their students will select and perform for their peers. Thanks to their collaborative efforts, fluency instruction has become not only purposeful but celebratory.

Questions for Reflection

Checking In with Yourself: Which of the misunderstandings in this shift did you find yourself thinking most deeply about? What might be the next step for you to shift your fluency instruction?

Weekly Whole-Class Routines: How can you adjust your instructional schedule to incorporate regular fluency practice? What predictable routines can you establish to support you and your students?

Text Selection: What sources do you have for gathering texts for fluency practice that are manageable in length, appropriate in difficulty, and interesting to read? How can you bring more variety and interest into your text selections, considering poetry, speeches, plays, excerpts from read-alouds, articles, songs, et cetera?

Components: How will you support students in becoming more reflective about all three aspects of their fluency—accuracy, rate, and prosody? As you identify students with specific fluency needs, how will you adapt instruction to be responsive?

Authenticity: How will you incorporate different performance opportunities into your instructional routines to make repeated reading more authentic, purposeful, and joyful for students?

Assessment: How do you know what students need to work on to improve their fluency? How will you document student progress? How will you support students in keeping track of and reflecting on their fluency progress?

Integration: In what ways could fluency practice become part of your various instructional contexts, such as conferring with readers or working with small groups? How might you bring content area texts into your fluency practice?

Differentiation: Who do your current fluency practices serve? Who will benefit the most from this shift in practice? Which techniques or assists from this shift could you incorporate to differentiate fluency instruction? How will you engage your students who already read fluently?

Reimagining Independent Practice in the Literacy Classroom

M r. Taylor is passionate about getting his fifth-grade students to think deeply about big topics and social issues. So, every day he shares carefully selected texts during interactive text experiences. For example, earlier this week they spent two days unpacking the topic of rainforest deforestation.

During read-aloud, he depends on turn-and-talk to let students share and deepen their thinking with a partner. These brief discussions are usually driven by his carefully crafted, open-ended questions. His students seem to appreciate these opportunities for thinking and connecting. Although they are cooperative about shifting their attention when time is up, it's often clear that they have much more to say than time will allow. And while it would be nice to offer students more time to actively engage with the complex ideas, universal themes, and compelling language of these powerful texts, he feels the pressure of trying to "fit everything in."

Following read-aloud each day, students move to forty minutes of independent reading, a school-wide minimum set by the literacy leadership team for upper elementary readers. Despite his crunched literacy block, Mr. Taylor appreciates this protected time. He has long been an advocate of student book choice, as long as the choices are "just right" for each student's current level of reading development. Engagement during independent reading is tricky enough, it seems, and he doesn't want to add the layers of frustration or the need for "fake reading" that might result if students choose books beyond their reach.

To support "just-right" book choice, Mr. Taylor has organized his classroom library by levels. Within each range of levels, he's also separated the texts into baskets of fiction and nonfiction, ensuring that there is a mix of both available within the collection for each range. Each fall, once he knows a baseline reading level for each student, he lets them know which level book baskets they should choose from, making adjustments to their assignments across the year as he reevaluates.

While students read their self-selected texts, Mr. Taylor meets with small groups, teaching from books at their instructional reading level. Mr. Taylor is committed to the idea of gathering readers with similar needs and providing guided practice in leveled texts. And since Mr. Taylor is known by his students to be "firm but fair," his students work hard to be respectful by maintaining quiet while he works with groups. But, despite the fact that he and his students are working hard, he wishes he could help them deepen their thinking when they read independently.

As he considers the opportunities students have for reflecting on their independent reading, he has to admit that meaningful reader response is definitely getting short shrift. He loves the idea of giving students more time to talk or write about what they are reading, but by the time he's met with two small groups each day, there just aren't enough minutes left. The reality is that the most frequent connecting thread for bringing closure to the time invested in independent reading is when he says, "Readers, I see we're running late for P.E. It's time to put your books away and line up at the door."

Yesterday, as Mr. Taylor took a few minutes to observe independent reading during the windows of time between his small groups, he couldn't help but feel a little disheartened, although the room was quiet and everyone had a book in their hands. Students like Jerome and Erin, who had started the school year already excited about reading, were obviously deeply engaged with their books. But many others clearly were not. Marta, who is still in the earliest stages of reading and writing English, was sitting quietly with a book propped in front of her, but she was actually looking around the room. Toby and Rolf, both skilled readers, had books in hand but were engaged in a bit of covert communication with nonverbal gestures that clearly had nothing to do with the texts they were "reading."

And although Tia was very engaged, Mr. Taylor couldn't help but notice she was reading the same graphic novel series she's been reading since the first week of school. Last week, Mr. Taylor was hopeful that she had found something new when he overheard her excitement over Oma's book, *Wishtree* by Katherine Applegate (2017). But he was as disappointed as she was when she sighed and said, "Oh. I can't read that level yet."

At lunch with his teammates, Mr. Taylor shares his recent disillusionment with independent reading and is surprised to hear others express similar concerns. Then, before he knows it, Ms. Parker proposes a month-long, class-to-class reading challenge across the grade, with a pizza party for the class that reads the most and individual prizes for the top readers in each class. His team seems intrigued by this idea as a potential way to invigorate independent reading after the recent winter break. And although Mr. Taylor has never been a fan of hoopla, parties, or prizes, he's trying to keep an open mind because he's just not sure what else to try.

A COMMON PRACTICE TO RECONSIDER

▼ ▼ ▼ ▼ ▼ ▲

We assume that self-selected, independent reading practice is meaningful because students are compliant, quiet, and busy.

We all want to help students discover the purpose and benefits of a vibrant reading life, both within our classroom walls *and* beyond them. We want to help children see reading as a path for expanding their world view, getting lost in a good story, solving their problems, feeling less alone, and pursuing their passions. Most of all, we want children to read because they *want* to! We certainly don't want to put all of our energy into helping students become proficient readers without also helping them come to know the benefits and joy of leveraging reading as a tool for enriching their lives.

Throughout this book, we've explored the factors that contribute to students *being able* to read for meaning. It's clear—as we've learned from various reading models—that becoming an active reader takes both skill *and* motivation. Aware of these two goals, many of us have come to believe that giving students lots of time for self-selected reading practice is the best way to support both.

But the fact that our classrooms are filled with energetic, social beings whose skills are as varied as their interests intensifies the challenge of making reading practice meaningful. And despite our best efforts toward supporting dedicated time and student choice for independent reading practice, most classrooms still contain only small handfuls of strong readers who are also fired up about reading. Although recent research confirms some of our worst suspicions about kids' perceptions of reading by third grade and beyond (Parsons et al. 2018), reading research also offers us some hope for how to implement instructional changes that can make the most of students' reading practice, increasing the likelihood that students both *can* and *want* to read.

Clearing Up Some Confusion

In this final shift we want to help you create a learning environment that provides all readers meaningful ways to engage with texts, ideas, and each other. You don't have to choose between joyful learning and effective reading practice. We can embrace both as vital elements of a learning environment that draws children in, keeping them connected and engaged as learners while also helping them become expert readers.

So, what are the most important considerations for helping children engage in independent reading practice that is meaningful? Let's dig in one last time and examine a few common misunderstandings about reading practice, as we consider a number of related factors from text-selection to reading levels to student choice.

MISUNDERSTANDING:

Self-selected independent reading is the most important use of time in the literacy block.

A huge body of research has found that students who read more become better readers (Anderson et al. 1985; Anderson, Wilson, and Fielding 1988; Cunningham and Stanovich 1998; Fielding and Pearson 1994; Guthrie et al. 1999; Schoonover 1938; Watkins and Edwards 1992).

Based on that research, it makes intuitive sense that if we give children lots of time to read on their own, they'll get better at reading. After all, whether it's learning to cook, learning to swim, or learning to read, it sure seems logical that the more you do something, the better you'll get at it. Then, of course, it also seems like a fair assumption that the better we are at something, the more motivated we are to actually keep doing it.

Free-choice independent reading not only provides students with lots of time for eyes-on-text but it also allows them to follow their interests as readers. No wonder it has seemed like the perfect open-ended task for students while we work with small groups or individuals! For its flexibility and appeal, large blocks of full-choice independent reading time are prominently featured as the central component of many intermediate literacy classrooms.

But the relationship between lots of time spent with books and becoming a good reader is not as straightforward or direct as we may have hoped. And while reading volume *is* beneficial, it is simply not sufficient (Duke, Ward, and Pearson 2021; Fielding and Pearson 1994; Watkins and Edwards 1992).

What's easy to misunderstand about the research on independent reading is that although there is a strong *correlation* between students' reading scores and the amount of time that they choose to spend reading on their own, this isn't the same as a *causal*, or cause-and-effect, relationship. And if you wanted to cherry-pick studies to make a case for independent reading, you may be able to mount a pretty persuasive argument, since the term "independent reading" appears frequently in the literature. But when you read more closely you can see that these studies often refer to something other than self-selected, independent, sustained silent reading as many of us understand it. What's more, "although there are considerable differences in amount of reading volume *in* school, it is likely that differences in out-of-school reading volume are an even more potent source of the rich-get-richer and the poor-get-poorer achievement pattern" (Cunningham and Stanovich 1994, 4).

What the research hasn't really teased out yet is whether some children are better readers *because* they read more, or whether they read more *because* reading came easier to them in the first place and led to more success and inclination to read. It's another chicken-and-egg dilemma.

So, yes, large doses of self-selected independent reading seem to be both beneficial and engaging for *some* students, especially those with well-developed word-reading skills, strong language comprehension, and solid reader identities in place. These are active readers whose strands of both the upper and lower halves of the reading rope (Scarborough 2001) are strong. These are the kids who don't *just* read because it's reading time; they read because they love reading.

But what about the students who aren't automatic with decoding and word recognition, who have gaps in background knowledge about everyday topics, who are emerging bilinguals, or who don't think of themselves as "good" readers? These are students whose reading rope strands may be frayed in some places or just not fully strengthened yet. And what about the students who can read pretty well but still don't *love* (or even like) to read? We've known lots of students—and we're guessing you have, too—who participate grudgingly in extended blocks of self-selected independent reading time every day but make little progress and show little inclination toward falling in love with reading. These are often the students who begin to exhibit resistance to books and reading, and this resistance shows up in the classroom as frustration, boredom, distraction, and even disruption. For these kids—those who struggle, skim, or even pretend to read texts—independent reading time is often time lost. They are anything but engaged as readers.

Think about it this way: if you don't know how to swim, simply spending time in the water—without adequate instruction, modeling, or feedback— likely won't make you a better swimmer. In fact, winding up with an accidental mouthful of water, practicing strokes incorrectly, or finding you've miscalculated the distance to the safety of the pool's edge will probably *demotivate* you from getting back in the water. Yet, with the right coaching and scaffolds to help you develop some strong foundational swimming skills, swimming every day can help you become a better swimmer, and your progress may even motivate you to keep improving. But *knowing how* to swim doesn't necessarily mean you will *choose* to.

So, if you've been thinking, "Uh-oh, these authors are about to advocate that I abandon independent reading altogether," please don't panic. We're not going to do that. Choice-driven, high-volume independent reading can still play an important role in helping children become proficient and engaged readers. But traditional independent reading isn't the *only* way, or necessarily the best way, to support *all* readers. And in light of lackluster research to support current practices, we are advocating that it's time to rethink putting too many of our reading success eggs in the independent-choice reading basket.

2 MISUNDERSTANDING:

Independent reading and self-selected reading are the same thing.

Researchers agree: if we want students to become fluent readers, we *do* want them to actively process lots of print every day (Castles, Rastle, and Nation 2018; Stanovich and West 1989). And independent reading *can* play a role in making that happen. But the key to leveraging independent reading more effectively likely lies in letting go of some of our assumptions about what independent reading *must be*—that is, dedicated classroom time when everyone is reading silently from self-selected texts. Instead, we can broaden our definition of what meaningful independent reading practice can become in light of the reading science.

Yes, independent reading practice can rely on self-selected texts, but it can also unfold with teacher-selected texts and some narrowed choice. Yes, it can be a chance to practice silent reading, but it can also be an opportunity to engage in oral reading practice in preparation for a Reader's Theater performance. Yes, it can draw on texts that are new to the reader, but it can also be an opportunity for repeated or close reading of texts that you have scaffolded in other instructional contexts, such as read-aloud, shared reading, and small groups. And yes, independent reading practice can happen in isolation, but it can also take place with partners or small groups.

Basically, our paradigm for independent reading can expand beyond a single reader silently reading a single, completely self-selected book. And by stretching our definition and assumptions of independent reading, we can make space for more effective and science-aligned literacy practice for all children.

Reading researchers are still determining how to best combine reading *instruction* and reading *practice* in the right doses to motivate readers. Instruction and practice go hand in hand, whether we're learning how to knit or how to play tennis. But practice in and of itself is not enough. Keep practicing a flawed tennis serve dozens of times a day, and soon it will be hard to unlearn your habits and relearn how to serve any other way.

In the same way, if students are skipping words instead of decoding them or reading words without really working to unlock deep meaning, practice without coaching and feedback can lock those habits in place without really elevating the reading. Current insights from research suggest the need for a *balance* of high-volume independent reading with scaffolded instructional reading of more challenging text (Kim and White 2008; Morgan, Wilcox, and Eldredge 2000; Stahl and Heubach 2005).

But independent reading is also a mainstay for engaging students while we are otherwise occupied with small groups. So how can we both scaffold the students who are reading independently, so that their practice is meaningful, *and* teach small groups? We certainly don't want to fill students' time with worksheets or other mind-numbing busywork.

As we consider all of the aspects of more brain-friendly literacy instruction, we recognize there is an opportunity to provide students different ways to engage in meaningful reading practice (McBreen and Savage 2021; Hruby et al. 2016), taking *some* (not all) of our eggs out of the basket of entirely self-selected, silent, independent reading.

So, what if we open our minds to possibilities beyond our traditional definition of independent reading? What if we take a fresh look at those minutes dedicated to independent reading and reframe them more inclusively as "meaningful literacy practice," intentionally making space for other brain-friendly practice routines alongside some self-selected reading? Consider that meaningful reading practice might include more opportunities for students to do the following:

- ▲ Expand their reading diets by having some free choice, some narrowed-choice opportunities, and even some assigned reading or rereading

- ▲ Write to process or respond to texts, even texts that have been read during other parts of the day

- ▲ Gather with peers in book clubs, poetry clubs, or expertise groups

- ▲ Engage in rich discussion to process text

- ▲ Build and strengthen foundational skills by practicing in decodable or skill-based texts

- ▲ Stretch into more challenging texts with the benefit of peer assistance or technology, such as reading with a partner or following along with an audio recording

- ▲ Reread complex texts they have already been introduced to during read-aloud, shared reading, and small-group instruction

If we want to avoid independent reading becoming the sink-or-swim experience it is for many kids, we need to provide opportunities for reading practice that is less isolated, more scaffolded, more varied, more purposeful, and ultimately more meaningful.

MISUNDERSTANDING:

The most important way to help readers fill gaps and gain confidence is through the use of "just-right" texts.

We applaud Mr. Taylor's commitment to small-group instruction, especially when it comes to the Filling-the-Gaps Challenge, which many intermediate teachers grapple with. Motivation and engagement for many children will hang in the balance as long as they continue to feel the angst, struggle, and even shame of not yet being able to read grade-level texts with proficiency.

If you're like Mr. Taylor (and us), chances are you've engaged in the practice of level-based text selection, with only the best of intentions. We've wanted to engage students by meeting them where they are, avoiding texts that might frustrate, dishearten, or demotivate them as readers.

So, the appeal of using a leveled system is easy to see, and it certainly seems like a logical approach to meeting the varied needs of the readers we serve. The logic of organizing books according to complexity, administering assessments to determine students' "independent" and "instructional" reading levels, and then matching students to texts that are presumably "just right" for them—the Goldilocks metaphor—can seem nearly irresistible.

Many of us have given text levels center stage across instructional contexts. We've learned to rely on "instructional" levels to guide text selection for reading in small groups. We've shared "independent" reading levels with students, for them to consider when making personal reading selections. Sometimes we've even let levels drive our text selection at the expense of offering children texts that are really worthwhile.

But there is a problem with consistency when it comes to levels. It might be easy to assume that text levels are exact. A level is a level is a level, right? Well, unfortunately, it's just not so. Brabham and Villaume (2002) explain that "some [leveling systems] are based on readability formulas; others apply multiple criteria related to language predictability, text formatting, and content; still others present progressions of letter-sound relationships. These progressions also reflect varying degrees of precision" (438). This means that one leveling system may focus on particular attributes of a text over others, causing leveling confusion.

For example, *The Old Man and the Sea* (1952) by Ernest Hemingway is written on 5.1 grade-level according to Accelerated Reader and a 940 (the equivalent of fifth grade) by Lexile, but it is listed as Z+ (eighth grade and above) by guided reading systems. Similarly, do a quick search for the levels of *Harry Potter and the Sorcerer's Stone* (Rowling 1997) and you will find that Accelerated Reader assigns it a higher level than *The Old Man and the Sea* while guided reading systems assign it a lower level. Goodness! It's easy to be confused by how levels are determined and what that means for students' text selections.

But inconsistency isn't the only problem with levels.

Levels can be a very limiting type of shorthand, giving children perceptions of who they are as readers, even as people. With labels such as "proficient," "not proficient," "below grade level," and so on, we can create an unintended connection between leveling books and leveling children. This can easily give way to a "compare-despair" effect (Noon 2020), with children comparing themselves to others and feeling like they come up short. Whether it's children comparing their own reading level to a peer's with statements like "I'm an S, but Henry is only an M," or a child like Tia from Mr. Taylor's classroom, eager to try out a new book only to discover it's not on her level, the negative effects on children are not hard to find.

What's more, when we create a system where the texts children have access to are limited to those at a specific level that is presumably comfortable for them to read, then we set some students up to be forever stuck in books below grade level. These parameters reduce students' opportunities to read complex text, to develop new knowledge, and to be exposed to more sophisticated vocabulary and language structures. Low expectations often follow, creating more fertile ground for the "rich to get richer," or the Matthew effect (Stanovich 1986).

Don't get us wrong. We appreciate systems that give us some clues to the complexity and readability of a text. It is kind of like the way we are glad there are sizes on pants. Even though we still try them on before we buy them, the sizes give us a reference point and a place to start.

We definitely see value in teachers understanding the characteristics that make texts more or less complex in their word-reading demands, language complexity, and structural and literary features. And of course we're supportive of scaffolds that can make a teacher's work easier. After all, we don't have time to read and analyze every text our students will encounter.

But rather than focus on text levels for grouping and text selection, we recommend that you use a variety of assessment data sources to help you—or your students—select texts that are best aligned (Burkins and Yates 2021) to the reading purpose.

Glasswell and Ford (2011) succinctly remind us, "Instructional levels are not the same as instructional needs, and they are not magic bullets that ensure quality teaching around the small group reading table" (211). If we are offering students decoding practice with specifically taught sound-spellings as the focus, for example, we might select a passage because it is written with more controlled spellings and provides lots of practice for the target sound. You might choose a text that is more challenging—beyond instructional reading level—as the focus of repeated reading practice, or a text that is less challenging—below instructional reading level—as a starting point for knowledge building (Velcro) related to a complex topic. Basically, "just right" for any given child will involve a number of different factors depending on the nature of the reading task and the background knowledge of the reader (Burkins and Yaris 2016; RAND 2002).

Finally, and maybe even most importantly, one of the biggest challenges with putting too much faith in these metrics is that the leveling systems behind them can't take into account the interests, motivations, background experiences, knowledge, purposes, and perspectives that children bring to the book selection process (RAND 2002). Remember the baseball study from Shift 1? Background knowledge on a topic can completely upset the whole text-matching equation—in a good way! Not to mention that different contexts make different demands on a reader, further complicating the "just-right" text idea.

The RAND Reading Study Group (2002) offers us a helpful model that explains that reading comprehension is dependent on the *reader*, the *text*, the *task*, and the *context*. Think about how motivated a Minecraft-loving student might be to discover a book containing tips from the experts about how to design your world and outmaneuver creepers. That's a really different context, or reading purpose, from unwinding before bed with the next intriguing title from the Land of Stories (Colfer 2017) series, or researching the Navajo code talkers for a class presentation. These contexts all place different demands on the reader. For each, the reader will bring different motivation, focus, and energy to make sense of the text.

So text complexity can inform instructional decisions across read-aloud, shared reading, small-group instruction, and independent reading. But we may want to rethink the process of forming groups and selecting texts mostly by text level. When we vary the difficulty of the texts we select according to the reading purpose, there is room for a range of "just-right" reading (rather than a single "level") and we minimize the risk of students defining themselves by text levels.

MISUNDERSTANDING:

Offering choice means turning students loose to read whatever they want.

One of the things we find most promising in schools today is the increased recognition that our students' identities matter and that none of us are "single stories" (Adichie 2009). Students walk into our classrooms each morning with their own aspirations, passions, lived experiences, and challenges. And these identities shape their preferences about which books they want to read.

This is a good thing. Research has shown that choice—following those preferences—leads to higher levels of engagement and motivation for readers (Guthrie and Humenick 2004; Guthrie et al. 1999), including choosing to read outside of school (Ivey and Broaddus 2001; Reis et al. 2007)! In fact, 89 percent of children aged six to seventeen report that their favorite books are those they have chosen for themselves (Scholastic 2019). And the opposite is also true. A lack of student choice can be a primary factor in undermining both reading motivation *and* achievement (Dolezal et al. 2003; Pressley 2003).

What's more, there is evidence to suggest that letting students follow their interests results in them paying more attention, persisting longer, learning more, and showing more enjoyment (Ames 1992; Ames and Archer 1988; Hidi and Baird 1988; Hidi and Harackiewicz 2000). Who among us doesn't have these benefits on our wish list for children?

Entrusting students with choosing texts for themselves is an important way to affirm and support both their engagement and their identities as readers. But offering choice in text selection doesn't mean simply turning students loose to pick any book that might appeal to them, whether they can really decode and understand it or not. On the other hand, setting rigid restrictions based on levels isn't the best way to support text selection, either. So where is the sweet spot between these two extremes?

Finding worthwhile texts that match your interests and your reading skills requires a nuanced but critical skill set. We think of this as not just choice but *informed choice* (Yates and Nosek 2018). And supporting students in becoming agentive enough to make informed choices comes with a teacher commitment to patiently coaching students as they develop these skills over time. Of course, in order to learn to successfully make informed book choices, students will need access to a thoughtfully curated and well-maintained classroom library. Such a library houses a vibrant and appealing collection of texts with lots of variety in genre, topic, authors, series, degrees of complexity, and diverse representations of people, perspectives, communities, and lived experiences.

As adults, we appreciate the freedom and autonomy to make choices for ourselves and follow our individual interests. Children are no different. But we certainly don't want to overgeneralize opportunities for choice in ways that actually interfere with meaningful literacy practice. So, here are three ways to offer choice while still maximizing learning.

▲ **Guide text choices sometimes.** Choice doesn't have to be unlimited. In fact, limitless choice can actually be a bit paralyzing at times. So, sometimes—for individual and instructional reasons—you can narrow students' choices a bit. This might mean having students choose a text from a teacher-created collection of content-specific texts you select to intentionally prime or extend their knowledge on a science or social studies topic. Or it might involve students choosing from three possible texts proposed by a classmate who wants to form a reading partnership. For a reluctant reader it might mean choosing from a short, teacher-created book stack (Burkins and Yaris 2014; Miller 2009) built of texts hand-picked with the specific student's interests in mind.

▲ **Offer students other choices.** Offering readers choice doesn't have to only mean that they are deciding *what* to read. Even if the text and the task are chosen by the teacher ("Reread yesterday's shared reading article about Daylight Saving Time and then write out at least two reasons you think DST should continue or end"), it doesn't mean that there isn't still room for student choice. For example, students might choose whom to read with (a partner or on their own), where to read (in their seat, in the soft seating area, or on the floor), and/or in what order to complete their reading practice (start with the repeated reading text or with a self-selected text) (Shanahan et al. 2010).

6

▲ **Think more broadly about what it means to let children follow their interests.** With pressure through the years to make self-selected independent reading the cornerstone of the literacy classroom, many teachers actually feel as though they *can't* or *shouldn't* choose independent reading texts for, or even with, students. But following interests doesn't necessarily mean that interest-related texts must *only* be selected by the students themselves. Sometimes it's our job to suggest, present, and—yes— even select texts for students as we work to make sure they get a healthy reading diet with the right mix of more comfortable and more complex texts. And we also want to be careful that we don't limit the interests children pursue to only those they already had in place when we met them. When you think about it, how can students develop interest in a topic they don't yet know anything about? So, sometimes our knowledge-building efforts need to include stretching and expanding student interests, introducing them to new and engaging ideas and topics that can spill over into independent reading and eventually even become a part of what they choose for themselves.

There's no question that we want students to have access to books for independent reading that will pique their interest, bolster their confidence, expand their knowledge, and make them want to turn page after page to see what happens next! But reaching the goal of such meaningful practice may require us to reconsider some elements of our current independent reading practices. In the instructional recommendations, we'll offer additional suggestions for the essential work of coaching students toward informed book choice.

MISUNDERSTANDING:

5

Self-selected reading time should only be spent reading.

We agree that getting in the "reading zone" (Atwell 2007) requires time to read. This is confirmed by research. In fact, the single most effective pathway to fluent reading is children getting their eyes on a lot of print (Stanovich and West 1989)! Castles, Rastle, and Nation (2018) remind us that "children need to see as many words as possible, as frequently as possible" (26). So, yes, time for meaningful reading practice matters.

But research has also shown that reading comprehension can be deepened when children have a chance to respond to texts through writing or through conversation. Let's take a closer look at these two options for making literacy practice more meaningful.

▲ **Written Responses: Putting Thinking on the Page**

When literacy instruction amplifies both reading *and* writing by making the most of them as reciprocal and interdependent processes, it results in significantly improved *reading* comprehension (Graham et al. 2018), and what purpose is there for reading if not to deeply comprehend? In fact, writing "summaries"—not necessarily formal paragraphs, but simply processing what you can remember about a text you've read—can improve comprehension even more than answering questions (Hebert, Simpson, and Graham 2013).

Of course, it would be arduous to ask students to write summaries about everything they read, even if it would boost comprehension. But there are other forms of writing that children can engage in to deepen their thinking. And their responses don't have to be limited to the texts they are reading on their own. Meaningful literacy practice time can actually include writing in response to interactive reading experiences that have taken place during *other* times of the day. For example, Mr. Taylor, from the opening scenario, might extend the conversation about deforestation by inviting students to share more of their opinions in writing during literacy practice time.

▲ **Student Discussion:**
Leveraging Children's Natural Desire to Connect

For many children, the too-isolated feeling of independent reading day after day—reading practice that is usually both silent and alone—is one more reason for disengagement. But few things can make a book experience as rich and engaging as a conversation with a friend. This is as true of the children in your classroom as it is of participants in Oprah's Book Club. In fact, just like written summaries, conversations about text can deepen a reader's comprehension, literate dispositions, motivation, and engagement (De Naeghel, Van Keer, and Vanderlinde 2014; Protacio 2019;

Jones 2020) and self-efficacy (Venegas 2018). That's a lot of reasons to make time for meaningful conversations about texts. And it's no surprise that Mr. Taylor's students are anxious to discuss and debate the ideas in the complex texts he shares about deforestation. Children are, after all, social creatures, so discussion can bring engagement and energy that can make reading practice meaningful.

Wilkinson and Nelson (2020) describe discussion as "the open-ended, collaborative exchange of ideas for the purpose of furthering students' thinking, understanding, learning, or appreciation of text" (231). You might be wondering, "Really, what makes for a good discussion among third, fourth, or fifth graders?" Well, what sets some discussions apart from others is making space for students to share multiple points of view, including responding to and reflecting on each other's ideas.

So, yes, meaningful practice should certainly include time for self-selected reading. But it doesn't need to stop there. We can also look for ways to bring writing or talking about texts into self-selected reading, negotiating the push and pull between time for reading and time for processing. You can design the options for reading and for responding to text in ways that offer lots of opportunities for choice, challenge, and connection. In the instructional recommendations for this chapter, we will further explore both written responses to texts and student discussions about what they are reading.

MISUNDERSTANDING:

Extrinsic rewards are a good way to motivate students to read.

While it's easy to get caught up in the idea, as Mr. Taylor's team has, that pizza parties, points, and prizes will incentivize students to read, we should be cautious about dangling carrots to entice readers. In his book *The Reading Mind*, cognitive scientist Daniel Willingham (2017) explains that rewarding children for reading can paradoxically lead to negative consequences for their long-term progress as a reader.

Even though the buzz created by an upcoming pizza party may motivate students to read in the short-run, students can end up only focusing on the unsustainable good feelings that come from winning a contest and eating pizza, while they also infer that reading isn't worth doing for its own sake. Research shows that extrinsic rewards actually make students *less* likely to engage in the rewarded activities without an incentive attached (Deci, Koestner, and Ryan 1999). Basically, "meaningful" reading practice actually loses meaning when stickers, contests, and pizza overshadow the more subtle joys of falling in love with a particular character, finding it impossible to put down a mystery, or discovering the power of informational texts to feed a personal passion.

If we don't motivate with parties and points and prizes, then how can we get reticent or simply unmotivated readers to read more? In the section below we share three alternatives to external motivators. These options all offer more nuanced contributions to helping children make their reading practice truly meaningful.

▲ **Thoughtfully design your interactive text experiences as an advertisement for the power of becoming a reader.** The power of these scaffolded experiences with texts is that they can be both instructional and motivating. The texts we select for read-aloud and shared reading become advertisements for children, showing them the power of reading and how it can help/change/ inspire/entertain/inform them. With every text we choose to share with children, we are essentially saying, "Hey, look at this! This is an example of what reading can be." Sometimes we show them that reading is a path to adventure or discovery. Sometimes we show them that reading is a way to make sense of our lives and to feel connected to others. Sometimes we show them that books provide a path to becoming more expert on a topic that matters to them. During interactive text experiences, the alchemy of the words, the illustrations, the voices, and the collective thoughts of children work together to create a magic and mystery that isn't achieved through any other medium we know.

▲ **Honor diverse choices in self-selected reading.** Not every bit of a child's reading practice needs to be in a book. And not every book they choose has to be literature with a capital L. Engaging all readers means making space for lots of types of self-selected texts. This commitment to textual variety means valuing graphic novels and choose-your-own-adventure books alongside the latest Newbery Medal or Coretta Scott King Book Award winner.

6

And it means validating reading the sports page of the newspaper as much as reading a nonfiction book from cover to cover. It means stocking your library both with books that include representations of people that will remind children of themselves and their own lives and with books that broaden their understanding of people with different lived experiences. It means making choice reading genuinely about choice, while continually feeding students new possibilities to expand their reading lives through book trailers, peer-to-peer recommendations, and regular teacher book talks.

▲ **Show students how to set and work hard toward meaningful goals.** There are lots of ways to approach goal setting, but at the heart of this research-backed instructional strategy (Hattie 2009) is ensuring that students are very clear on *what* they are working to improve and *how* they will know when they have reached their goal. Teachers can help students set and achieve goals specifically related both to content and processes, such as reading with phrasing, stopping to comprehend text chunk by chunk, or bringing more variety into their self-selected reading choices. The key is that goals should be challenging yet achievable.

And although goals related to reading volume can play an important role in some students' growth, broadening our ideas about goals can give students even more options for making their reading practice more purposeful. Of course, there's no real magic in goal setting in and of itself. The power comes from opportunities to personally reflect on progress and receive process-oriented feedback. This feedback is where coaching from the teacher, and even other readers, can offer insights into what is working, as well as how to improve.

In this age of movie streaming, video games, and social media, it would be easy to fall into thinking that engagement is synonymous with entertainment and that our classrooms need to have revolving doors of novel and fast-paced activities.

But it's not true.

Creating an engaging and motivating context that supports the diverse readers in your classroom doesn't require a lot of frenzy and amusement. Ultimately, children are motivated more because they have real reasons to read (Guthrie and Humenick 2004), because they see themselves as capable readers (Mol and Bus 2011; Willingham 2017), and because they have texts that enrich their experience. In other words, they find reading (and writing) practice meaningful.

A Short Summary of the Science

- ▲ Students who read more are better readers, but reading research isn't clear about the best ways to support choice-driven independent reading.

- ▲ In addition to self-selected independent reading, there are other ways to support meaningful reading practice.

- ▲ Text selection should be guided by the text, the reader, the task, and the context.

- ▲ Text leveling isn't an exact or perfect science.

- ▲ Leveling systems can't take into account the ways interest, motivation, and background knowledge affect a text match.

- ▲ Reader motivation and engagement are important factors in making reading practice meaningful, and student choice can increase both.

- ▲ Written responses to texts deepen comprehension.

- ▲ Discussion increases both comprehension and engagement.

- ▲ Extrinsic rewards for reading actually make students less interested in reading in the long run.

- ▲ Goal setting, with coaching and feedback, can both motivate students and contribute to reading growth.

6

THE SIMPLE AND SCIENTIFICALLY SOUND SHIFT

▼ ▼ ▼ ▼ ▼ ▲

Expand your definition of independent reading to include multiple ways of engaging in meaningful practice.

Recommendations for Making the Shift

Understandably, independent reading practice has long been a staple of intermediate literacy classrooms. But in light of the misunderstandings we untangled in the first half of this chapter, we hope you will find some of the instructional routines in Table 6.1 helpful as you work to make reading practice even more engaging and more impactful. In the sections following the table, we zoom in on supporting student text choices, writing in response to reading, and responding to texts through discussion.

TABLE 6.1

HIGH-LEVERAGE INSTRUCTIONAL ROUTINES FOR MAKING INDEPENDENT READING PRACTICE MEANINGFUL

The What: *Routine*	The Why: *Purpose*	The How: *Example(s)*
Organizing Classroom Libraries	To support opportunities for meaningful literacy practice by providing access to a diverse, vibrant, and well-stocked classroom library	The classroom library is organized in ways that make sense and appeal to students. Books are sorted by topic ("under the sea," "tales of friendship"), genre (poetry, biographies), author, series, etc. Special topics or texts are displayed strategically throughout the year. Student suggestions for new titles are valued and included.
Supporting Informed Text Choices	To entrust students with choosing texts for themselves in order to strengthen engagement, increase motivation, and affirm reader identity	See "Zooming In on Supporting Informed Text Choice."
Aligning Texts with Instructional Purpose	To offer texts of varying difficulty by selecting them based on instructional context and purposes	In order to provide fluency practice for a group of four students, you use a short poem. Students engage in repeated reading across several days. In order to support three students who need practice decoding words with basic vowel teams, you find short passages that offer lots of practice with the target phonics patterns and use these passages in a small-group lesson. Students then reread the passages during independent reading practice. In order to pre-build background knowledge, you read aloud a relatively simple text related to an upcoming content topic and introduce basic concepts and vocabulary.

continues

The What: *Routine*	The Why: *Purpose*	The How: *Example(s)*
Reading Partnerships	To support language comprehension, reading comprehension, and engagement through the less complex social interaction of a two-person dialogue	Two students choose a book from a designated library of "read together" titles, planning a schedule for their reading and conversations. They take their books home to complete the reading. On certain days, partners use a simple conversation protocol, meeting for the first half of the designated independent reading time.
Book Clubs	To support language comprehension, reading comprehension, and engagement through the more complex social interaction of a multi-person dialogue	Groups of three to five students choose a historical fiction book from four titles you've preselected. These groups, whether organic or teacher-matched, are formed for a particular purpose. Students read the agreed-upon sections on their own and come together for a portion of reading practice time to discuss.
Writing in Response to Reading	To utilize the reciprocal relationship between reading and writing to engage students in deeper thinking about a text	See "Zooming In on Writing in Response to Reading."
Responding to Texts Through Discussion	To help students process their thinking about what they read by discussing it with a partner or a small group	See "Zooming In on Responding to Texts Through Discussion."
Personal Goal Setting and Feedback	To help students identify specific content or process goals, reflect on their learning, and consider—through reflection and/or feedback—what's working and next steps	Every Monday morning students set and/or refine their personal learning goals for the week. You provide sentence starters that can be helpful, but students are not limited to these. On Wednesdays, students check in with a classmate to share their progress toward their goal, reflect, and get feedback. On Fridays, students do a quick-write on their current goal, share their reflections, and celebrate progress.

Zooming In on Supporting Informed Text Choices

Cultivating the skills children need to consistently find their way to books that will match their interests takes time and patience. A rich and vibrant library that is organized in a student-friendly way and stocked with a diversity of topics, genres, and representations of people and perspectives provides the backdrop for successful book choice. We acknowledge that helping all readers become skilled with text choice is anything but a simple process. However, in the section below we offer a collection of suggestions that can help you scaffold and patiently coach students toward making wise text selections independently.

▲ **Coach toward a healthy variety of texts.** This includes text complexity, genre, purpose, length, and other characteristics. Encourage students to intentionally stretch themselves to broaden their scope. You might consider engaging the class in a specific challenge related to expanding their reading repertoire, such as the "Reading Without Walls" challenge created by former National Ambassador of Young People's Literature Gene Luen Yang, which challenges students to read a book about a character who doesn't look or live like them; to read a book about a topic they don't know much about; or to read a book in a format they don't usually read (Yang 2016).

▲ **Help children notice and name their preferences, interests, and reasons for reading.** Teach students to make "I" statements about their choices. For example, "*I* notice some of my favorite books have been realistic fiction with strong female characters," or "*I* really like informational text with lots of facts and full-color photographs," or "*I* chose this book because I'm trying to learn all I can about natural disasters."

▲ **Take advantage of the power of book recommendations and reviews from other readers.** There is power in readers spreading the word to other readers about the books they are discovering. This can include book talks from classmates or from you, author video trailers, "shelfie" pictures with books posted in the classroom, star ratings on a 1–5 scale, and more.

▲ **Teach children to effectively use Switch on What You Know and begin to Map the Text.** Students can practice these two strategic processes by studying a book's cover, reading the blurb, previewing the table of contents to find clues to the superstructure, sampling the text for content (and readability), and examining the overall structure (superstructure). This effort before reading will help them make decisions regarding a book's interest for them and its reading demands, and it will set them up to better understand the text if they do decide to read it.

▲ **Teach a student-friendly metaphor for thinking about text difficulty.** In *Reading Wellness* (2014), Jan and her co-author Kim Yaris offer a weightlifting metaphor that quickly gets students thinking about how the "weight" (difficulty) of a text they choose affects the work necessary to "lift" it. We offer a download that further explains this metaphor at TheSixShifts.com/Downloads.

▲ **Encourage and celebrate *rereading*.** This can include whole texts, and even parts of texts, for a variety of purposes. Rereading— as you already know—deepens understanding and builds fluency. So, one way to support text selection is to let go of the idea that every reading experience needs to be a "new read" and instead affirm and support rereading worthwhile texts for a variety of reasons.

▲ **Help children learn from their choices—even the imperfect ones.** Book choice can be tricky for students. Affirm and celebrate the ones that seem to really work, while also making space for children to learn from (and even abandon) some texts that don't turn out to be a good match. In *To Know and Nurture a Reader* (2018), Kari and her co-author Christina Nosek offer a Book Choice Reflection Tool, designed to help students consider how both interest and challenge intersect in ways that can inform current and future book choices. We offer a download that elaborates on the interactive use of this tool at TheSixShifts.com /Downloads.

▲ **Teach children to follow one book into another.** Following a book involves making a choice about your future reading that is influenced by some aspect of your *current* reading. This momentum may include reading the next title from a series, finding another book by the author you just enjoyed, or building a personalized text set to develop expertise on a topic you just learned about.

Zooming In on Writing in Response to Reading

Writing about what they've read gives students opportunities to engage language to arrive at insights as they practice translating speech into print. These two processes are, of course, the two sides of the Simple View of Reading (Gough and Tunmer 1986).

Fortunately, the responding process doesn't have to be rigid. It is possible to offer choice within reading response, making space for students to respond to the things *they* find compelling about a text. Sharing the responses with the class or in small groups—especially with other students that are reading the same text—can elevate both the practice and the level of engagement. In Table 6.2 we offer a few different ways students might respond to texts in writing.

TABLE 6.2

IDEAS FOR STUDENTS' WRITTEN RESPONSES TO TEXTS

Description and Purpose	Examples, Ideas, and Prompts
Writing Summaries	
To support students in attending to the sequence of events, main ideas, and details in texts To encourage students to build a strong mental model as they read	"In your own words, sum up what you have read." "What do you think is most important to remember from this story/text and why?" "How would you explain/describe to a friend what's most important?"
Writing About Personal Reactions	
To support personal responses from students *after* the reading, giving them the opportunity to focus on what they do or don't find appealing about the story, the information, the craft, etc.	"How was your experience of reading this text? What did you like? Dislike? Agree with? Disagree with? Why?" "What seems important to this author? How do you know?" "What (or whom) does the author leave out? How would the story change if this was included?" "What would you change about this text? Why?"

continues

Description and Purpose	Examples, Ideas, and Prompts
Writing Reviews	
To support students in both summarizing text and in sharing their thoughts about what makes it appealing (or unappealing)	"Would you recommend this book to a friend? Why or why not?" "What kind of reader might like this book? Why?" "Whom does this book remind you of? Why? What can you tell them about the book to entice them to read it?"
Asking and Answering Questions	
To encourage students to ask questions of the text—particularly those that require inferring—and to develop a habit of thinking deeply about what they read	"What questions do you have about the characters, events, or ideas in the text?" "Write and answer a thought-provoking fill-in-the-missing-pieces (inferential) question that will really make your classmates think. You will pose this question to your discussion group tomorrow."

While "Writing Summaries" has its own row in the table above, you may have noticed that summarizing is really a part of many of these response options. Perhaps you remember that writing summaries—or reflecting on the mental model they've created—helps children comprehend texts even better than answering questions about a text (Hebert, Simpson, and Graham 2013). But the kind of summaries that lead to this deep comprehension do not need to involve weeks of modeling and practice so that children can write perfect, five-sentence summary paragraphs. These research-based summaries are simply children recounting important events or ideas from the text in their own words. Summing up the high points of a text (structure, perspective, important ideas, etc.) gets kids thinking deeply and critically (Hare and Borchart 1984; Rinehart, Stahl, and Erickson 1986; Taylor and Beach 1984).

Finally, while students should definitely have opportunities to respond to texts they read during independent reading time, remember they can also use that "reading" time to do writing in response to the more complex texts or experiences they've encountered during other times of the day (Misunderstanding 5), such as a science experience or a read-aloud text. Of course, not every text (or even most texts) needs a written response! It's not all-or-nothing. But written responses—especially those that include an element of summarizing—are actually a worthwhile way to improve *reading comprehension*.

Zooming In on Responding to Texts Through Discussion

Although independent reading is typically a solitary and silent activity, humans are social creatures. What if there was someone to talk to about what you were reading? What if you could read thought-provoking texts simultaneously with others and then hear their thinking and share your own? And what if you were reading some texts—whether selected completely through free choice or narrowed by the teacher—that introduced you to ideas, dilemmas, and unresolved debates that left you itching to talk to your classmates?

Conversation *about* texts is a legitimate part of meaningful *reading* practice. A large body of research supports more dialogic teaching (Alexander 2017). If you read *Shifting the Balance K–2* (Burkins and Yates 2021), you'll remember that Shift 1 includes a dialogic conversation tool (Whitehurst et al. 1988) to help elevate the conversations of younger readers during read-aloud. Research points to benefits of the same kind of practices for our upper elementary students who are clamoring to talk about their experiences with worthwhile texts (Murphy et al. 2009; Murphy et al. 2016). And opportunities for social interaction around texts can support the development of positive attitudes toward reading and can enhance reading motivation and engagement (Sainsbury and Schagen 2004; De Naeghel, Van Keer, and Vanderlinde 2014; Protacio 2019; Jones 2020) as well as self-efficacy, especially among students identified as struggling or reluctant (Venegas 2018).

Of course, not all talk is equally valuable when it comes to reading comprehension. The most productive and engaging discussions for enhancing comprehension are both structured and focused but not monopolized by the teacher (Wilkinson and Nelson 2020; McKeown, Beck, and Blake 2009). Here are five things to keep in mind as you create opportunities for students to participate in engaging discussions.

▲ **Ensure students have access to worthwhile texts.** Great discussions start with great texts, so make sure the texts students are responding to through discussion give them lots to think and talk about. To ensure that all students can access texts prior to the discussion, you may also need to provide some student scaffolds, such as shared reading with a partner, repeated reading, audio recordings, and so on.

▲ **Use dyads to teach the basics.** Learning to navigate a meaningful text discussion happens gradually over time. We find it works best to first introduce and nurture discussion in partnerships. The simple two-person turn-and-talk can serve as a runway for eventual small-group discussions among three to five students who manage themselves.

▲ **Provide scaffolds for the specific discussion behaviors you want students to practice.** Whether a class anchor chart or laminated cards for individuals, many students will benefit from clear reminders of how to participate: *Look at the speaker. Wait for your turn.* Sentence starters like the following can serve as helpful scaffolds:

- "I agree/disagree with what you said about _____ because . . ."
- "I want to add on to what you said about _____ . . ."
- "I heard you say _____ but I understood that differently."
- "One part I found confusing/interesting/funny/concerning was _____."
- "I wonder why _____."

▲ **Provide a structured focus for the discussion.** Offer students a few structured questions or other entry points to both focus the discussion and take it beyond surface level. Questions like "What character did you identify with most closely and why?" or "What did the text leave you really thinking about?" can initiate rich conversations. You can make the questions in the "Writing about Reading" section above do double duty by using them to launch meaningful group discussions as well.

▲ **Support turn-taking and listening.** Establish a discussion protocol that guides students in deciding who will start and how the discussion will proceed in ways that ensure everyone's voice is heard. In the early stages, a physical scaffold like a talking stick can serve as a concrete reminder of whose turn it is to have the floor.

Like any skill worth building, developing the tools and mindset for productive group conversations takes time. Let students practice, practice, and practice some more. Don't give up if all the group discussions don't go smoothly, especially at first. Even after lots of practice, conversations will sometimes get off track. Just try it out. Reflect and adjust.

Meanwhile, Back in the Classroom . . .

Although the first couple of weeks of February's Fabulous Reading Frenzy created a bit of a spike in at-home reading for many of the students in Mr. Taylor's classroom, the overall experience of the reading competition was far from transformative.

By week three many students actually became discouraged by the hallway scoreboard that showed Ms. Romero's class with a sizable lead. One day Mr. Taylor even overheard Caden say, "What's the big deal anyway? We have pizza for dinner every single Friday night!" And nobody seemed surprised that Jerome and Erin were leading the class for total pages read. In fact, even as Mr. Taylor was first introducing the competition to the class, Tia blurted out, "Erin is going to win, for sure."

And it wasn't just his students. Mr. Taylor and his team could see early on that this competition would likely do little to alleviate their ongoing concerns about the depth and quality of thinking that was happening during daily independent reading time. In fact, the rush to accumulate points seemed to actually lead them to read less thoughtfully. So, Mr. Taylor and his colleagues are back to the drawing board, exploring some other options for making independent reading more meaningful, especially for those who seem disenchanted, if not downright resistant.

One thing they all want to do is increase opportunities for readers to respond to what they read, especially with regard to read-aloud texts. Since they've learned that summing up a text actually helps students comprehend, they've decided that they'll have their students write short synopses of a read-aloud text once a week.

Because he's long appreciated the power of repeated reading, and in order to experiment a bit with "breaking the silence" during independent reading time, Mr. Taylor chooses to embed repeated reading practice—a "not-so-silent" routine—into each day's independent reading practice.

Students are free to choose from one of three texts for their daily repeated reading practice: a three-paragraph segment from the current unit of study in their science or social studies textbook, a text from their small-group instruction that week, or a passage from their shared reading binder. And on Fridays, students meet in small groups to read expressively for each other, coach each other with encouragement and feedback, and discuss the meaning of the text. With the help of other students, Mr. Taylor makes sure that students new to English have access to an audio recording of the passages they want to practice.

It's only been a few weeks, but he's a bit blown away at how much energy this uncomplicated little routine seems to infuse into their reading practice.

Another exciting development has come from Ms. Jones and Mrs. Collin. They pulled together a mini-library on wheels that they call the Partner Cart. This collection contains two copies of texts across a variety of genres, difficulties, and topics, along with a familiar prompt card for pairs that need a bit of support. The texts are organized in large baggies within baskets. The cover-out organization makes them easy to browse. The cart moves to a different classroom in the grade level each day. Students eagerly await their turn with the cart, and partnership conversations are both bringing new life to independent reading and helping students develop academic discussion skills like listening, questioning, connecting, and adding on.

Seeing the level of interest and engagement that partner reading is creating, the fifth-grade team is scrambling to add even more varied and engaging text pairs to the cart, pooling their book order bonus points, completing their book fair wish lists, and even scouting out area thrift stores. They plan to build on conversations with partners, treating them as a stepping-stone to book clubs with small groups.

Finally, Mrs. Dahli has taken a bold step that they are all watching with interest. Although they have all been long invested in sorting books onto shelves and into bins by level, she is beginning to redesign her classroom library to support a different approach to student choice. She is reorganizing by author, genre, series, and topic in an attempt to support more authentic and interest-based book choices. Since it's the middle of the year, she's bought herself some time by pulling together a few content-specific and high-interest baskets, setting out a fresh one each day. She's also posted an "Under Construction" sign in the classroom library to pique student interest in the transformation.

Rethinking the routines and structures for independent literacy practice is definitely a work in progress for the team. But, bit by bit, they are elevating the engagement and motivation of their students. Maybe they'll try some things along the way that don't measure up to their expectations—like the competition for pizza and prizes. But, by pooling their experiences and expertise, reflecting and adjusting as they go, they're confident they'll also discover some instructional gems that truly make independent practice more meaningful for students.

Questions for Reflection

Checking In with Yourself: Which of the misunderstandings about independent practice did you find most thought-provoking? Which ones have you believed and how has your thinking changed? How will your independent practice time change as a result?

Classroom Library: How is your classroom library organized? How could your library better serve students? Is there an opportunity to de-level your library and instead focus on organization by genre, author, topic, series, and so on? Does your classroom library have a healthy mix of fiction and nonfiction offerings? Does it represent a diversity of people, topics, text types, perspectives, formats, and genres?

Student Text Choices: How can you support students in selecting texts for meaningful independent reading practice without relying heavily on levels? When and why will you sometimes narrow students' choices? When will you expect students to read something you choose for them, such as rereading a text from small-group instruction or a book related to the current science study?

Other Choices: Even beyond texts for independent reading, how can you give students more opportunities to make choices across the school day?

Interactive Text Experiences: In what ways do your text selections for read-aloud and shared reading help children stretch into complex texts? How can you use your whole class texts for rereading (or pre-reading) during meaningful independent practice?

continues

Engaging More Deeply with Texts: How can you bring in written responses and conversations to deepen understanding of texts and increase engagement during independent practice times? What role can partnerships, discussion groups, and book clubs play in raising engagement and motivation for your students?

Independence: What routines do you establish to support students in developing agency and taking ownership of their independent reading lives? And how can you help them continue this sense of ownership to also read at home?

Differentiation: Which techniques from this shift could you incorporate to differentiate your support of meaningful reading practice for all students? What next steps will you take?

AFTERWORD

Dear Readers,

t has been a true honor to have you join this conversation and take this journey with us.

We know that it would be easy to read a book like this and come away feeling a bit overwhelmed. After all, just as a new item of clothing can easily get lost in an already stuffed-to-overflowing closet, there is nothing easy about adding a bit of this and a bit of that to an already crowded schedule with established practices in place.

But when we are thinking about adding something new, it is often the perfect time to reflect on what we might be able to let go of. We suspect that in most of our teaching "closets"—just as in most of our bedroom closets—there are likely some things we are ready to reconsider. Some simply don't serve us well anymore. Some have gone out of style. Some don't really fit well. Some we realize when we're honest, never really worked the way we'd hoped, even though we may still love the fabric or the style. So, whether you are ready to let go of strategy-based text selection or of sending students around tricky words rather than learning to decode all the way through them, moving something out of the closet is often a necessary step for making space for something new.

But of course, examining our current wardrobe (or practices) is not just about replacing the old with the new. In every closet (and every classroom) there are sure to be timeless and foundational pieces—like that white button-down blouse or that gray pencil skirt—that continue to stand the test of time, season after season, year after year. We certainly don't want these staples to slip into the discard pile by accident, any more than we want mainstays of our instruction—like read-aloud, selecting quality texts, and honoring home languages—to get lost in the shuffle.

And sometimes the new thing we decide to bring into our wardrobe, or our practice, doesn't replace anything at all. Instead it becomes the very thing that makes other pieces work better. It's like finally finding the ideal black pants, which can be dressed up for work and are also comfortable enough for Saturday morning errands but look great no matter what you pair them with.

Sometimes we discover there is just such a versatile missing piece in our instructional practices. Maybe for you that missing piece is leveraging meaningful fluency practice as the bridge that supports both word recognition and comprehension. Or maybe it's bringing more varied practices into your independent reading time. Whatever it is, sometimes a thoughtful addition can really make existing pieces shine!

Research also continues to evolve, much like fashion. As new developments inform our thinking about how reading happens in the brain and how that translates to classroom practice, we will continue to need to make decisions about what to keep and what to let go of.

And if learning both the why and the how of more science-aligned practices has left you feeling like you have a whole lot in your wardrobe that needs updating, be kind to yourself, and remember that you don't have to change everything all at once. Even the most transformative change begins with a single first step. And each successive step keeps momentum going.

So, as you use what we've shared on these pages to inventory your closet and try things on in front of your mirror, think of this book as that trusted friend you rely on when it's time for honest feedback.

We believe in taking stock. We believe in making space. We believe in following both research and students. We believe in continually refining practices until everything in your instructional closet truly works. And most of all, we believe in you.

With love,
Katie, Jan, and Kari

We are @TheSixShifts on Facebook, Instagram, and Twitter. You can also contact us directly through TheSixShifts.com.

REFERENCES

Adams, Marilyn J. 1990. *Beginning to Read: Thinking and Learning About Print.* Cambridge, MA: MIT Press.

Adams, Marilyn J. 2005. "Comment." *Brookings Papers on Education Policy.* Washington, DC: Brookings Institution.

Adams, Marilyn J. 2015. "Preface." In *Knowledge for Literacy: Literacy Ladders* (pp. 4–10). Washington, DC: Albert Shanker Institute. https://www.shankerinstitute.org/resource/literacy-ladders.

Adichie, Chimamanda N. 2009, July. "The Danger of a Single Story" (video). TED Conferences. https://www.ted.com/talks/chimamanda_ngozi_adichie_the_danger_of_a_single_story.

Alexander, Patricia A., Jonna M. Kulikowich, and Sharon K. Schulze. 1994. "How Subject-Matter Knowledge Affects Recall and Interest." *American Educational Research Journal* 31 (2): 313–337.

Alexander, Robin. 2017. "Dialogic Teaching in Brief." https://coleridgeprimary.org/wp-content/uploads/2019/11/Dialogc-teaching-in-brief-170622.pdf.

Álvarez-Cañizo, Marta, Paz Suárez-Coalla, and Fernando Cuetos. 2015. "The Role of Reading Fluency in Children's Text Comprehension." *Frontiers in Psychology* 6: 1810. https://www.frontiersin.org/articles/10.3389/fpsyg.2015.01810/full.

Alvermann, Donna E., Lynn C. Smith, and John E. Readence. 1985. "Prior Knowledge Activation and the Comprehension of Compatible and Incompatible Text." *Reading Research Quarterly* 20: 420–436.

Ames, Carole. 1992. "Classrooms: Goals, Structures, and Student Motivation." *Journal of Educational Psychology* 84 (3): 261–271.

Ames, Carole, and Jennifer Archer. 1988. "Achievement Goals in the Classroom: Students' Learning Strategies and Motivation Processes." *Journal of Educational Psychology* 80 (3): 260–267.

Anderson, Richard C., Elfrieda H. Hiebert, Judith A. Scott, and Ian A. G. Wilkinson. 1985. *Becoming a Nation of Readers: The Report of the Commission on Reading.* Washington, DC: National Academy of Education.

Anderson, Richard C., and William E. Nagy. 1992. "The Vocabulary Conundrum." *American Educator* 16 (4): 14–18, 44–47.

Anderson, Richard C., Paul T. Wilson, and Linda G. Fielding. 1988. "Growth in Reading and How Children Spend Their Time Outside of School." *Reading Research Quarterly* 23 (3): 285–303.

Armbruster, Bonnie, Thomas H. Anderson, and Joyce Ostertag. 1989. "Teaching Text Structure to Improve Reading and Writing." *The Reading Teacher* 43 (2): 130–137.

Armbruster, Bonnie, Fran Lehr, and Jean Osborn. 2001. *Put Reading First: The Research Building Blocks for Teaching Children to Read: Kindergarten Through Grade 3.* Washington, DC: National Institute for Literacy.

Ash, Gwynne E., and Melanie R. Kuhn. 2006. "Meaningful Oral and Silent Reading in the Elementary and Middle School Classroom: Breaking the Round Robin Reading Addiction." In *Fluency Instruction: Research-Based Best Practices*, edited by Tim Rasinski, Camille Blachowicz, and Kristin Lems (pp. 155–172). New York: Guilford Press.

Ashby, Jane, Marion McBride, Shira Naftel, Lucy Hart Paulson, David Kilpatrick, and

Louisa Cook Moats. 2022. "Teaching Phoneme Awareness in 2022: A Guide for Educators." https://static1.squarespace.com/static/5c38560bb98a78f7ba7097bd/t/62cc9f1023f93b0e6bdb3450/1657577235258/Teaching-PA-in-2022_A-Guide-for-Educators.pdf.

Atwell, Nancie. 2007. *The Reading Zone: How to Help Kids Become Skilled, Passionate, Habituate, Critical Readers*. New York: Scholastic.

Aukerman, Maren, and Lorien Chambers Schuldt. 2021. "What Matters Most? Toward a Robust and Socially Just Science of Reading." *Reading Research Quarterly* 56 (S1): S85–S103.

Barnes, Marcia A., Maureen Dennis, and Jennifer Haefele-Kalvaitis. 1996. "The Effects of Knowledge Availability and Knowledge Accessibility on Coherence and Elaborative Inferencing in Children from Six to Fifteen Years of Age." *Journal of Experimental Child Psychology* 61 (3): 216–224.

Baumann, James F. 1986. "Teaching Third-Grade Students to Comprehend Anaphoric Relationships: The Application of a Direct Instruction Model." *Reading Research Quarterly* 21 (1): 70–90. https://doi.org/10.2307/747961.

Baumann, James F., Elizabeth C. Edwards, George Font, Cathleen A. Tereshinski, Edward J. Kame'enui, and Stephen Olejnik. 2002. "Teaching Morphemic and Contextual Analysis to Fifth-Grade Students." *Reading Research Quarterly* 37 (2): 150–176.

Baumann, James F., Nancy Seifert-Kessell, and Leah A. Jones. 1992. "Effect of Think-Aloud Instruction on Elementary Students' Comprehension Monitoring Abilities." *Journal of Reading Behavior* 24 (2): 143–172.

Beck, Isabel L., Margaret McKeown, and Linda Kucan. 2013. *Bringing Words to Life: Robust Vocabulary Instruction*. New York: Guilford Press.

Beck, Isabel L., Charles A. Perfetti, and Margaret McKeown. 1982. "The Effects of Long-term Vocabulary Instruction on Lexical Access and Reading Comprehension." *Journal of Educational Psychology* 74: 506–520.

Berkeley, Sheri, Thomas E. Scruggs, and Margo A. Mastropieri. 2009. "Reading Comprehension Instruction for Students with Learning Disabilities, 1995–2006: A Meta-Analysis." *Remedial and Special Education* 31 (6): 423–436.

Bhattacharya, Alpana, and Linnea C. Ehri. 2004. "Graphosyllabic Analysis Helps Adolescent Struggling Readers Read and Spell Words." *Journal of Learning Disabilities* 37 (4): 331–348.

Biber, Douglas, and Susan Conrad. 2019. *Register, Genre, and Style*. 2nd ed. Cambridge, UK: Cambridge University Press.

Blachowicz, Camille, and John J. Lee. 1991. "Vocabulary Development in the Literacy Classroom." *The Reading Teacher* 45: 188–195.

Blachowicz, Camille, Peter J. L. Fisher, Donna Ogle, and Susan Watts-Taffe. 2006. "Vocabulary: Questions from the Classroom." *Reading Research Quarterly* 41 (4): 524–539.

Block, Cathy C., Linda B. Gambrell, and Michael Pressley, eds. 2002. *Improving Comprehension Instruction: Rethinking Research, Theory, and Classroom Practice*. Newark, DE: International Reading Association.

Boon, Richard, Michael Paal, Anne-Marie Hintz, and Cornelius Freyre. 2015. "A Review of Story Mapping Instruction for Secondary Students with LD." *Learning Disabilities: A Contemporary Journal* 13 (2): 117–140.

Bowers, Jeffrey S., and Peter N. Bowers. 2017. "Beyond Phonics: The Case for Teaching Children the Logic of the English Spelling System." *Educational Psychologist* 52: 124–141.

Bowers, Peter, John Kirby, and Hélène Deacon. 2010. "The Effects of Morphological

Instruction on Literacy Skills: A Systematic Review of the Literature." *Review of Educational Research* 80 (2): 144–179.

Brabham, Edna G., and Susan K. Villaume. 2002. "Leveled Text: The Good News and the Bad News." *The Reading Teacher* 55: 438–441.

Brady, Susan. 2020. "A 2020 Perspective on Research Findings on Alphabetics (Phoneme Awareness and Phonics): Implications for Instruction (Expanded Version)." *The Reading League Journal*. https://www .thereadingleague.org/wp-content/uploads /2020/10/Brady-Expanded-Version-of -Alphabetics-TRLJ.pdf.

Brody, Sara. 2001. *Teaching Reading Language, Letters, and Thought.* 2nd ed. Milford, NH: LARC.

Burkins, Jan Miller, and Kim Yaris. 2014. *Reading Wellness: Lessons in Independence and Proficiency.* Portsmouth, NH: Stenhouse Publishers.

Burkins, Jan, and Kim Yaris. 2016. *Who's Doing the Work: How to Say Less So Readers Can Do More.* Portsmouth, NH: Stenhouse.

Burkins, Jan, and Kari Yates. 2021. *Shifting the Balance: 6 Ways to Bring the Science of Reading into the Balanced Literacy Classroom.* Portsmouth, NH: Stenhouse.

Burns, Matthew K., Jennifer Hodgson, David C. Parker, and Kathryn Fremont. 2011. "Comparison of the Effectiveness and Efficiency of Text Previewing and Preteaching Keywords as Small-Group Reading Comprehension Strategies with Middle-School Students." *Literacy Research and Instruction* 50 (3): 241–252.

Burns, Matthew K., Nell Duke, and Kelly Cartwright. 2023. "Evaluating Components of the Active View of Reading as Intervention Targets: Implications for Social Justice." School Psychology 38 (1): 30–41. https:// doi.org/10.1037/spq0000519.

Cain, Kate, Jane V. Oakhill, and Kate Lemmon. 2004. "Individual Differences in the Inference of Word Meanings from Context: The Influence of Reading Comprehension, Vocabulary Knowledge, and Memory Capacity." *Journal of Educational Psychology* 96: 671–681.

Calderón, Margarita, Diane August, Daniel Durán, Nancy Madden, Robert Slavin, and M. Gil. 2003. *Spanish to English Transitional Reading: Teacher's Manual.* Baltimore, MD: Success for All Foundation.

Camp, Deanne. 2000. "It Takes Two: Teaching with Twin Texts of Fact and Fiction." *The Reading Teacher* 53: 400–408.

Cappiello, Mary A., Katie E. Cunningham, Denise Davila, Erika Thulin Dawes, and Grace Enriquez. 2022. *The Classroom Bookshelf* [blog]. https://classroombookshelf .wordpress.com/.

Cappiello, Mary Ann, and Erika Thulin Dawes. 2015. *Teaching to Complexity: A Framework for Text Evaluation.* Huntington Beach, CA: Shell Education.

Cappiello, Mary Ann, and Erika Thulin Dawes. 2021. *Text Sets in Action: Pathways Through Content Area Literacy.* Portsmouth, NH: Stenhouse.

Carlisle, Joanne F., Elfrieda H. Hiebert, and Devin Kearns. 2015. "Characteristics of Complex Words in Early Elementary Texts." Paper presented at the Annual Meeting of the Society of Scientific Study of Reading. https://www.academia.edu/29968605 /Characteristics_of_Complex_Words _in_Early_Elementary_Texts.

Carlo, Mara S., Diane August, Barry McLaughlin, Catherine E. Snow, Cheryl Dressler, David N. Lippman, Teresa J. Lively, and Claire E. White. 2004. "Closing the Gap: Addressing the Vocabulary Needs of English-Language Learners in Bilingual and Mainstream Classrooms." *Reading Research Quarterly* 39 (2): 188–215.

Castles, Anne, Kathleen Rastle, and Kate Nation. 2018. "Ending the Reading Wars: Reading Acquisition from Novice to Expert." *Psychological Science in the Public*

Interest 19 (1): 5–51. doi: 10.11/77 /1529100618772271.

Catts, Hugh W. Winter 2021/2022. "Rethinking How to Promote Reading Comprehension." *American Educator* 45 (4): 26–33.

Cervetti, Gina N., Miranda S. Fitzgerald, Elfrieda H. Hiebert, and Michael Hebert. 2023. "Meta-Analysis Examining the Impact of Vocabulary Instruction on Vocabulary Knowledge and Skill." *Reading Psychology*, 44 (6): 672–709, doi: 10.1080 /02702711.2023.2179146.

Cervetti, Gina N., Jacquline Barber, Rena Dorph, P. David Pearson, and Peter G. Goldschmidt. 2012. "The Impact of an Integrated Approach to Science and Literacy in Elementary School Classrooms." *Journal of Research in Science Teaching* 49 (5): 631–658.

Cervetti, Gina N., Tanya S. Wright, and Hyejin Hwang. 2016. "Conceptual Coherence, Comprehension, and Vocabulary Acquisition: A Knowledge Effect?" *Reading and Writing* 29 (4): 761–779.

Chall, Jeanne S., Vicki A. Jacobs, and Luke E. Baldwin. 1990. *The Reading Crisis: Why Poor Children Fall Behind.* Cambridge, MA: Harvard University Press.

Cohen, R. 1983. "Students Generate Questions as an Aid to Reading Comprehension." *Reading Teacher* 36 (8): 770–775.

Coltheart, Max, Kathleen Rastle, Conrad Perry, Robyn Langdon, and Johannes Ziegler. 2001. "DRC: A Dual Route Cascaded Model of Visual Word Recognition and Reading Aloud." *Psychological Review* 108 (1): 204–256. doi: 10.1037//0033-295x.108.1.204.

Cromley, Jennifer G., and Roger Azevedo. 2007. "Testing and Refining the Direct and Inferential Mediation Model of Reading Comprehension." Journal of *Educational Psychology* 99 (2): 311–325. doi:10.1037/0022-0663.99 .2.311.

Cunningham, Anne E. 2005. "Vocabulary Growth Through Independent Reading and Reading Aloud to Children." In *Teaching and Learning Vocabulary: Bringing Research to Practice*, edited by Elfrieda H. Hiebert and Michael L. Kamil (pp. 45–68). Mahwah, NJ: Lawrence Erlbaum Associates.

Cunningham, Anne E., and Keith E. Stanovich. 1994. "What Reading Does for the Mind." *Journal of Direct Instruction* 1 (2): 8–15.

Cunningham, Anne E., and Keith E. Stanovich. 1997. "Early Reading Acquisition and Its Relation to Reading Experience and Ability 10 Years Later." *Developmental Psychology* 33 (6): 934–945. https://doi.org/10.1037 /0012-1649.33.6.934.

Cunningham, Anne E., and Keith E. Stanovich. 1998. "The Impact of Print Exposure on Word Recognition." In *Word Recognition in Beginning Literacy*, edited by Jamie L. Metsala and Linnea C. Ehri (pp. 235–262). Mahwah, NJ: Lawrence Erlbaum Associates.

Cunningham, Katie Egan. 2019. *Start with Joy: Designing Literacy Learning for Student Happiness.* Portsmouth, NH: Stenhouse.

Davey, Beth, and Susan McBride. 1986. "Effects of Question-Generation on Reading Comprehension." *Journal of Educational Psychology* 22: 2–7.

Deci, Edward L., Richard Koestner, and Richard M. Ryan. 1999. "A Meta-analytic Review of Experiments Examining the Effects of Extrinsic Rewards on Intrinsic Motivation." *Psychological Bulletin* 125 (6): 627–668. https://doi.org/10.1037/0033 -2909.125.6.627.

Dehaene, Stanislas. 2013. "Inside the Letter Box: How Literacy Transforms the Human Brain." *Cerebrum* 7: 1–16. https:// www.ncbi.nlm.nih.gov/pmc/articles /PMC3704307/.

De Naeghel, Jessie, Hilde Van Keer, and Ruben Vanderlinde. 2014. "Strategies for Promoting Autonomous Reading Motivation: A Multiple Case Study Research in Primary Education." *Frontline Learning Research* 2 (1): 83–101.

Denner, Peter R., John P. Rickards, and Andrew J. Albanese. 2003. "The Effect of

Story Impressions Preview on Learning from Narrative Text." *Journal of Experimental Education* 71: 313–332.

Dewitz, Peter, Eileen Carr, and Judythe P. Patberg. 1987. "Effects of Inference Training on Comprehension and Comprehension Monitoring." *Reading Research Quarterly* 22 (1): 99–121. https://doi.org/10.2307/747723.

Diliberto, Jennifer A., John R. Beattie, Claudia P. Flowers, and Robert F. Algozzine. 2009. "Effects of Teaching Syllable Skills Instruction on Reading Achievement in Struggling Middle School Readers." *Literacy Research and Instruction* 48 (1): 14–27.

Doignon-Camus, Nadège, and Daniel Zagar. 2014. "The Syllabic Bridge: The First Step in Learning Spelling-to-Sound Correspondences." *Journal of Child Language* 41 (5): 1147–1165.

Dolezal, Sarah E., Lindsay M. Welsh, Michael Pressley, and Melissa M. Vincent. 2003. "How Nine Third-Grade Teachers Motivate Student Academic Engagement." *Elementary School Journal* 103 (3): 239–267.

Duff, Dawna, Bruce J. Tomblin, and Hugh Catts. (2015). "The Influence of Reading on Vocabulary Growth: A Case for a Matthew Effect." *Journal of Speech, Language, and Hearing Research* 58 (3): 853–864.

Duke, Nell K. 2000. "3.6 Minutes Per Day: The Scarcity of Informational Text in First Grade." *Reading Research Quarterly* 35 (2): 202–224.

Duke, Nell, and Kelly Cartwright. 2021. "The Science of Reading Progresses: Communicating Advances Beyond the Simple View of Reading." *Reading Research Quarterly* 56 (S1): S25–S44.

Duke, Nell, and P. David Pearson. 2002. "Effective Practices for Developing Reading Comprehension." In *What Research Has to Say About Reading Instruction*, edited by Alan E. Farstrup and S. Jay Samuels (3rd ed., pp. 205–242). Newark, DE: International Reading Association, Inc.

Duke, Nell, Alessandra E. Ward, and P. David Pearson. 2021. "The Science of Reading Comprehension Instruction." *The Reading Teacher* 74 (6): 663–672.

Duran, Nicholas D., Philip McCarthy, Art C. Graesser, and Danielle S. McNamara. 2007. "Using Temporal Cohesion to Predict Temporal Coherence in Narrative and Expository Texts." *Behavior Research Methods* 39 (2): 212–223. https://doi.org/10.3758/BF03193150.

Durkin, Dolores. 1978/1979. "What Classroom Observations Reveal about Reading Comprehension Instruction." *Reading Research Quarterly* 14 (4). 481–533.

Dymock, Susan. 2007. "Comprehension Strategy Instruction: Teaching Narrative Text Structure Awareness." *The Reading Teacher* 61 (2): 161–167.

Dyson, Hannah, Wendy Best, Jonathan Solity, and Charles Hulme. 2017. "Training Mispronunciation Correction and Word Meanings Improves Children's Ability to Learn to Read Words." *Scientific Studies of Reading* 21 (5): 392–407.

Edwards, Ashley, Laura Steacy, Noam Siegelman, Valeria M. Rigobon, Devin M. Kearns, Jay Rueckl, and Donald Compton. 2022. "Unpacking the Unique Relationship Between Set for Variability and Word Reading Development: Examining Word- and Child-Level Predictors of Performance." *Journal of Educational Psychology* 114 (6): 1242–1256.

Ehri, Linnea C. 1984. "How Orthography Alters Spoken Language Competencies in Children Learning to Read and Spell." In *Language Awareness and Learning to Read*, edited by J. Downing and R. Valtin (pp. 119–147). New York: Springer Verlag.

Ehri, Linnea C. 1987. "Learning to Read and Spell Words." *Journal of Reading Behavior* 14: 5–31.

Ehri, Linnea C. 1995. "Phases of Development in Learning to Read Words by Sight." *Journal of Research in Reading* 18 (2): 116–125.

Ehri, Linnea C. 1998. "Grapheme-Phoneme Knowledge Is Essential for Learning to Read Words in English." In *Word Recognition in Beginning Literacy*, edited by J. L. Metsala and L. C. Ehri (pp. 3–40). Mahwah, NJ: Erlbaum.

Ehri, Linnea C. 2005a. "Learning to Read Words: Theory, Findings, and Issues." *Scientific Studies of Reading* 9 (2): 167–188. doi: 10.1207/s1532799xssr0902_4.

Ehri, Linnea C. 2005b. "Development of Sight Word Reading: Phases and Findings." In *The Science of Reading: A Handbook*, edited by M. J. Snowling and C. Hume (pp. 135–154). Oxford, UK: Blackwell.

Ehri, Linnea C. 2014. "Orthographic Mapping in the Acquisition of Sight Word Reading, Spelling Memory, and Vocabulary Learning." *Scientific Studies of Reading* 18 (1): 5–21. https://eric.ed.gov/?id=EJ1027413.

Ehri, Linnea. 2017. "Orthographic Mapping and Literacy Development Revisited." In *Theories of Reading Development*, edited by Kate Cain, Donald L. Compton, and Rauno K. Parrila (pp. 127–146). Amsterdam: John Benjamins. https://doi.org/10.1075/swll.15.

Ehri, Linnea C., and Lee Wilce. 1980. "The Influence of Orthography on Readers' Conceptualization of the Phonemic Structure of Words." *Applied Psycholinguistics* 1: 371–385.

Eide, Denise. 2012. *Uncovering the Logic of English: A Common-Sense Approach*. Minneapolis, MN: Pedia Learning.

Elbaum, Batya, Sharon Vaughn, Marie Tejero Hughes, and Sally Watson Moody. 2000. "How Effective Are One-to-One Tutoring Programs in Reading for Elementary Students at Risk for Reading Failure? A Meta-Analysis of the Intervention Research." *Journal of Educational Psychology* 92 (4): 605–619.

Elbro, Carston, and Ida Buck-Iverson. 2013. "Activation of Background Knowledge for Inference Making: Effects on Reading Comprehension." *Scientific Studies of Reading* 17 (6): 435–452. https://doi.org/10.1080/10888438.2013.774005.

Elhassan, Zena, Shelia G. Crewther, Edith L. Bavin, and David P. Crewther. 2015. "Preliminary Validation of FastaReada as a Measure of Reading Fluency." *Frontiers of Psychology* 6: 1634. doi: 10.3389/fpsyg.2015.01634.

Elkonin, Daniil B. 1973. "Methods of Teaching Reading." In *Comparative Reading: Cross National Studies of Behavior and Processing in Reading and Writing*, edited by J. Downing (pp. 551–579). New York: Macmillan.

Elleman, Amy M. 2017. "Examining the Impact of Inference Instruction on the Literal and Inferential Comprehension of Skilled and Less Skilled Readers: A Meta-analytic Review." *Journal of Educational Psychology* 109 (6): 761–781.

Englert, Carol S., and Elfrieda H. Hiebert. 1984. "Children's Developing Awareness of Text Structures in Expository Materials." *Journal of Educational Psychology* 76 (1): 65–74. https://doi.org/10.1037/0022-0663.76.1.65.

Fielding, Linda, and P. David Pearson. 1994. "Reading Comprehension: What Works." *Educational Leadership* 51 (5): 62–68.

Fisher, Douglas, Nancy Frey, and John Hattie. 2016. *Teaching Literacy in the Visible Learning Classroom, Grades K–5*. Dallas, TX: Corwin.

Fisher, Douglas, Nancy Frey, and Diane Lapp. 2008. "Shared Readings: Modeling Comprehension, Vocabulary, Text Structures, and Text Features for Older Readers." *The Reading Teacher* 61 (7): 548–556.

Flood, James, and Diane Lapp. 1986. "Types of Texts: The Match Between What Students Read in Basals and What They Encounter in Tests." *Reading Research Quarterly* 21 (3): 284–297.

Foorman, Barbara, Nicholas Beyler, Kelly Borradaile, Michael Coyne, Caroline Denton, Joseph Dimino, Joshu Ferguson,

Lynda Hayes, Juliette Henke, Laura Justice, Betsy Keating, Warnick Lewis, Samina Sattar, Andre Streck, Richard Wagner, and Sarah Wissel. 2016. *Foundational Skills to Support Reading for Understanding in Kindergarten Through 3rd Grade.* NCEE 2016-4008. Washington, DC: U.S. Department of Education, Institute of Education Sciences, National Center for Education Evaluation and Regional Assistance. https://ies.ed.gov/ncee/wwc/PracticeGuide/21.

Fuchs, Lynn S., Douglas Fuchs, Michelle K. Hosp, and Joseph R. Jenkins. 2001. "Oral Reading Fluency as an Indicator of Reading Competence: A Theoretical, Empirical, and Historical Analysis." *Scientific Studies of Reading* 5 (3): 239–256.

Fukkink, Ruben G., and Kees de Glopper. 1998. "Effects of Instruction in Deriving Word Meaning from Context: A Meta-Analysis." *Review of Educational Research* 68 (4): 450–469.

Gabriel, Rachel. 2020. "The Future of the Science of Reading." *The Reading Teacher* 74 (1): 11–18.

Gajria, Meenakshi, Asha Jitendra, Sheetal Sood, and Gabriell Sacks. 2007. "Improving Comprehension of Expository Text in Students with LD: A Research Synthesis." *Journal of Learning Disabilities* 40 (3): 210–225.

Gambrell, Linda, and Ruby J. Bales. 1986. "Mental Imagery and the Comprehension-Monitoring Performance of Fourth and Fifth-Grade Poor Readers." *Reading Research Quarterly* 21 (4): 454–464.

García-Madruga, Juan A., Maria Rosa Elosúa, Laura Gil, Isabel Gómez-Veiga, José Óscar Vila, Isabel Orjales, Antonio Contreras, María Ángeles Melero, and Gonzalo Duque. 2013. "Reading Comprehension and Working Memory's Executive Processes: An Intervention Study in Primary School Students." *Reading Research Quarterly* 48 (2): 155–174. https://doi.org/10.1002/rrq.44.

Gerbier, Emilie, and Thomas Toppino. 2015. "The Effect of Distributed Practice: Neuroscience, Cognition, and Education." *Trends in Neuroscience and Education* 4 (3): 49–59.

Glasswell, Kath, and Michael Ford. 2011. "Let's Start Leveling About Leveling." *Language Arts* 88 (3): 208–216.

Goodwin, Amanda P., and Soyeon Ahn. 2013. "A Meta-Analysis of Morphological Interventions in English: Effects on Literacy Outcomes for School-Age Children." *Scientific Studies of Reading* 17 (4): 257–285.

Gough, Philip B., and William E. Tunmer. 1986. "Decoding, Reading, and Reading Disability." *Remedial and Special Education* 7 (1): 6–10. doi: 10.1177/074193258600700104.

Graesser, Arthur C., Danielle S. McNamara, Zhiqang Cai, Mark Conley, Haiying Li, and James Pennebaker. 2014. "Coh-Metrix Measures Text Characteristics at Multiple Levels of Language and Discourse." *Elementary School Journal* 115 (2): 210–229. https://doi.org/10.1086/678293.

Graesser, Arthur C., Murray Singer, and Tom Trabasso. 1994. "Constructing Inferences During Narrative Text Comprehension." *Psychological Review* 101 (3): 371–395. https://doi.org/10.1037/0033-295X.101.3.371.

Graham, Steve, Xinghua Liu, Angelique Aitken, Clarence Ng, Brendan Bartlett, Karen R. Harris, and Jennifer Holzapfel. 2018. "Effectiveness of Literacy Programs Balancing Reading and Writing Instruction: A Meta-Analysis." *Reading Research Quarterly* 53 (3): 279–304.

Graves, Michael F. 2000. "A Vocabulary Program to Complement and Bolster a Middle-Grade Comprehension Program." In *Reading for Meaning: Fostering Comprehension in the Middle Grades*, edited by Barbara M. Taylor, Michael F. Graves, and Paul van Den Broek (pp. 116–135). New York: Teachers College Press.

Graves, Michael F. 2006. *The Vocabulary Book.* New York: Teachers College Press.

Graves, Michael F., Cheryl L. Cooke, and Michael J. Laberge. 1983. "Effects of Previewing Difficult Short Stories on Low Ability Junior High School Students' Comprehension, Recall, and Attitudes." *Reading Research Quarterly* 18 (3): 262–276.

Graves, Michael, and Susan Watts-Taffe. 2002. "The Place of Word Consciousness in a Research-Based Vocabulary Program." In *What Research Has to Say About Reading Instruction*, edited by Alan E. Farstrup and S. Jay Samuels (pp. 140–165). Newark, DE: International Reading Association.

Guthrie, John T., and Nicole M. Huminick 2004. "Motivating Students to Read: Evidence for Classroom Practices That Increase Reading Motivation and Achievement." In *The Voice of Evidence in Reading Research*, edited by P. McCardle and V. Chhabra (pp. 329–354). Baltimore: Paul H. Brookes.

Guthrie, John T., Allen Wigfield, Pedro Barbosa, Kathleen C. Perencevich, Ana Taboada, Marcia H. Davis, Nicole T. Scaffidi, and Stephen Tonks. 2004. "Increasing Reading Comprehension and Engagement Through Concept-Oriented Reading Instruction." *Journal of Educational Psychology* 96: 403–423.

Guthrie, John T., Allan Wigfield, Jamie Metsala, and Kathleen E. Cox. 1999. "Motivational and Cognitive Predictors of Text Comprehension and Reading Amount." *Scientific Studies of Reading* 3 (3): 231–256. https://doi.org/10.1207/s1532799xssr0303_3.

Hall, Kendra M., Brenda L. Sabey, and Michelle McClellan. 2005. "Expository Text Comprehension: Helping Primary-Grade Teachers Use Expository Texts to Full Advantage." *Reading Psychology* 26 (3): 211–234.

Hall, Sophie S., Rebecca Kowalski, Kevin B. Paterson, Jaskaran Basran, Ruth Filik, and John Maltby. 2015. "Local Text Cohesion, Reading Ability and Individual Science Aspirations: Key Factors Influencing Comprehension in Science Classes." *British Educational Research Journal* 41 (1): 122–142. https://doi.org/10.1002/berj.3134.

Halloran, Clare, Rebecca Jack, James Okun, and Emily Oster. 2021. "Pandemic Schooling Mode and Student Test Scores: Evidence from US States." National Bureau of Economic Research. https://www.nber.org/papers/w29497.

Hansen, Jane, and P. David Pearson. 1983. "An Instructional Study: Improving the Inferential Comprehension of Good and Poor Fourth-Grade Readers." *Journal of Educational Psychology* 75 (6): 821–829. https://doi.org/10.1037/0022-0663.75.6.821.

Hare, Victoria C., and Kathleen M. Borchardt. 1984. "Direct Instruction of Summarization Skills." *Reading Research Quarterly* 20 (1): 62–78. https://doi.org/10.2307/747652.

Hasbrouck, Jane, and Gerald Tindal. 2006. "Oral Reading Fluency Norms: A Valuable Assessment Tool for Reading Teachers." *The Reading Teacher* 59 (7): 636–644.

Hasbrouck, Jane, and Gerald Tindal. 2017. "An Update to Compiled ORF Norms." Technical Report No. 1702. Behavioral Research and Teaching, University of Oregon.

Hattan, Courtney. 2019. "Prompting Rural Students' Use of Background Knowledge and Experience to Support Comprehension of Unfamiliar Content." *Reading Research Quarterly* 54 (4): 451–455. https://doi.org/10.1002/rrq.270.

Hattan, Courtney, and Patricia A. Alexander. 2020. "Prior Knowledge Activation in Elementary Classroom Discourse." *Reading and Writing* 33: 1617–1647. https://doi.org/10.1007/s11145-020-10022-8.

Hattan, Courtney, and Sarah M. Lupo. 2020. "Rethinking the Role of Knowledge in the Literacy Classroom." *Reading Research Quarterly* 55 (S1): S283–S298.

Hattan, Courtney, Lauren M. Singer, Sandra Loughlin, and Patricia A. Alexander. 2015.

"Prior Knowledge Activation in Design and in Practice." *Literacy Research: Theory, Method, and Practice* 64 (1): 478–497.

Hattie, John. 2003. "Teachers Make a Difference: What Is the Research Evidence?" Paper presented at the ACER Research Conference, Melbourne, Australia. http://research.acer.edu.au/research_conference_2003/4.

Hattie, John. 2009. *Visible Learning: A Synthesis of Over 800 Meta-analyses Relating to Achievement.* London: Routledge.

Hayden, Emily, Elfrieda H. Hiebert, and Guy Trainin. 2019. "Patterns of Silent Reading Rate and Comprehension as a Function of Developmental Status, Genre, and Text Position." *Reading Psychology* 40 (8): 731–767.

Hayes, Donald P., and Margaret G. Ahrens. 1988. "Vocabulary Simplification for Children: A Special Case of 'Motherese'?" *Journal of Child Language* 15 (2): 395–410. https://doi.org/10.1017/S0305000900012411.

Heath, Melissa A., Kathryn Smith, and Ellie L. Young. 2017. "Using Children's Literature to Strengthen Social and Emotional Learning." *School Psychology International* 38 (5): 541–561.

Hebert, Michael, Janet J. Bohaty, J. Ron Nelson, and Jessica Brown. 2016. "The Effects of Text Structure Instruction on Expository Reading Comprehension: A Meta-Analysis." *Journal of Educational Psychology* 108 (5): 609–629. https://doi.org/10.1037/edu0000082.

Hebert, Michael, Amy Simpson, and Steve Graham. 2013. "Comparing Effects of Different Writing Activities on Reading Comprehension: A Meta-Analysis." *Reading and Writing: An Interdisciplinary Journal* 26 (1): 111–138. doi: 10.1007/s11145-012-9386-3.

Hemingway, Ernest. 1952. *The Old Man and the Sea.* New York: Simon & Schuster.

Hennessey, Nancy L. 2020. *The Reading Comprehension Blueprint: Helping Students Make Meaning from Text.* Baltimore, MD: Paul H. Brookes.

Hidi, Suzanne, and William Baird. 1986. "Interestingness—A Neglected Variable in Discourse Processing." *Cognitive Science* 10: 179–194.

Hidi, Suzanne, and William Baird. 1988. "Strategies for Increasing Text-Based Interest and Students' Recall of Expository Texts." *Reading Research Quarterly* 23 (4): 465–483. https://doi.org/10.2307/747644.

Hidi, Suzanne, and Judith M. Harackiewicz. 2000. "Motivating the Academically Unmotivated: A Critical Issue for the 21st Century." *Review of Educational Research* 70 (2): 151–179. https://doi.org/10.2307/1170660.

Hiebert, Elfrieda H., Amanda P. Goodwin, and Gina N. Cervetti. 2018. "Core Vocabulary: Its Morphological Content and Presence in Exemplar Texts." *Reading Research Quarterly* 53 (1): 29–49.

Hiebert, Elfrieda H., and D. Ray Reutzel. 2010. *Revisiting Silent Reading: New Directions for Teachers and Researchers.* Newark, DE: International Reading Association.

Hilden, Katherine R., and Michael Pressley. 2007. "Self-Regulation Through Transactional Strategies Instruction." *Reading and Writing Quarterly* 23 (1): 51–75.

Hilfrank, Elizabeth. 2022. "Endangered Species Act: How This 1973 Law Protects Animals." *National Geographic Kids.* https://kids.nationalgeographic.com/history/article/endangered-species-act.

Hirsch, E. D., Jr. 2003. "Reading Comprehension Requires Knowledge of the Words and the World: Scientific Insights into the Fourth-Grade-Slump and the Nation's Stagnant Comprehension Scores." *American Educator* 27: 10–29.

Honig, Bill, Linda Diamond, and Linda Gutlohn. 2018. *Teaching Reading Sourcebook.* 3rd ed. Oakland, CA: Core.

Hoover, Wesley A., and Philip B. Gough. 1990. "The Simple View of Reading." *Reading and Writing: An Interdisciplinary Journal,* 2 (2): 127–160. https://doi.org/10.1007/BF00401799.

Hoover, Wesley A., and William E. Tunmer. 2021. "The Primacy of Science in Communicating Advances in the Science of Reading." *Reading Research Quarterly* 57 (2): 1–10.

Hruby, George G., Leslie Burns, Stergios Botzakis, Susan L. Groenke, Leigh A. Hall, Judson Laughter, and Richard L. Allington. 2016. "The Metatheoretical Assumptions of Literacy Engagement: A Preliminary Centennial History." *Review of Research in Education* 40 (1): 588–643. https://doi.org/10.3102/0091732X16664311.

Hudson, Roxanne, Holly Lane, and Paige Pullen. 2005. "Reading Fluency Assessment and Instruction: What, Why, and How?" *The Reading Teacher* 58 (8): 702–714.

Ivey, Gay, and Karen Broaddus. 2001. "Just Plain Reading: A Survey of What Makes Students Want to Read in Middle Schools." *Reading Research Quarterly* 36 (4): 350–377.

Jeong, Jongseong, Janet S. Gaffney, and Jin-Oh Choi. 2010. "Availability and Use of Informational Texts in Second-, Third-, and Fourth-Grade Classrooms." *Research in the Teaching of English* 44: 435–456.

Johnson-Laird, P. N. 1983. *Mental Models: Towards a Cognitive Science of Language, Inference and Consciousness.* Cambridge, UK: Cambridge University Press.

Jones, Sara. 2020. "Measuring Reading Motivation: A Cautionary Tale." *The Reading Teacher* 74 (1): 79–89.

Kaefer, Tanya, Susan B. Neuman, and Ashley M. Pinkham. 2015. "Pre-Existing Background Knowledge Influence Socioeconomic Differences in Preschoolers' Word Learning and Comprehension." *Reading Psychology* 36 (3): 203–231.

Juel, Connie, and Rebecca Deffes. 2004. "Making Words Stick: What Research Says About Reading." *Educational Leadership* 61 (6): 30–35.

Kearns, Devin M. 2020. "Does English Have Useful Syllable Division Patterns?" *Reading Research Quarterly* 55 (S1): S145–S160.

Kearns, Devin M., Cheryl Lyon, and Shannon L. Kelley. 2022. "Structured Literacy Interventions for Reading Long Words." In *Structured Literacy Interventions: Teaching Students with Reading Difficulties, Grades K–6*, edited by Louise Spear-Swerling (pp. 43–66). New York: Guilford Press.

Kearns, Devin M., and Victoria M. Whaley. 2019. "Helping Students with Dyslexia Read Long Words: Using Syllables and Morphemes." *Teaching Exceptional Children* 51 (3): 212–225.

Kendeou, Panayiota, and Peter van den Broek. 2007. "The Effects of Prior Knowledge and Text Structure on Comprehension Processes During Reading of Scientific Texts." *Memory and Cognition* 35 (7): 1567–1577. https://doi.org/10.3758/BF03193491.

Kessler, Brett, and Rebecca Treiman. 2001. "Relationship Between Sounds and Letters in English Monosyllables." *Journal of Memory and Language* 44 (4): 592–617. https://doi.org/10.1006/jmla.2000.2745.

Kieffer, Michael J., and Nonie K. Lesaux. 2007. "Breaking Down Words to Build Meaning: Morphology, Vocabulary, and Reading Comprehension in the Urban Classroom." *The Reading Teacher* 61 (2): 134–144.

Kilpatrick, David. 2015. *Essentials of Assessing, Preventing, and Overcoming Reading Difficulties.* Hoboken, NJ: Wiley.

Kilpatrick, David. 2016. *Equipped for Reading Success.* Syracuse, NY: Casey & Kirsch.

Kim, James, and Thomas G. White. 2008. "Scaffolding Voluntary Summer Reading for Children in Grades 3 to 5: An Experimental Study." *Scientific Studies of Reading* 12 (1): 1–23. https://doi.org/10.1080/10888430701746849.

Kim, James, Mary A. Burkhauser, Jackie E. Relyea, Joshua B. Gilbert, Ethan Scherer, Jill Fitzgerald, Douglas Mosher, and Joseph McIntyre. 2023. "A Longitudinal Randomized Trial of a Sustained Content Literacy Intervention from First to Second Grade:

Transfer Effects on Students' Reading Comprehension." *Journal of Educational Psychology* 115 (1): 73–98. https://doi.org/10.1037/edu0000751.

Kim, Min K., Diane P. Bryant, Brian R. Bryant, and Yujeong Park. 2017. "A Synthesis of Interventions for Improving Oral Reading Fluency of Elementary Students with Learning Disabilities." *Preventing School Failure: Alternative Education for Children and Youth* 61: 116–125.

Kim, Young-Suk Grace. 2015. "Developmental, Component-Based Model of Reading Fluency: An Investigation of Predictors of Word Reading Fluency, Text-Reading Fluency, and Reading Comprehension." *Reading Research Quarterly* 50 (4): 459–481. doi: 10.1002/rrq.107.

Kim, Young-Suk Grace, Jamie M. Quinn, and Yaacov Petscher. 2021. "What Is Text Reading Fluency and Is It a Predictor or an Outcome of Reading Comprehension? A Longitudinal Investigation." *Developmental Psychology* 57 (5): 718–732. https://doi.org/10.1037/dev0001167.

Kintsch, Walter. 1998. *Comprehension: A Paradigm for Cognition.* Cambridge, UK: Cambridge University Press.

Kintsch, Walter, and Teun A. van Dijk. 1978. "Toward a Model of Text Comprehension and Production." *Psychological Review* 85 (5): 363–394. https://doi.org/10.1037/0033-295X.85.5.363.

Kosmoski, Georgia J., Geneva Gay, and Edward L. Vockell. 1990. "Cultural Literacy and Academic Achievement." *Journal of Experimental Education* 58 (4): 265–272.

Kostons, Danny, and Greetje van der Werf. 2015. "The Effects of Activating Prior Topic and Metacognitive Knowledge on Text Comprehension Scores." *British Journal of Educational Psychology* 85: 264–275.

Kuhfeld, Megan, Karyn Lewis, and Tiffany Peltier. 2022. "Reading Achievement Declines During the COVID-19 Pandemic: Evidence from 5 Million U.S. Students in Grades 3–8." *Reading and Writing* 36: 245–261. https://link.springer.com/article/10.1007/s11145-022-10345-8.

Kuhn, Melanie R. 2020. "Whole Class or Small Group Fluency Instruction: A Tutorial of Four Effective Approaches." *Education Sciences* (Special Issue: Reading Fluency) 10: 145.

Kuhn, Melanie R., Paula J. Schwaneflugel, Robin D. Morris, Lesley M. Morrow, Deborah G. Woo, Elizabeth B. Meisinger, Rose A. Cevcik, Barbara A. Bradley, and Steven A. Stahl. 2006. "Teaching Children to Become Fluent and Automatic Readers." *Journal of Literacy Research* 38 (4): 357–387.

Kuhn, Melanie R., and Steven A. Stahl. 1998. "Teaching Children to Learn Word Meanings from Context: A Synthesis and Some Questions." *Journal of Literacy Research* 30 (1): 119–138.

Kuhn, Melanie R., and Steven A. Stahl. 2003. "Fluency: A Review of Developmental and Remedial Practices." *Journal of Educational Psychology* 95 (1): 3–21. https://doi.org/10.1037/0022-0663.95.1.3.

LaBerge, David, and S. Jay Samuels. 1974. "Toward a Theory of Automatic Information Processing in Reading." *Cognitive Psychology* 6 (2): 293–323. doi: 10.1016/0010-0285(74)90015-2.

Lane, Holly B., and Stephanie Allen. 2010. "The Vocabulary-Rich Classroom: Modeling Sophisticated Word Use to Promote Word Consciousness and Vocabulary Growth." *The Reading Teacher* 63 (5): 362–370.

Laufer, Batia 1989. "What Percentage of Text-Lexis is Essential for Comprehension?" In *Special Language: From Humans Thinking to Thinking Machines*, edited by C. Lauren and M. Nordman (pp. 316–323). Clevedon, UK: Multilingual Matters.

Lee, Sung H., and Shu-Fei Tsai. 2017. "Experimental Intervention Research on Students with Specific Poor Comprehension: A Systematic Review of Treatment Outcomes." *Reading and Writing* 30: 917–943.

Lennox, Sandra. 2013. "Interactive Read-Alouds: An Avenue for Enhancing Children's Language for Thinking and Understanding: A Review of Recent Research." *Early Childhood Education Journal* 41 (5): 381–389.

Lewis, Karyn, Megan Kuhfeld, Erik Ruzek, and Andrew McEachin. 2021. "Learning During COVID-19: Reading and Math Achievement in the 2020–21 School Year." NWEA Research Brief. https://www.nwea .org/content/uploads/2021/07/Learning -during-COVID-19-Reading-and-math -achievement-in-the-2020-2021-school -year.research-brief.pdf.

Lubliner, Shira, and Linda Smetana. 2005. "The Effects of Comprehensive Vocabulary Instruction on Title I Students' Metacognitive Word-Learning Skills and Reading Comprehension." *Journal of Literacy Research* 37 (2): 163–200. https://doi.org /10.1207/s15548430jlr3702.

Lyon, G. Reid. 1998. "Why Reading Is Not a Natural Process." *Educational Leadership* 55 (6): 14–18.

MacKay, Elizabeth, Elise Lynch, Tamara Sorenson Duncan, and Hélène Deacon. 2021. "Informing the Science of Reading: Children's Awareness of Sentence-Level Information Is Important for Reading Comprehension." *Reading Research Quarterly* 56: 1–10. doi.10.1002/rrq.397.

Maki, Kathrin, and Stephanie Hammerschmidt-Snidarich. 2022. "Reading Fluency Intervention Dosage: A Novel Meta-Analysis and Research Synthesis." *Journal of School Psychology* 92: 148–164.

Manzo, Ula C., and Anthony V. Manzo. 2008. "Teaching Vocabulary-Learning Strategies: Word Consciousness, Word Connection and Word Prediction." In *What Research Has to Say About Vocabulary Instruction*, edited by Alan E. Farstrup and S. Jay Samuels (pp. 80–105). Newark, DE: International Reading Association.

Marzano, Robert. 2004. *Building Background Knowledge for Academic Achievement: Research on What Works in Schools.* Alexandria, VA: ASCD.

Marzano, Robert, and James D. Pickering. 2005. *Building Academic Vocabulary: A Teacher's Manual.* Alexandria, VA: ASCD.

Marulis, Loren M., and Susan B. Neuman. 2013. "How Vocabulary Interventions Affect Young Children at Risk: A Meta-Analytic Review." *Journal of Research on Educational Effectiveness* 6: 223–262.

McBreen, Miriam, and Robert Savage. 2021. "The Impact of Motivational Reading Instruction on the Reading Achievement and Motivation of Students: A Systematic Review and Meta-analysis." *Educational Psychology Review* 33 (3): 1125–1163. https:// doi.org/10.1007/s10648-020-09584-4.

McKenna, Michael C., Dennis J. Kear, and Randolph A. Ellsworth. 1995. "Children's Attitudes Toward Reading: A National Survey." *Reading Research Quarterly* 30 (4): 934–956. https://doi.org/10.2307/748205.

McKeown, Margaret. G. 1993. "Creating Effective Definitions for Young Word Learners." *Reading Research Quarterly* 28: 16–33.

McKeown, Margaret G. 2019. "Effective Vocabulary Instruction Fosters Knowing Words, Using Words, and Understanding How Words Work." *Language Speech, and Hearing Services in Schools* 50: 466–476.

McKeown, Margaret G., Isabel L. Beck, and Ronette G. K. Blake. 2009. "Rethinking Reading Comprehension Instruction: A Comparison of Instruction for Strategies and Content Approaches." *Reading Research Quarterly* 44 (3): 218–253.

McKeown, Margaret. G., Isabel Beck, Richard C. Omanson, and Martah T. Pople. 1985. "Some Effects of the Nature and Frequency of Vocabulary Instruction on the Knowledge and Use of Words." *Reading Research Quarterly* 20 (5): 522–535. https://doi.org /10.2307/747940.

Meier, Margaret. 1984. "Comprehension Monitoring in the Elementary Classroom." *Reading Teacher* 37 (8): 770–774.

Miller, Donalyn. 2009. *The Book Whisperer: Awakening the Inner Reader in Every Child.* Hoboken, NJ: Jossey-Bass.

Minor, Cornelius. 2018. *We Got This: Equity, Access, and the Quest to Be Who Our Students Need Us to Be.* Portsmouth, NH: Heinemann.

Moats, Louisa. 2001. "Overcoming the Language Gap." *American Educator*, 5–9.

Moats, Louisa. 2004. "Efficacy of a Structured, Systematic Language Curriculum for Adolescent Poor Readers." *Reading and Writing Quarterly* 20: 145–159.

Moats, Louisa, and Carol Tolman. 2009. *Language Essentials for Teachers of Reading and Spelling (LETRS): The Challenge of Learning to Read (Module 1).* Boston: Sopris West.

Mokhtari, Kouider, and H. Brian Thompson. 2006. "How Problems of Reading Fluency and Comprehension Are Related to Difficulties in Syntactic Awareness Skills Among Fifth Graders." *Reading Research and Instruction* 46 (1): 73–94. https://doi.org/10.1080/19388070609558461.

Mol, Suzanne E., and Adriana G. Bus. 2011. "To Read or Not to Read: A Meta-Analysis of Print Exposure from Infancy to Early Adulthood." *Psychological Bulletin* 137 (2): 267–296. https://doi.org/10.1037/a0021890.

Morgan, Alisa, Bradley R. Wilcox, and J. Lloyd Eldredge. 2000. "Effect of Difficulty Levels on Second Grade Delayed Readers Using Dyad Reading." *Journal of Educational Research* 94 (2): 113–119.

Moss, Barbara. 2008. "The Information Text Gap: The Mismatch Between Non-Narrative Text Types in Basal Readers and 2009 NAEP Recommended Guidelines." *Journal of Literacy Research* 40 (2): 201–219.

Moss, Barbara, and Evangeline Newton. 2002. "An Examination of the Informational Text Genre in Basal Readers." *Reading Psychology* 23: 1–13.

Muhammad, Gholdy. 2020. *Cultivating Genius: An Equity Framework for Culturally and Historically Responsive Literacy.* New York: Scholastic.

Murphy, P. Karen, Ian A. Wilkinson, Anna O. Soter, and C. M. Firetto. 2016. "Instruction Based on Discussion." In *Handbook of Research on Learning and Instruction*, edited by Richard E. Mayer and Patricia A. Alexander. 2nd ed. New York: Routledge.

Murphy, P. Karen, Ian A. Wilkinson, Anna Soter, Maeghan Hennessey, and John Alexander. 2009. "Examining the Effects of Classroom Discussion on Students' Comprehension of Text." *Journal of Educational Psychology* 101 (3): 740–764.

Nagy, William E., and Richard C. Anderson. 1984. "How Many Words Are There in Printed School English?" *Reading Research Quarterly* 19 (3): 304–330.

Nagy, William E., Virginia W. Berninger, and Robert D. Abbott. 2006. "Contribution of Morphology Beyond Phonology to Literacy Outcomes of Upper Elementary and Middle-School Students." *Journal of Educational Psychology* 98: 134–147.

Nagy, William E., Patricia Herman, and Richard C. Anderson. 1985. "Learning Words from Context." *Reading Research Quarterly* 20 (2): 233–253.

Nathan, Ruth G., and Keith E. Stanovich. 1991. "The Causes and Consequences of Differences in Reading Fluency." *Theory into Practice* 30 (3): 176–184.

Nation, Paul, and Robert Waring. 1997. "Vocabulary Size, Text Coverage, and Word Lists." In *Vocabulary: Description, Acquisition and Pedagogy*, edited by N. Schmitt and M. McCarthy (pp. 6–19). Cambridge, UK: Cambridge University Press.

National Governors Association Center for Best Practices and Council of Chief State School Officers. 2010. *Common Core State*

Standards for English Language Arts and Literacy in History/Social Studies, Science, and Technical Subjects. Washington, DC: National Governors Association.

National Institute of Child Health and Human Development. 2000. *Report of the National Reading Panel: Teaching Children to Read: An Evidence-Based Assessment of the Scientific Research Literature on Reading and Its Implications for Reading Instruction: Reports of the Subgroups.* NIH Publication No. 004754. Washington, DC: U.S. Government Printing Office.

National Reading Panel. See National Institute of Child Health and Human Development.

Nese, Joseph F. T., Gian Biancarosa, Kelli Cummings, Patrick Kennedy, Julia Alonzo, and Gerald Tindal. 2013. "In Search of Average Growth: Describing Within-Year Oral Reading Fluency Growth Across Grades 1–8." *Journal of School Psychology* 51: 625–642. doi: 10.1016/j.jsp.2013.05.006.

Neuman, Susan B. 2006. "How We Neglect Knowledge—and Why." *American Educator*, 24–27. https://www.aft.org/periodical/american-educator/spring-2006/how-we-neglect-knowledge-and-why.

Neuman, Susan B., Carol Copple, and Sue Bredekamp. 2000. *Learning to Read and Write: Developmentally Appropriate Practices for Young Children.* Washington, DC: National Association for the Education of Young Children.

Newton, Joanna, Nancy Padack, and Timothy Rasinski. 2008. *Evidence-Based Instruction in Reading: A Professional Development Guide to Vocabulary.* New York: Pearson.

NICHD. See National Institute of Child Health and Human Development.

Noon, Edward. 2020. "Compare and Despair or Compare and Explore? Instagram Social Comparisons of Ability and Opinion Predict Adolescent Identity Development." *Cyberpsychology* 14 (2): article 1. doi: 10.5817/CP2020-2-1.

Nystrand, Martin. 2006. "Research on the Role of Classroom Discourse as it Affects Reading Comprehension." *Research in the Teaching of English* 40: 392–412.

Oczkus, Lori D. 2010. *Reciprocal Teaching at Work: Strategies for Improving Reading Comprehension.* 2nd ed. Newark, DE: International Reading Association.

Okkinga, Mariska, Roel van Steensel, Amos J. S. van Gelderen, and Peter J. C. Sleegers. 2018. "Effects of Reciprocal Teaching on Reading Comprehension of Low-Achieving Adolescents: The Importance of Specific Teacher Skills." *Journal of Research in Reading* 41 (1): 20–41.

Opitz, Michael F., and Timothy Rasinski. 2008. *Good-Bye Round Robin: 25 Effective Oral Reading Strategies.* Portsmouth, NH: Heinemann.

Palincsar, Annemarie S., and Ann L. Brown. 1984. "Reciprocal Teaching of Comprehension-Fostering and Comprehension-Monitoring Activities." *Cognition and Instruction* 1 (2): 117–175.

Palincsar, Annemarie S., and Nell K. Duke. 2004. "The Role of Text and Text-Reader Interactions in Young Children's Reading Development and Achievement." *The Elementary School Journal* 105 (2): 183–197.

Palincsar, Annemarie S., and Laura Klenk. 1992. "Fostering Literacy Learning in Supportive Contexts." *Journal of Learning Disabilities* 25 (4): 211–225.

Parsons, Seth A., Margaret Vaughn, Roya Q. Scales, Melissa A. Gallagher, Allison W. Parsons, Stephanie G. Davis, Melissa Pierczynski, and Melony Allen. 2018. "Teachers' Instructional Adaptations: A Research Synthesis." *Review of Educational Research* 88 (2): 205–242. https://doi.org/10.3102/0034654317743198.

Pearson, P. David, Annemarie A. Palincsar, Gina Biancarosa, and Amy I. Berman. 2020. *Reaping the Rewards of the Reading for Understanding Initiative.* Washington, DC: National Academy of Education.

Perfetti, Charles, and Joseph Stafura. 2014. "Word Knowledge in a Theory of Reading Comprehension." *Scientific Studies of Reading* 18 (1): 22–37. https://doi.org /10.1080/10888438.2013.827687.

Pikulski, John, and David Chard. 2005. "Fluency: Bridge Between Decoding and Reading Comprehension." *The Reading Teacher* 58 (6): 510–519.

Pressley, Michael. 2003. "Psychology of Literacy and Literacy Instruction." In *Handbook of Psychology: Educational Psychology*, edited by W. M. Reynolds and G. E. Miller (pp. 333–355). Hoboken, NJ: John Wiley & Sons.

Pressley, Michael, Sonya Symons, Barbara L. Snyder, and Teresa Carilgia-Bull 1989. "Strategy Instruction Research Comes of Age." *Learning Disability Quarterly* 12: 16–31.

Protacio, Maria S. 2019. "How Positioning Affects English Learners' Social Interactions Around Reading." *Theory into Practice* 58 (3): 217–225.

Pyle, Nicole, Ariana C. Vasquez, Benjamin Lignugaris/Kraft, Sandra L. Gillam, D. Ray Reutzel, Abbie Olszewski, Hugo Segura, Daphne Hartzheim, Woodrow Laing, and Daniel Pyle. 2017. "Effects of Expository Text Structure Interventions on Comprehension: A Meta-Analysis." *Reading Research Quarterly* 52 (4): 469–501.

RAND *Reading Study Group. 2002. Reading for Understanding: Toward an R&D Program in Reading Comprehension.* Santa Monica, CA: RAND.

Raphael, Taffy E., and Jean McKinney. 1983. "An Examination of Fifth- and Eighth-Grade Children's Question-Answering Behavior: An Instructional Study in Metacognition." *Journal of Reading Behavior* 15 (3): 67–86.

Rasinski, Timothy V. 1990. "Effects of Repeated Reading and Listening-While-Reading on Reading Fluency." *The Journal of Educational Research* 83 (3): 147–151, doi:10.1080 /00220671.1990.10885946.

Rasinski, Timothy V. 2012. "Why Reading Fluency Should Be Hot!" *The Reading Teacher* 65 (8): 516–522.

Rasinski, Timothy V. 2017. "Readers Who Struggle: Why Many Struggle and a Modest Proposal for Improving Their Reading." *The Reading Teacher* 70 (5): 519–524.

Rasinski, Timothy V., Nancy Padak, Christine McKeon, Lori G. Krug-Wilfong, Julie A. Friedauer, and Patricia Heim. 2005. "Is Reading Fluency a Key for Successful High School Reading?" *Journal of Adolescent and Adult Literacy* 49: 22–27.

Rasinski, Timothy V., Kasim Yildirim, and James Nageldinger. 2011. "Building Fluency Through the Phrased Text Lesson." *The Reading Teacher* 65 (4): 252–255.

The Reading League. 2021. "Science of Reading: Defining Guide." https://www .thereadingleague.org/what-is-the-science -of-reading/.

Recht, Donna R., and Lauren Leslie. 1988. "Effect of Prior Knowledge on Good and Poor Readers' Memory of Text." *Journal of Educational Psychology* 80: 16–20.

Reis, Sally M., D. Betsy McCoach, Michael Coyne, Fredric J. Schreiber, Rebecca D. Eckert, and E. Jean Gubbins. 2007. "Using Planned Enrichment Strategies with Direct Instruction to Improve Reading Fluency, Comprehension, and Attitude Toward Reading: An Evidence-Based Study." *Elementary School Journal* 108 (1): 3–24.

Reutzel, D. Ray, and Robert Cooter. 2015. *Teaching Children to Read: The Teacher Makes the Difference.* New York: Pearson.

Reutzel, D. Ray, Cindy D. Jones, and T. Newman. 2010. "Scaffolded Silent Reading." In *Revisiting Silent Reading: New Directions for Teachers and Researchers*, edited by Elfrieda H. Hiebert and D. Ray Reutzel (pp. 129–150). Newark, DE: International Reading Association.

Rinehart, Steven D., Steven A. Stahl, and Lawrence G. Erickson. 1986. "Some Effects of Summarization Training on Reading and

Studying." *Reading Research Quarterly* 21 (4): 422–438.

Rosenshine, Barak, and Carla Meister. 1994. "Reciprocal Teaching: A Review of the Research." *Review of Educational Research* 64 (4): 479–530.

Rosenshine, Barak, Carla Meister, and Saul Chapman. 1996. "Teaching Students to Generate Questions: A Review of the Intervention Studies." *Review of Educational Research* 66 (2): 181–221.

Rowe, Deborah W., and Lawrence Rayford. 1987. "Activating Background Knowledge in Reading Comprehension Assessment." *Reading Research Quarterly* 22 (2): 160–176. https://doi.org/10.2307/747663.

Rupley, William H., John W. Logan, and William D. Nichols. 1998/1999. "Vocabulary Instruction in a Balanced Reading Program." *The Reading Teacher* 52 (4): 114–124.

Saat, Ferhat, and Emine G. Özenç. 2022. "Effect of Self-Evaluation-Based Oral Reading Method in Elementary School on Reading Fluency and Reading Comprehension." *Participatory Educational Research* 9 (2): 437–462.

Sainsbury, Marian, and Ian Schagen. 2004. "Attitudes to Reading at Ages Nine and Eleven." *Journal of Research in Reading* 27 (4): 373–386. https://doi.org/10.1111/j.1467-9817.2004.00240.x.

Samuels, Jay. 1979. "The Method of Repeated Readings." *The Reading Teacher* 32(4): 403–408.

Sanders, Ted, and Joost Schilperoord. 2008. "Text Structure as a Window on the Cognition of Writing." In *Handbook of Writing Research*, edited by Charles McArthur, Steve Graham, and Jill Fitzgerald (pp. 386–405). New York: Guilford Press.

Scarborough, Hollis S. 2001. "Connecting Early Language and Literacy to Later Reading (Dis)abilities: Evidence, Theory, and Practice." In *Handbook for Research in Early Literacy*, edited by Susan Neuman

and D. Dickinson (pp. 97–110). New York: Guilford Press.

Schmitz, Anke, Cornelia Gräsel, and Björn Rothstein. 2017. "Students' Genre Expectations and the Effects of Text Cohesion on Reading Comprehension." *Reading and Writing: An Interdisciplinary Journal* 30 (5): 1115–1135. https://doi.org/10.1007/s11145-016-9714-0.

Schneider, Wolfgang, Joachim Körkel, and Franz E. Weinert. 1989. "Domain-Specific Knowledge and Memory Performance: A Comparison of High- and Low-Aptitude Children." *Journal of Educational Psychology* 81: 306–312.

Scholastic. 2019. "Kids and Family Reading Report, 7th Edition." https://www.scholastic.com/content/corp-home/kids-and-family-reading-report.html.

Schoonover, Ruth C. 1938. "The Case for Voluminous Reading." *The English Journal* 27 (2): 114–118.

Schwanenflugel, Paula J., Steven A. Stahl, and Elisabeth L. McFall. 1997. "Partial Word Knowledge and Vocabulary Growth during Reading Comprehension." *Journal of Literacy Research* 29 (4): 531–553.

Scott, Cheryl, and Catherine Balthazar. 2013. "The Role of Complex Sentence Knowledge in Children with Reading and Writing Difficulties." *Perspectives on Language and Literacy* 39: 18–30.

Scott, Judith A., Diane Jamieson-Noel, and Marlene Asselin. 2003. "Vocabulary Instruction Throughout the Day in Twenty-Three Canadian Upper-Elementary Classrooms." *The Elementary School Journal* 103 (3): 269–286.

Scott, Judith A., and William E. Nagy. 1997. "Understanding the Definitions of Unfamiliar Verbs." *Reading Research Quarterly* 32 (2): 184–200.

Seidenberg, Mark, and James L. McClelland. 1989. "A Distributed, Developmental Model of Word Recognition and Naming."

Psychological Review 97 (4): 523–568. doi: 10.1037//0033-295X.96.4.523.

Serravallo, Jennifer. 2015. *The Reading Strategies Book: Your Everything Guide to Developing Skilled Readers.* Portsmouth, NH: Heinemann.

Shanahan, Timothy. 2017, July 23. "Everything You Wanted to Know About Repeated Reading." *Shanahan on Literacy* (blog). https://www.shanahanonliteracy.com/blog /everything-you-wanted-to-know-about -repeated-reading#sthash.gs4ARrJA.dpbs.

Shanahan, Timothy. 2018, May 28. "Where Questioning Fits in Comprehension Instruction: Skills and Strategies, Part II." *Shanahan on Literacy* (blog). https:// shanahanonliteracy.com/blog/where -questioning-fits-in-comprehension -instruction-skills-and-strategies-part -ii#sthash.WPkhpK4D.dpbs.

Shanahan, Timothy, Kim Callison, Christine Carriere, Nell K. Duke, P. David Pearson, Christopher Schatschneider, and Joseph Torgesen. 2010. *Improving Reading Comprehension in Kindergarten Through 3rd Grade: A Practice Guide.* NCEE 2010–4038. Washington, DC: National Center for Education Evaluation and Regional Assistance, Institute of Education Sciences, U.S. Department of Education.

Shapiro, Amy. 2004. "How Including Prior Knowledge as a Subject Variable May Change Outcomes of Learning Research." *American Education Research Journal* 41 (1): 159–189. https://doi.org/10.3102 /00028312041001159.

Sims Bishop, R. 1990. "Mirrors, Windows, and Sliding Glass Doors. *Perspectives* 1 (3): ix–xi.

Sindelar, Paul T., Lisa E. Monda, and Lawrence J. O'Shea. 1990. "Effects of Repeated Readings on Instructional- and Mastery-Level Readers." *The Journal of Educational Research* 83 (4): 220–226. https://doi.org /10.1080/00220671.1990.10885959.

Singson Maria, Diana Mahony, and Virginia Mann. 2000. "The Relation Between Reading Ability and Morphological Skills: Evidence from Derivational Suffixes." *Reading and Writing* 12: 219–252.

Smith, Reid, Pamela Snow, Tanya Serry, and Lorraine Hammond. 2021. "The Role of Background Knowledge in Reading Comprehension: A Critical Review." *Reading Psychology* 42 (3): 214–240. doi: 10.1080/02702711.2021.1888348.

Solari, Emily, Nicole Patton Terry, Nadine Gaab, and Tiffany P. Hogan. 2020. "Translational Science: A Road Map for the Science of Reading." *Reading Research Quarterly* 55 (S1): S347–S360.

Sorenson Duncan, Tamara, Catherine Mimeau, Nikita Crowell, and Hélène Deacon, S. H. 2021. "Not All Sentences are Created Equal: Evaluating the Relation between Children's Understanding of Basic and Difficult Sentences and their Reading Comprehension." *Journal of Educational Psychology* 113 (2): 268–278. https://doi .org/10.1037/edu0000545.

Souto-Manning, Mariana, and Jessica Martell. 2017. "Committing to Culturally Relevant Literacy Teaching as an Everyday Practice: It's Critical!" *Language Arts* 94 (4): 252–256.

Spencer, Mercedes, and Richard K. Wagner. 2017. "The Comprehension Problems for Second-Language Learners with Poor Reading Comprehension Despite Adequate Decoding: A Meta-Analysis." *Journal of Research in Reading* 40 (2): 199–217. doi: 10.1111/1467-9817.12080.

Spichtig, Alexandra N., Elfrieda H. Hiebert, Christian Vorstius, Jeffrey P. Pascoe, P. David Pearson, and Ralph Radach. 2016. "The Decline of Comprehension-Based Silent Reading Efficiency in the United States: A Comparison of Current Data with Performance in 1960." *Reading Research Quarterly* 51 (2): 239–259.

Stahl, Steven. 1986. "Three Principles of Effective Vocabulary Instruction." *Journal of Reading* 29: 662–668.

Stahl, Steven, and Kathleen M. Heubach. 2005. "Fluency-Oriented Reading Instruction." *Journal of Literacy Research* 37 (1): 25–60.

Stahl, Steven, Kathleen Heubach, and Angelia Holcomb. 2005. "Fluency-Oriented Reading Instruction." *Journal of Literacy Research* 37: 25–60. doi: 10.1207/s15548430jlr3701_2.

Stahl, Steven, and Marilyn Fairbanks. 1986. "The Effects of Vocabulary Instruction: A Model-Based Metaanalysis." *Review of Educational Research* 56: 72–110.

Stanovich, Keith E. 1986. "Matthew Effects in Reading: Some Consequences of Individual Differences in the Acquisition of Literacy." *Reading Research Quarterly* 21 (4): 360–407. http://www.jstor.org/stable/747612.

Stanovich, Keith E., and Richard F. West. 1989. "Exposure to Print and Orthographic Processing." *Reading Research Quarterly* 24 (4): 402–433. https://doi.org/10.2307/747605.

Suggate, Sebastian P. 2010. "Why What We Teach Depends on When: Grade and Reading Intervention Modality Moderate Effect Size." *Developmental Psychology* 46 (6): 1556–1579.

Steacy, Laura M., Lesly Wade-Woolley, Jay G. Rueckl, Kenneth R. Pugh, James D. Elliott, and Donald L. Compton. 2019. "The Role of Set for Variability in Irregular Word Reading: Word and Child Predictors in Typically Developing Readers and Students At-Risk for Reading Disabilities." *Scientific Studies of Reading* 23 (6): 523–532.

Sternberg, Robert J. 1987. "Most Vocabulary Is Learned from Context." In *The Nature of Vocabulary Acquisition*, edited by M. G. McKeown and M. E. Curtis (pp. 89–106). Hillsdale, NJ: Erlbaum.

Taberski, Sharon. 2011. *Comprehension from the Ground Up: Simplified, Sensible Instruction for the K–3 Reading Workshop.* Portsmouth, NH: Heinemann.

Talbott, Elizabeth, John W. Lloyd, and Melody Tankersley. 1994. "Effects of Reading Comprehension Interventions for Students with Learning Disabilities." *Learning Disability Quarterly* 17 (3): 223–232.

Taylor, Barbara M., and Richard W. Beach. 1984. "The Effects of Text Structure Instruction on Middle-Grade Students' Comprehension and Production of Expository Text." *Reading Research Quarterly* 19 (2): 134–146. doi: 10.2307/747358.

Therrien, William J. 2004. "Fluency and Comprehension Gains as a Result of Repeated Reading: A Meta-Analysis." *Remedial and Special Education* 25: 252–261.

Tunmer, William E., and James W. Chapman. 2012. "Does Sct for Variability Mediate the Influence of Vocabulary Knowledge on the Development of Word Recognition Skills?" *Scientific Studies of Reading* 16 (2): 122–140. https://doi.org/10.1080/10888438.2010.542527.

Turner, Franklin N. 2010. "Evaluating the Effectiveness of Fluency-Oriented Reading Instruction with Increasing Black and Latino Reading Fluency, as Compared to Asian and White Second-Grade Students' Reading Fluency." *Journal of Negro Education* 79 (2): 112–124.

Valencia, Sheila W., and Marsha R. Buly. 2004. "Behind Test Scores: What Struggling Readers Really Need." *The Reading Teacher* 57 (6): 520–531.

VanFossen, Phillip J. 2005. "Reading and Math Take So Much of the Time: An Overview of Social Studies Instruction in Elementary Classrooms in Indiana." *Theory and Research in Social Education* 33: 376–403.

Van Keer, Hilde, and Jean P. Verhaeghe. 2005. "Effects of Explicit Reading Strategies Instruction and Peer Tutoring on Second and Fifth Graders' Reading Comprehension and Self-Efficacy Perceptions." *Journal of Experimental Education* 73 (4): 291.

VanWagenen, Margaret A., Randy L. Williams, and T. F. McLaughlin. 1994. "Use of Assisted Reading to Improve Reading Rate, Word Accuracy, and Comprehension with ESL Spanish-speaking Students." *Perceptual and*

Motor Skills 79 (1, Pt. 1): 227–230. https:// doi.org/10.2466/pms.1994.79.1.227.

Vaughn, Sharon, Russel Gersten, Joseph Dimino, Mary J. Taylor, Rebecca Newman-Gonchar, Sarah Krowka, Michael J. Kieffer, Margaret McKeown, Deborah Reed, Michele Sanchez, Kimberly St. Martin, Jade Wexler, Seth Morgan, Armando Yañez, and Madhavi Jayanthi. 2022. *Providing Reading Interventions for Students in Grades 4–9.* WWC 2022007. Washington, DC: National Center for Education Evaluation and Regional Assistance (NCEE), Institute of Education Sciences, U.S. Department of Education.

Venegas, Elena M. 2018. "Strengthening the Reader Self-Efficacies of Reluctant and Struggling Readers Through Literature Circles." *Reading and Writing Quarterly* 34 (5): 419–435. doi: 10.1080/10573569 .2018.1483788.

Wagner, Richard K., and Caitlin Ridgewell. 2009. "A Large-Scale Study of Specific Reading Comprehension Disability." *Perspectives on Language and Literacy* 35 (5): 27–31.

Wagoner, Shirley A. 1983. "Comprehension Monitoring: What It Is and What We Know About It." *Reading Research Quarterly* 18 (3): 328–346.

Walker, Carol H. 1988. "Relative Importance of Domain Knowledge and Overall Aptitude on Acquisition of Domain-Related Information." *Cognition and Instruction* 4: 25–42.

Walpole, Sharon, Michael McKenna, Zoe A. Philippakos, and John Z. Strong. 2020. *Differentiated Literacy Instruction in Grades 4 and 5: Strategies and Resources.* 2nd ed. New York: Guilford Press.

Watkins, Marley, and Vicki Edwards. 1992. "Extracurricular Reading and Reading Achievement: The Rich Stay Rich and the Poor Don't Read." *Reading Improvement* 29: 236–242.

Wexler, Natalie. 2019. *The Knowledge Gap: The Hidden Cause of America's Broken Education System—and How to Fix It.* New York: Penguin Random House.

Wexler, Natalie. 2022, October 25. "New Podcast Examines Why Teachers Have Been 'Sold a Story' on Reading Instruction." *Minding the Gap* (blog). https:// nataliewexler.substack.com/p/new -podcast-examines-why-teachers.

White, Sheida, John Sabatini, Birnara J. Park, Jing Chen, Jared Bernstein, and Mengyi Li. 2021. *The 2018 NAEP Oral Reading Fluency Study.* NCES 2021-025. U.S. Department of Education. Washington, DC: Institute of Education Sciences, National Center for Education Statistics. https://nces.ed.gov /pubsearch/pubsinfo.asp?pubid=2021025.

Whitehurst, Grover, Francine L. Falco, Christopher J. Lonigan, Janet E. Fischel, Barbara D. DeBaryshe, Marta C. Valdez-Menchaca, and Marie B. Caulfield. 1988. "Accelerating Language Development through Picture Book Reading." *Developmental Psychology* 24 (4): 552–559. doi: 10.1037/0012-1649.24.4.552.

Wikipedia. 2022. "Battle of Thermopylae." Wikimedia Foundation. https://en.wikipedia .org/wiki/Battle_of_Thermopylae.

Wilkinson, Ian, and Kathryn Nelson. 2020. "Role of Discussion in Reading Comprehension." In *Visible Learning Guide to Student Achievement*, edited by John Hattie and Eric M. Anderman (pp. 231–237). New York: Routledge.

Wilkinson, Ian, and E. H. Son. 2011. "A Dialogic Turn in Research on Learning and Reaching to Comprehend." In *Handbook of Reading Research*, edited by M. L. Kamil, P. Afflerbach, P. D. Pearson, and E. B. Moje (pp. xiii–xxvi). London: Routledge.

Williams, Joanna, Kenda M. Hall, and Kristen D. Lauer. 2004. "Teaching Expository Text Structure to Young At-Risk Learners: Building the Basics of Comprehension Instruction." *Exceptionality* 12 (3): 129–144.

Willingham, Daniel T. 2006a, Spring. "How Knowledge Helps." *American Educator.*

https://www.aft.org/periodical/american-educator/spring-2006/how-knowledge-helps.

Willingham, Daniel T. 2006b. "The Usefulness of Brief Instruction in Reading Comprehension Strategies." *American Educator* 30 (4): 39–50.

Willingham, Daniel. 2007. "Critical Thinking: Why Is It So Hard to Teach?" *American Educator* 31: 8–19. https://www.aft.org/sites/default/files/media/2014/Crit_Thinking.pdf.

Willingham, Daniel. 2012, April 30. "Collateral Damage of Excessive Reading Comprehension Instruction." *Science and Eduction* (blog). http://www.danielwillingham.com/daniel-willingham-science-and-education-blog/collateral-damage-of-reading-comprehension-strategy-instruction.

Willingham, Daniel. 2017. *The Reading Mind: A Cognitive Approach to Understanding How the Mind Reads.* San Francisco: Jossey-Bass.

Willingham, Daniel, and Gail Lovette. 2014, September 26. "Can Reading Comprehension Be Taught?" *Teachers College Record.* http://www.danielwillingham.com/uploads/5/0/0/7/5007325/willingham&lovette_2014_can_reading_comprehension_be_taught_.pdf.

Winograd, Peter N. 1984. "Strategic Difficulties in Summarizing Texts." *Reading Research Quarterly* 19 (4): 404–425. https://doi.org/10.2307/747913.

Wissinger, Daniel R., Adrea J. Truckenmiller, Amber E. Konek, and Stephen Ciullo. 2023. "The Validity of Two Tests of Silent Reading Fluency: A Meta-Analytic Review." *Reading and Writing Quarterly.* doi: 10.1080/10573569.2023.2175340.

Wolf, Maryanne. 2007. *Proust and the Squid: The Story and Science of the Reading Brain.* New York: Harper Perennial.

Wyse, Dominic, and Alice Bradbury. 2022. "Reading Wars or Reading Reconciliation? A Critical Examination of Robust Research Evidence, Curriculum Policy, and Teachers' Practices for Teaching Phonics and Reading." *Review of Education* 10 (1): 1–53. doi: 10.1002/rev3.3314.

Yang, Gene Luan 2016. "The Reading Without Walls Challenge." https://geneyang.com/the-reading-without-walls-challenge.

Yates, Kari, and Christina Nosek. 2018. *To Know and Nurture a Reader: Conferring with Confidence and Joy.* Portsmouth, NH: Stenhouse.

Yeomans-Maldonado, Gloria. 2017. "Development of Comprehension Monitoring in Beginner Readers." *Reading and Writing* 9 (30): 2039–2067.

Young, Chase, David Paige, and Timothy V. Rasinski. 2022. *Artfully Teaching the Science of Reading.* New York: Routledge.

Zwaan, Rolf A., and Gabriel Radvansky. 1998. "Situation Models in Language Comprehension and Memory." *Psychological Bulletin* 123 (2): 162–185. https://doi.org/10.1037/0033-2909.123.2.162.

Children's Literature Cited

Alston, B. B. 2021. *Amari and the Night Brothers.* New York: HarperCollins.

Applegate, Katherine. 2017. *Wishtree.* New York: Feiwel and Friends.

Beason, Pamela. 2016. *Endangered: A Sam Weston Mystery.* Bellingham, WA: Wild-Wing Press.

Bryant, Jen. 2020. *Above the Rim: How Elgin Baylor Changed Basketball.* New York: Harry N. Abrams.

Colfer, Chris. 2017 *The Land of Stories: Worlds Collide.* Little, Brown Books for Young Readers.

Davies, Nicola. 2016. *Tiny Creatures: The World of Microbes.* Somerville, MA: Candlewick Press.

Deary, Terry. 1998. *Horrible Histories: The Measly Middle Ages.* New York: Scholastic.

FintekCafe. 2021. *Business Basics for Kids: Learn with Lemonade Stand Series.* n.p.: FintekCafe.

Furgang, Kathy. 2013. *National Geographic Kids Everything Money: A Wealth of Facts, Photos, and Fun!* Washington, DC: National Geographic Kids.

Gibbons, Gail. 2000. *Alligators and Crocodiles.* New York: Holiday House.

Jackson, Ty Allen. 2021. *Make Your Own Money: How Kids Can Earn It, Save It, Spend It, and Dream Big.* North Adams, MA: Storey.

Jenkins, Martin. 2014. *Can We Save the Tiger?* Somerville, MA: Candlewick Press.

Jenkins, Martin. 2017. *Exploring Space: From Galileo to the Mars Rover and Beyond.* Somerville, MA: Candlewick Press.

Keller, Tae. 2020. *When You Trap a Tiger.* New York: Random House Books for Young Readers.

Lewis, J. Patrick, ed. 2012. *The Book of Animal Poetry: 200 Poems with Photographs That Squeak, Soar, and Roar!* Washington, DC: National Geographic Kids.

Marotta, Millie. 2019. *A Wild Child's Guide to Endangered Animals.* San Francisco: Chronicle Books.

PBS. 2007. *Science Trek: DK4 Endangered Species.* https://www.pbs.org/video/d4k-endangered-species-9yfzbv/.

Reynolds, Peter. 2018. *The Word Collector.* New York. Scholastic.

Rowling, J. K. 1997. *Harry Potter and the Sorcerer's Stone.* New York: Scholastic.

Sorell, Traci. 2021. *We Are Still Here! Native American Truths Everyone Should Know.* Watertown, MA: Charlesbridge.

Tarshis, Lauren. 2015. *I Survived the Great Chicago Fire.* New York: Scholastic.

White, E. B. 1952. *Charlotte's Web.* New York: HarperCollins.

INDEX

LOOKING FOR MORE?

Shifting the Balance: The Online Classes

- 2 courses (1 aligned to each book)
- 12 weeks of anytime access
- 6 learning modules per class
- Downloadable guidebooks
- 2+ hours of video instruction per shift
- 2 one-hour Q&A sessions with the authors
- Custom course options for large groups
- Satisfaction guarantee

GRADUATE CREDIT AVAILABLE

TheSixShifts.com/online-class/

SHIFTING THE BALANCE

6 Ways to Bring the Science of Reading into the Upper Elementary Classroom

Katie Egan Cunningham
Jan Burkins · Kari Yates